THE SILENT SERVICE

John Parker, a journalist and former Fleet Street editor, has undertaken many investigative projects in his writing career with topics ranging from the Mafia to Northern Ireland. His numerous books include several military bestsellers including *SBS: The Inside Story of the Special Boat Service*; *The Gurkhas: The Inside Story of the World's Most Feared Soldiers*; *The Killing Factory: The Secrets of Germ and Chemical Warfare*; *Death of a Hero: Captain Robert Nairac GC and the Undercover War in Northern Ireland* and *Commandos: The Inside Story of Britain's Most Elite Fighting Force*.

Investigative and Military books by John Parker:

SBS: The Inside Story of the Special Boat Service
The Gurkhas: The Inside Story of the World's Most
Feared Soldiers
Inside the Foreign Legion
Commandos: The Inside Story of Britain's Most Elite Fighting
Force
Death of a Hero: Captain Robert Nairac, GC, and the
Undercover War in Northern Ireland
The Killing Factory: The Secrets of Germ and
Chemical Warfare
The Walking Dead: Judge Liliana Ferraro, Mafia Hunter
At the Heart of Darkness: The Myths and Truths of Satanic
Ritual Abuse
King of Fools: The Duke of Windsor and his Fascist Friends

THE SILENT SERVICE

The Inside Story of The Royal Navy's
Submarine Heroes

John Parker

headline

Copyright © 2001 John Parker

The right of John Parker to be identified as the Author of
the Work has been asserted by him in accordance with the
Copyright, Designs and Patents Act 1988.

First published in 2001
by HEADLINE BOOK PUBLISHING

First published in paperback in 2002
by HEADLINE BOOK PUBLISHING

10 9 8 7 6 5 4 3 2

John Parker would be happy to hear from readers with their
comments on the book at the following e-mail address:
johnparker@wyndham.freeserve.co.uk

ISBN 0 7472 3805 7

Typeset by
Letterpart Limited, Reigate, Surrey

Printed and bound in Great Britain by
Mackays of Chatham plc, Chatham, Kent

HEADLINE BOOK PUBLISHING
A division of Hodder Headline
338 Euston Road
London NW1 3BH

www.headline.co.uk
www.hodderheadline.com

CONTENTS

ACKNOWLEDGEMENTS

The year 2001 saw the celebration of a hundred years of British submarines, and from the earliest beginnings to the present day a fascinating, dangerous, courageous and at times exceedingly tragic story unfolds. Year upon year, a unique relentlessness emerges in the growing pains, as such there certainly were, in the development of the Silent Service, one that bears no comparison with any other arm of the British military or naval forces. But their history is indeed shared. It embraces two vast bodies of men, the sailors and the shipbuilders who were pioneers of skills that have been passed on and enhanced decade after decade through that century of naval history. A remarkably close bond was established between the thousands of men of the Royal Navy, who went into submarines, sometimes reluctantly, to sail beneath the waves of the world's oceans in truly intrepid style, and the army of shipyard employees, metalworkers, engineers, craftsmen, designers, naval architects, mathematicians, oceanographers and eventually nuclear scientists engaged on the creation of 'ships, submersible'. And no wonder. One loose bolt or bad weld could spell disaster.

It has been a dramatic journey, one that takes us from the first-ever British submarine, the tiny seven-man *Holland 1* launched in October 1901 at a cost of £35,000, to today's multimillion-pound nuclear boats staffed by 140 officers and ratings, which can circumnavigate the world 40 times without having to refuel and carry more explosive power in one submarine than all the bombs dropped by both sides in the whole of the Second World War, including the two atomic bombs.

Stories abound. Without wishing to over-gild the lily, it is no overstatement to say that to the layman they may sound incredible, occasionally horrific. Yet, submariners by nature, it would appear, are a cool, calm bunch who can lay quietly reading in their bunks while all about them is mayhem, their submarine resting on the bottom pounded by depth charges from which there is no escape or who, in more modern times, were the frontiersmen of the Cold War in which they might face the prospect of firing missiles that could flatten whole cities and kill millions of their fellow human beings. And so it is to the men themselves that I have turned for their personal recollections from these hundred years of action-packed history. As with my previous books in this series for Headline, I rely heavily on personal testimony, over and above the dry facts and politics of history, and once again I am deeply indebted to many who contributed their time and effort in bringing this story to life. As before, the quoted recollections are based on interviews conducted either with myself or taped for the Sound Archive of the Imperial War Museum. I am also indebted to Rosemary Tudge (now retired) and other members of the staff of the IWM for their help and cooperation in research. This was especially valuable in searching out tapes and personalities related to specific incidents arising in the chronology of events, including the real truth about Enigma, famous wartime stories such as the Man Who Never Was, and the frank recollections of a nuclear boat commander recounted in these pages in his own words. Mention must also be made of another great British resource, the Royal Navy Submarine Museum, which has supplied the entire photographic illustrations herein from its extensive archive, and of its director, Commander Jeff Tall, OBE, RN, for his personal help. Other research material was gleaned from the Public Records Office at Kew, the Royal Marines Museum at Southsea, the IWM document archives and from previously viewed material relating to the Special Boat Service, who were and still are comrades in arms of the Submarine Service.

CHAPTER ONE

Britain's First Submarine, with a Little Help from the IRA

To most officers and ratings of the proud nineteenth-century navies of the world, the very idea of submarines was anathema, a truly cursed invention, against which one angry French naval expert complained 'no human foresight can guard us'. The prospect of dark, shadowy vessels lurking silently in the deep, ready to blast their capital ships out of the water, filled them with both horror and loathing. If battles there were to be, let them be face to face, in the true man o' war traditions of seafaring nations. Their feelings were adequately summed up at the turn of the twentieth century by Admiral Sir Arthur Wilson, then Third Sea Lord at the British Admiralty, at a time when such craft were showing signs of becoming a reality rather than some unachievable dream by a heady collection of inventors. Soon after the French had opened a competition for designs of a submarine of 200 tonnes and with a range of 100 miles on the surface, Sir Arthur declared with forthright vigour that such boats were 'underhand, under water and damned un-English, certainly no occupation for a gentleman. Submarine crews, if captured, should be hanged as pirates.'

The Admiralty had steadfastly kept the lid on submarine development for more than a hundred years because its successive leaders believed the vessels represented an immense threat to the nation's maritime superiority. In that they were right, but to ignore them soon became impossible. New plans, new schemes kept on coming to the fore and, curiously enough, the best were developed by inventors and backers who hated the British with a passion, such as the Fenian Society – forerunners of the IRA. Yet it was this group's funds in America that initially backed the man who designed Britain's first submarine.

Like many of the elements of mechanical warfare that began to emerge among the colonising nations as they spread their influence across the globe, the thought of boats that could travel under water had been around for centuries. Alexander the Great was supposedly lowered to the bottom of the sea in a glass barrel in 337 BC, but it was not until 1578 that anything like a truly submersible craft, remarkably close to the first submarines, appeared in the writings of Englishman William Bourne. Whether it was ever built remains unclear.

The earliest recorded workable solution to diving beneath the waves was a wooden rowing boat covered with greased hide, designed by Dutch scientist Cornelius van Drebbel and demonstrated in England in 1624. He built at least three, having been sponsored by King James I, who was reportedly given a submerged trip along the Thames from Westminster to Greenwich. The boat was driven by manpower: twelve oarsmen, six each side, in a craft around four and a half metres long. Detail of this boat is sketchy and no drawings survive, but it appeared that Drebbel used goatskin bags filled with water to submerge; the bags would be emptied by squeezing the sides for returning to the surface.

Various designers built numerous prototypes of a more sturdy nature in the years ahead, but naval commanders showed not the slightest enthusiasm for them. The earliest record of a submersible being used in hostilities is the one that really stung the British and encouraged their mind-set against production of such a craft. During the War of American Independence (1775–83), a young Yale graduate named David Bushnell, inspired by his devotion to the independence cause, designed a one-man submarine, which he called *Turtle*. Built from wood in the shape of an egg, his machine was powered by a hand-cranked propeller. Its sole purpose was to damage the British fleet during its blockade of New York harbour in 1776. He also devised what might be considered their first torpedo, a 68-kilogramme keg of gunpowder, to do some serious damage to the 64-gun HMS *Eagle*, standing with her imposing might at the head of the British fleet. Given the speed in which she was built, the submarine was surprisingly effective.

A volunteer, Sergeant Ezra Lee, was to make the attack. He took off in darkness, bobbing along the surface towards his target. Unfortunately, a sudden change in the weather blew him off course, but he recovered well and managed to reach the frigate. At that point he submerged to get underneath the vessel. His bad luck continued, however. The task took longer than had been calculated. Running low on air, he had to return to the surface, where he was spotted by a British patrol boat. He unleashed his powder keg, which exploded with an almighty retort, and he escaped. Although the raid was aborted, George Washington went on to record that it was an 'effort of genius'. Indeed, there will be many similar events in the history of the submarine in these pages, notably some with remarkable similarity that won the coveted Victoria Cross for those who took part.

A more substantial vessel arrived in 1800 when a brilliant American inventor, Robert Fulton, of quite recent Irish descent, built the *Nautilus*, a copper-covered submarine. This, too, was inspired by the anti-British feelings of its creator, who travelled to England from his home in Pennsylvania in the 1780s to study painting but ended up harbouring an immense dislike for his hosts. His thoughts eventually turned from art to draughtsmanship, and he designed new canal systems before concentrating on the idea of a submarine. This, he perceived, might be used against the British fleet, and he was convinced that he had a solution to creating the ultimate weapon. In 1796 he travelled to France with his plans and made expansive claims that he had the means to destroy the ships of their traditional enemy, the British. Initially, the French rejected his plan but Fulton remained in France and persisted with his proposal. His patience was rewarded when Napoleon began his rise to power in 1799, just after Nelson had trounced the French in the Battle of Aboukir Bay. Napoleon commissioned Fulton to build his submarine, 6.4 metres long and shaped like a bullet. Propulsion under water was similar to Bushnell's, using a hand-cranked propeller.

In the first trials, Fulton and three mechanics descended to a depth of 7.5 metres, and later he added a detachable mine to demonstrate his theory of carrying out clandestine attacks on surface ships. The latter part of the equation failed. Napoleon himself became frustrated with lack of progress and eventually came to the conclusion that Fulton was no more than a common trickster.

Undaunted, Fulton returned to England under an assumed name and managed to bring his invention to the attention of Prime Minister William Pitt, no less. The Admiralty was instructed to investigate and to proceed to trials forthwith. Naval chiefs remained reluctant but did show interest in Fulton's ideas for mines, or torpedoes. Fulton gave a demonstration, attaching his mine to the hull of a 200-tonne Danish brig named *Dorothea* in 1805. The explosion blew the ship apart and Pitt, on hearing the results, wanted to buy Fulton's submarine plans immediately and approved an offer of £100,000. But the Admiralty mounted a stiff rearguard action. Its First Lord, Earl St Vincent, blasted the plan out of the water with a damning condemnation of submarines that was to remain the policy of the British for the remainder of the nineteenth century. He railed: 'Pitt was the greatest fool that ever existed to encourage a mode of war which they who commanded the seas did not want and which, if successful, would deprive them of it.'

Germany's naval chiefs were not impressed by the idea either. A former artillery sergeant named Wilhelm Bauer built a submarine, which he called *Fire Diver*, in 1850. Although its first voyage was successful, the submarine was barely a month old before it sank in Kiel harbour, and Bauer and two mechanics were lucky to escape with their lives. The German navy was quietly pleased, although Bauer did eventually build an ambitious 16-metre submarine for the Imperial Russian Navy, the fate of which has vanished into the mists.

The next stage in the development of submarines was an historical turning point: it was the first time such a craft had been used in a war. Although still very primitive, submarines were built by the Confederacy during the American Civil War (1861–5) to break the Federal blockade. A small fleet of them, believed to be nine in all and optimistically called *Davids*, were to be set against the Northern ships in a Goliath-like task. They were, in fact, more like torpedo boats, which were ballasted to steam along awash, so that only a minimal amount of the upper part of the boats was above water. They had an iron casing and were driven by steam power, which proved to be a built-in flaw. The hatch to the boiler had to remain open to provide an air intake. Naturally, in heavy seas or when confronting the waves left by other ships, the boat rapidly took on water and several of them went to the bottom. Their most spectacular raid was on the Union warship *Ironsides* as she stood in blockade of Charleston. A resounding explosion from one of the *Davids'* explosive cargo did little damage but instilled fear among the opposing sailors that remained throughout the conflict and beyond. That fear was heightened when the Confederacy rolled out another, more menacing craft, a massive cigar-shaped submarine, an incredible 18.25 metres in length.

Named the *Hunley*, she was powered when submerged by a hand-wound crankshaft running almost the entire length of the boat and which required the combined strength of eight members of the crew to propel it at 6 knots. But despite its cumbersome length and almost total uncontrollability when submerged, the *Hunley* became the first underwater vessel ever to sink a ship in wartime. This was not achieved without cost. During trials, the *Hunley* sank four times, twice killing all her crew. Even so, she was raised and sent back into commission. Her fifth journey was into real-life action in 1864 – to carry a spar-mounted torpedo to sink the Union warship *Housatonic* off the coast of South Carolina. The *Hunley* crew successfully achieved their mission, but in doing so went to the bottom with their victim. As water gushed into a gaping hole on the side of the *Housatonic*, the *Hunley* was pulled forward and her bow became lodged in the tangled metalwork. All aboard the submarine perished.

These early setbacks would not, of course, deter a world-wide search for a successful design that overcame the most difficult challenge of all, which was to find a workable means of propulsion under water. That these difficulties would eventually be overcome was more or less confirmed – as we now know with hindsight – by the appearance in 1870 of the latest novel by Jules Verne. He who would, through his fiction, forecast the invention of balloon travel, aeroplanes, television, guided missiles, space travel and even accurately predict their eventual uses took his readers beneath the sea as the widespread interest in science during that era took hold. This time it was Verne's *Twenty Thousand Leagues under the Sea*, the story of Captain Nemo who cruises beneath the oceans in a submarine, and the fantastic journeys that Jules Verne described could more or less be guaranteed to come to fruition in the fullness of time.

Indeed, it may well have been the story of Nemo that inspired the passion for the mysteries of the deep in the Reverend George Garrett, a determined young scholar who had followed his father into the Church but had his heart set on other things. After an education that took him to Manchester Grammar School, Trinity College, Dublin, and Trinity College, Cambridge, his interest in mechanical science consumed his thoughts far more than the Almighty into whose service he had committed himself. He began scribbling designs for various inventions on scraps of paper, and one of them was for a submarine he called ·*Resurgam* ('rise again') and which eventually dominated his thoughts. At the age of 26, he produced detailed plans for a bullet-shaped outer casing with pointed ends, powered under water by a single member of the crew operating a hand-cranked propeller. He raised more than £1,500 and had the submarine built on the banks of the Mersey.

Garrett decided that he would put her under tow to his rented steam yacht and sail around the coast to Portsmouth in time for the ceremonial Spithead Review and there give a demonstration of his boat's seaworthiness. He set off on 10 December 1879, with *Resurgam* under tow crewed by two men while Garrett himself directed operations from the yacht. They headed first to the coast of North Wales for further trials in the challenging winter waters of the Irish Sea. It was an eventful time. The submarine was powered by a coal-fired, single-cylinder steam engine for surface travel, which had to be shut down shortly before the submarine submerged. In theory, residual heat from the engine would keep the vessel under way for about an hour before the need to surface again. It was a dangerous and overpowering contraption, giving off a heat of between 100 and 150 degrees Fahrenheit and strong carbon monoxide fumes. The crew avoided death by poisoning by wearing a breathing device Garrett himself had invented and that was not entirely efficient. Lighting was by candles and, in a craft virtually devoid of instruments, it was difficult for the crew to establish exactly where they were because the periscope had not yet been invented. On more than one occasion during the trials off the coast at Rhyl, they had to surface and hail passing vessels or fishermen to ask where they were. Eventually, they were ready for the remainder of their journey around the lively seas off the western coast of the British Isles, and on 25 February 1880 *Resurgam* was taken under tow again behind the steam yacht heading south towards Portsmouth.

The weather took a turn for the worse with a heavy swell, and the hawser connecting the yacht to the submarine suddenly went slack. *Resurgam* had gone to the bottom and efforts to find her were unsuccessful. The submarine was to remain undiscovered for more than a century. As for Garrett, he never did get to give the British navy a demonstration, although a submarine built on his design and named the *Nordenfelt* was built in Stockholm and a second at Barrow-in-Furness. Turkey bought the first and awarded Garrett the title of Pasha Garrett, although the submarine never went into service. The second, 36.75 metres long and displacing 230 tonnes, sank during the delivery voyage to Russia. Garrett, dismayed at his lack of success, emigrated to America to become a farmer, went bust, and ended up in the US army. He died penniless in 1902 at the age of 42, some said from the effects of carbon monoxide poisoning. Bill Garrett, a descendent of the pioneering vicar, who lives in New Jersey, led an expedition to try to locate the wreck in 1989, without success. In 1995 trawlerman Dennis Hunt was fishing off Rhyl when his nets became snagged. A diver friend, Keith Hurley, came out to free his nets and became the first person to lay eyes on *Resurgam* since February 1880.

It was Irish-American pioneer John Philip Holland (1841–1914) who took the development of the submarine to a point where it would at last be accepted by the US and British naval authorities. It was his version that became the model for the first submarines to be built for the fleets of those two countries. Holland was born in County Clare, Ireland, and joined a religious order in Cork at the age of 17. But other ideas distracted him from a spiritual calling, and he began to draw sketches of submersible boats. He left the order to join the exodus to America, where he took a job as a teacher in New Jersey. He continued to work on his designs for a submarine and in 1873 submitted his drawings to the US navy. They were rejected out of hand. However, the American branch of the Irish patriots, the Fenian Society, heard of Holland's work and gave him $6,000 to build two submarines, which they planned to use against the British navy.

The Fenian brotherhood was founded in New York by veterans of the 1848 Irish uprising to raise funds for the recruitment and training of exiles to fight the British for Irish independence. The group had made headlines with cross-border attacks on Canada; across the Atlantic, the Fenians were becoming increasingly active on the British mainland with terrorist tactics and a succession of bombing outrages in the late nineteenth century, including an attempt to blow up Clerkenwell Prison. Holland, desperate for funds, was not in the least restrained by the possibility that his boats might be turned on British shipping because he, too, harboured strong anti-British feelings.

His first submarine was tested with mixed results in the Passaic River in 1878. She sank on her first outing because of loose-fitting plugs and had to be hauled back from the seabed. Holland himself took the controls on his second trip, and it was a successful run, although still leaky. His second submarine, *Fenian Ram*, was launched in 1881. Powered by one of the earliest internal-combustion engines, the boat was 9.5 metres long and displaced 19 tonnes. She went through a series of successful trials in the lower Hudson River and became the subject of close scrutiny by British spies, aware of the Fenian connection. Holland's backers, meanwhile, were becoming impatient and demanded action. When he persisted in continuing his rigorous trials they 'stole' the boat, which they said was rightfully theirs anyhow, and towed it to New Haven ready to begin blitzing British shipping. After several attempts to master the controls, however, they gave up and washed their hands of submarines. Only Holland himself could handle it, and in any event he had damaged the controls prior to the Irishmen's theft.

With Holland's paymasters gone, he had to seek employment while he worked on new plans. It was during this time that he came to the attention of a wheeler-dealer named Isaac Rice, a magazine publisher and industrialist who had already established a monopoly in the American storage battery industry. Rice financed the creation of the Holland Torpedo Boat Company – thus owning the company as well as the plans for Holland's latest submarine designs. He had correctly assessed that this time Holland had come up with a winner. The boat was 17 metres long and was powered by a petrol engine on the surface and an electric motor when submerged. Rice could also supply the batteries – and a complimentary stock of white mice, three of which were to be taken in cages on each voyage as a warning against toxic fumes. The United States government finally agreed, in April 1900, to purchase the prototype for $165,000 from the renamed Electric Boat Company, and the craft was commissioned as the USS *Holland*.

Rice then travelled to London, armed with the knowledge of highly successful trials in the USA where the *Holland* had 'sunk' a battleship in fleet exercises, and the Admiralty decided that it, too, must finally join the submarine age. The British agreed to buy five improved *Holland*s, capable of carrying a crew of seven and able to withstand pressure down to 30 metres. Each one cost £35,000 to build, although Holland himself saw little profit from his invention. Rice had taken the precaution of including the designs and patents when he established his company, and eventually Holland resigned. Blocked by legal ties from utilising his designs again, he died in obscurity while the Electric Boat Company went on to become one of the world's foremost manufacturers of submarines, celebrating its centennial in 1999. And so, finally, the British were to get a submarine fleet, although the

Admiralty stressed to newspapers at the time that the craft were for experimental purposes only. Lord Selborne, First Lord of the Admiralty, would only go as far as to say in his estimates to the Commons: 'What future value these boats may have in naval warfare can only be a matter of conjecture.'

This continued negative view at the Admiralty changed virtually overnight. In July 1901 newspaper reports from France brought a graphic account of dramatic developments. A dummy torpedo struck a French battleship as she left Ajaccio harbour during naval manoeuvres. It had been fired from a new French submarine, *Gustav Zède*, which had secretly been sent from Toulon for the express purpose of demonstrating to the navies of the world that the French had stolen a march on every one of them. They now possessed the weapon that all sailors feared – a submarine that actually worked. And it worked so well that the French had a dozen already in production. Vickers Son and Maxim, who were building the first British *Holland* at Barrow-in-Furness, were told to get a move on. Captain Reginald Bacon (later to be knighted and promoted to the rank of admiral) was 38 years old when he volunteered to join the fledgling submarine service. A man of proven technical ability, he was an immediate choice to become the first head of submarine development, with the title of Captain of Submarine Boats. He immediately set about recruiting the crew for the five *Holland*s – no easy task, given that few wanted anything to do with them. The Admiralty wanted the first one off the slipway by the autumn.

Other nations also began to hurry towards establishing a submarine section, although Germany held back to the very last. For a nation that eventually put such great effort into its submarine fleet, the first German Unterseeboot, *U1*, did not come into service until 1906. Among those who were vehemently against submarines was Admiral Alfred Friedrich von Tirpitz,* who was soon to become Lord High Admiral of the German navy. As a correspondent in the magazine *The Sphere* wrote at the time: 'The very uncertainty as to their capability of serious attack adds to the importance of fully experimenting with this latest engine of naval warfare. The capacity for our Goliaths of the line to resist these Davids of the sea is also a very doubtful quantity. Every advance in either direction will therefore be watched with great interest.'

Indeed it was: in Britain, the five new submarines for the Royal Navy were to roll off the slips at Barrow in rapid succession to begin rigorous trials under the critical gaze of the professionals and the fascination of the general public. They were quite small boats: 19.48 metres long with a 3.64-metre beam and a displacement of 120 tonnes submerged. They were capable of firing a torpedo with the boat at rest, during a run on the surface or submerged. When running on the surface, a petrol marine engine with a fuel-tank range of around 250 miles drove the boats. They had a maximum speed of about 7 knots and when submerged an electric waterproof motor powered by heavy storage batteries gave the vessel an identical maximum speed which could be maintained for four hours on fully charged batteries. The general operation of the boat was given in *The Sphere* as follows:

Before it is desired to make a dive the boat is brought to 'awash' condition with only the conning tower ports above the water. The dive is then made at a small angle

* That in itself was another touch of irony for history: as will be seen, a large chunk of the British submarine fleet spent most of the Second World War trying to sink a battleship which bore his name.

until the proper depth is reached, when by automatic means the boat is brought to a horizontal position. After the discharge of the torpedo from the fixed bow tube, the compensation for the weight of the torpedo is made automatically, causing only a slight change of trim for a few seconds. Provision is made for quick rising and diving, the time of appearance of the conning tower above the water being dependent on the skill of the navigator.

In the United States, the *Holland* had already undergone exacting trials. Admiral Hitchborn, chief constructor in the US navy, filed a complimentary report:

The *Holland* has shown herself capable of such complete control in the vertical plane that she may be kept within a few inches of any desired depth while moving, or brought to the surface and taken under again in a very short time. Her direction and control in the horizontal plane on the surface is effected with the same facility as any other craft, and submerged is limited only by the difficulties of vision. Her crew, just two officers and five ratings, are provided for on board with reasonable comfort and safety for such periods as she may be in service and working either upon the surface or submerged, and her armament, consisting entirely of torpedoes, gives her great offensive power.

It was pointed out that a small-sized submarine could be carried conveniently on the deck of a warship. Using lifting apparatus installed for handling steam launches, the submarines could be lowered into the water in the vicinity of a hostile fleet, primed and charged for attack with their crews inside. On returning from a reconnaissance or attack mission, the submarine might move easily alongside and be recovered to the deck.

The gunboat HMS *Hazard* was appointed depot ship for the British submarines, and she arrived at Barrow in October 1901, ready to accompany the first two *Holland*s on their first journey to Portsmouth. They now, incidentally, had the benefit of a periscope, primitive though it was, with only two positions, up or down. In the latter position it was lowered to lie horizontally on the casing. It was designed by Captain Bacon, who was supervising the construction of the craft at Vickers. Even as the remaining three *Holland*s were still being built, Bacon managed to persuade the government to build several more submarines in what was the beginning of a decade of dramatic and hasty production of the boats, clearly to keep up with the French and, soon, the Germans. They were to roll off the production line in rapid succession, and each was coded alphabetically and given a number. Equally rapid was the arrival of new designs.

These provided for longer, wider and better-equipped submarines in which the crew could stand up to their full height if they weren't too tall. Each new model had greater range, and they were given a code letter to denote type: A-class, B-class, C-class and so on. Almost from the beginning, improvements were carried out across the board. It was evident that the *Holland*s, for example, had only a very small conning tower (see the photograph of Holland himself standing inside his little tower). The use of a petrol engine and acid-filled batteries in such a confined space was also clearly a serious danger to the crews. The small, dark boats, filled with these dangerous fumes and other foul odours, as well as open, noisy machinery that had a nasty habit of breaking down at a critical moment, called for tough men

15

with plenty of courage and a touch of madness. The carrying of caged white mice to detect carbon monoxide was also still necessary; when the mice began dying, the submariners knew it was time to freshen the air.

Trials and experiments to improve both the performance and the safety of their crews were not achieved without some serious disasters and deplorable loss of life. There were numerous life-threatening incidents in the early days, ranging from engine or battery failure to gas explosions or leakage. Also, accidents occurred when the craft were simply run over by surface ships, and wireless communications were not introduced until the D-class arrived in 1908.

A1, the first all-British submarine built to specifications drawn up by the submarine flotilla's Captain Bacon, went into the history books for other reasons. She was laid down in February 1902 and was scheduled for launch the following August. But Captain Bacon hit trouble even before she was officially launched. An explosion of battery gas resulting from a sparking motor caused damage, and six men were severely injured. Another gas accident occurred on her first journey, to Portsmouth, when she suffered engine failure and, rolling in heavy seas, took on water, which entered the batteries. The submarine was filled with chlorine gas, and the crew was forced to abandon ship, half-choking to death. Superstition was always rife among sailors, and *A1* was not a lucky boat, although she had performed well. In fact, all six British submarines – five *Holland*s and *A1* – were said to have taken their parts brilliantly in the first full fleet exercises to involve submarines, off the south coast in March 1904. The submarines were such a novelty that George, Prince of Wales (later George V), a career sailor, went along to witness this landmark event in the navy he loved. He went aboard *A1* and congratulated all concerned with this first all-British submarine.

Scarcely had the prince left for London following the death of the Duke of Cambridge, however, than *A1* was reported missing to the east of the Nab Lightship. The submarine was last seen submerging close to the shore with her periscope protruding above the surface. A little later the SS *Berwick Castle*, a Union Castle steamer bound from Southampton to Hamburg, passed the Nab Lightship and made a signal by megaphone to the umpire's yacht, *Fire Queen*, that she had been struck by something. It turned out to be *A1*, which sank immediately, giving the crew of two officers and nine men no time to escape. Divers went down the following day and found the vessel lying on her port side in 13 metres of water. The conning tower had been struck. *A1* was under the command of Lieutenant Loftus Charles Mansergh, who had entered the navy in 1886. The other officer was Sub-Lieutenant John Preston Churchill, of the Marlborough family of Winston Churchill.

An unsettling number of other disasters in the years immediately ahead virtually halted the flow of volunteers into the submarine service. After the loss of *A1*, the log of disasters affecting the A-class boats, of which there were to be 13 in total, from the time of their launch to the beginning of the First World War, makes grim reading.

A3 was in collision with her own depot ship, the *Hazard*, and sank immediately. She was one of a number of submarines from the Portsmouth flotilla engaged in instructional exercises off the Isle of Wight. Several had gathered, while submerged, close to the depot ship and were carrying out mock attacks with dummy torpedoes. Men on board the *Hazard* saw her dive about 1,800 metres away, and a short while later they felt a thud on the starboard. From the air that bubbled up to the surface, it was evident that the submarine had probably struck her conning tower against the ship's side, but then, as the *Hazard* passed on, *A3* took a fatal blow from the vessel's propeller. Although other ships raced to her assistance, the extent of escaping air told the observers on *Hazard* that *A3* had flooded and her crew of 4 was lost without chance of saving a single life. 'All on board were overwhelmed by the battering inrush of the water,' stated a report on the incident. This report went on to say that strong currents also had to be reckoned with, adding, somewhat naïvely:

> It cannot be ignored that a submarine is peculiarly vulnerable and that even a little wound is peculiarly apt to prove fatal. She is the most delicate of the naval sisterhood, not by reason of frail construction but because of her very fitness for her peculiar duty. If she sinks easily, it must be remembered that it is her business to sink and the prison-like characteristics that make escape so hard when she sinks by accident are the condition of safety when she sinks by design. Nothing was being attempted which had not been done in the usual routine hundreds of times before. On an average, four submarines carry out similar exercises five days weekly, making as many as twenty attacks in succession.

A4 sank near Devonport on 16 October 1905 after taking on water from the wash of a passing ship through an open ventilator. The crew was saved and the boat recovered but sank twice again in the same month, fortunately without loss of life. She was later damaged by an explosion caused by petrol fumes in which four were injured.

A5 was badly damaged by two petrol explosions in February 1905; seven crew were killed and twelve badly injured.

A7 became stuck in mud while submerged in Whitsand

Bay on 16 January 1914; 11 crew died.

A8, which had a reputation for being unstable, sometimes diving without warning, foundered in Plymouth Sound on 8 June 1905. Water flooded through an open hatch and the battery exploded. Only four of the nineteen men aboard (including trainees) survived. She was later raised and transported to Devonport Docks, where the dead were evacuated by removing a metal plate. This was later used to make a metal cross for the men's funeral. The boat was recommissioned within months, in time for naval manoeuvres in 1906.

A9 foundered outside Plymouth after being hit by SS *Coath* in August 1906 but managed to resurface without loss of life. Petrol fumes killed four members of the crew two years later.

The next generation of submarines, the B-class boats, led charmed lives in comparison, and only one, *B2*, was lost to accident. She went to the bottom after being run over by SS *Amerika* in the Strait of Dover in October 1912. The liner was outward bound, sailing at 20 knots, and almost cut the submarine in half. Only one of the crew of sixteen escaped with his life.

On 14 July 1909 one of the new C-class was fatally damaged in a similar accident while travelling as part of a small flotilla of submarines and surface vessels led by the cruiser *Bonaventure* in the North Sea. Just off Cromer, the steamer *Eddystone*, bound for Hull, apparently struck the submerged *C11*; 13 members of her crew were lost.

So what was life like for early submariners, inside those quite tiny and ill-equipped vessels in which escape from fumes, fire or accident was heavily stacked against them? Walter Halter has left us a poignant memory of his experiences. He had joined the navy as a boy in 1908 and eventually went into training to join the fledgling wireless branch, which gave him the impetus to go into submarines, but, as he admitted, for all the wrong reasons:

> I was on the *Defiance*, which was our wireless school at that time. There was a boatswain there whose one hatred in life was an ordinary telegraphist and he used to really put us through it. *Defiance* was an old wooden ship and she had to be scrubbed from stem to stern every day. And that boatswain made sure that everyone with a wireless badge on his arm would get a turn, with a swab that was as big as myself, swabbing the decks. Well, one afternoon, a messenger came around bearing a call for volunteers for the submarine service. So myself and my chum Charlie Coles were smart lads and decided we were going to get out of this swabbing business and put our names forward. We spent the rest of the morning having a thorough medical checkup, and when we came back for dinner we announced we had passed the medical and we didn't have to do any more work. One of the chaps said, 'You bloody fools. What did you do that for? Why didn't you ask someone first?' He started telling us some terrible yarns about submarines and I started to feel a bit shaky. Charlie wrote to his parents and they somehow got him out of it. I told my mother and she didn't like it either. She wrote back and told me to cancel it, and I went to the office and asked to have my name crossed out. They said, 'No, you can't. You're on draft for Blockhouse tomorrow.'* And so I went to HMS *Dolphin*, the shore establishment, for training. It was a fort guarding the entrance to Portsmouth Harbour, quite a small place compared to what it eventually

---

* Fort Blockhouse, an ancient fort at the entrance to Portsmouth harbour, was the training centre for submariners and home for the submarine service.

became. It was heaven. Discipline was quite comfortable, and when you were off duty you could lie on the ramparts and sunbathe. It was a different navy altogether. And when we got into the submarines, you were so near to the officers. In fact, everyone was close to each other and all the red tape was gone. No falling in and out. We went into the classrooms for the first couple of days. On the blackboard they showed us the layout of a submarine and how they operated. The following morning they split us up, so many of us in each boat that was going out. We used to go out in the Solent and do some diving practice, probably fire a torpedo and come back. That was to last a fortnight, at the end of which we'd receive the extra submarine pay of two shillings a day.

I went to *C18* and that was it – a member of a boat's crew. There was no wireless equipment in any submarines at that time, and I had to take on able seaman's duties. Serving on the submarines at that period was quite different from service aboard surface ships, although you did not live on your boat. You worked in the boat all day but never stayed at sea after dark. We had no quarters in the boats then, no sleeping arrangements, no cooking facilities or anything. When we went out for the day, we'd take a dinner with us. When we went on manoeuvres in Scotland, we'd go up there, start in the morning and aim to be up there by nightfall. If we didn't make it, we'd anchor for the night and lie out on the deck to sleep. That's what we had to do in the war. We had nowhere to sleep in the war. You just had to lie on the deck or wherever you could. And there wasn't room really for everybody to be lying down on the deck at the same time because in those boats there was just one deck. It wasn't very pleasant, either – lack of air, lack of food, overcrowding. It was no wonder I had been warned against it.

When the air started to get thick, the second officer used to tap the compressed-air bottles. He would release air from them and at the same time they'd start up the low-power air compressor, pumping air from the boat into a spare set of bottles. They'd regulate the air pressure in the boat by the barometer. That was all there was. And that would only freshen the air. You couldn't really replace the air, and you'd know it was getting bad when everybody's eyes started to swell up. When we came to the surface and the conning tower was opened at the top, the rush of fresh air down there used to have the same effect as an alcoholic drink. You'd go dizzy for a bit with the fresh air coming down the boat.

Of course, as the newer boats came on stream we could stay out longer and longer on patrol, surface or dived. The longest I was ever down was 36 hours, in an E-boat, and they had 33 crew. So you can tell that the air was pretty thick by then. Then, of course, there was the problem of nature calling. In *E17* we did have a toilet aft. And one of the exhaust pipes ran through it and you used to get boiled if you went in there.

There were no toilets on the earlier boats, but really it wasn't very necessary. We got so little food and so little to drink that you'd go days without wanting to go. The conning towers were hollow and there was a bucket there that we could use. If you were going to dive, there was no worry about any mess; it was just washed away. Otherwise you'd have to bring it up and throw it over the side. But if you were only passing water, you would just stand on lee side and do it over the bridge. When we were down below, doing extended diving, we used to use a bucket quarter filled with oil so you had a combination of smells.

Water supplies were always a problem. We could only carry a tonne and a quarter of fresh water and that might have to last for up to 14 days, which we had to do as the war approached. That isn't much for 33 men. So it was cut down to the very bone. Making tea could also be difficult because we had to heat the hotplate and often the captain wouldn't let you juice it because he needed to conserve the battery. The battery was the life of a submarine, absolutely the life of it, so we had to get the captain's permission to boil a kettle or do any cooking in our home-made oven. We used to take out fresh food to last us two or three days. But with the atmosphere inside a submarine, fresh food or bread or meat wouldn't keep. So then it was tinned corned beef, tinned salmon, and tinned oxtail soup and biscuits.

Batteries had a limited capacity, and when there was any extended diving to be done the batteries were almost flat by the time we could surface and charge them by running the engine. And, you see, if you were in enemy waters you could only charge at night, and it would need three or four hours of engine to power it up.

In the summer, when the night wasn't very long, we'd come up to the surface and just have our conning tower above water. Of course, they could do it much later on with a snorkel (at the end of the Second World War), but we used to have just our conning tower above water and a couple of lookouts up there and everybody on top line for a crash dive. I served on C-, D- and E-type submarines. My favourite was *D4*. I was on her for two years. I said at the beginning of the war, 'Oh, we're all right. This boat will survive any war. And she did . . .'

CHAPTER TWO

The Germans Berate 'Underhand British Pirates'

As the navies of the world moved towards building up a credible submarine force during the first decade of the twentieth century, the pace of growth was both remarkable and dramatic. It gathered momentum towards the First World War in a scenario in which submarines were to become universally recognised as great weapons of war, levellers of odds. In a curious way, too, they might be compared with the effects of the nuclear age on military strategy a half-century later. New designs and thoughts were being developed with such speed that some of the early boats were becoming obsolete even before the orders for their delivery had been completed. After the 13 A-class submarines ordered by the Royal Navy came 11 B-class boats, which subsequently made way for the building of 38 C-class – all launched prior to 1910. These first three British designs were more or less built around the *Holland* model. They were still fairly primitive machines, and their use remained essentially for short endurance tasks, such as coastal and harbour defence work. By 1908, totally new concepts were already on the drawing board. The next generation of submarines, the D- and E-boats, saw considerable advances in technology and capacity, which overnight gave the British submarine force an ocean-going capability with a range, in the case of the E-class, of 2,500 miles.

Much of this progress was due to visionary campaigning by the young submarine commanders in cooperation with Vickers Son and Maxim, who together saw the early stages of development into fruition. Even so, many in the higher echelons of both government and the Admiralty, in the years prior to the First World War, were still vehemently opposed to a build-up of submarines, and nor could they see the need.

Admiral Sir John 'Jackie' Fisher, Commander-in-Chief at Portsmouth, was among the leaders of the pro-submarine movement, and his influence on developments was to have a profound effect on the proliferation of British submarines. He can also be credited with greatly influencing the thoughts of Winston Churchill. Apart from the regular meetings resulting from their respective positions, the two men became firm friends and kept up a remarkable correspondence for a number of years through which Fisher fearlessly expounded his views. Although with the fleet as a whole to contend with, he famously fought for submarines to be recognised as weapons of the future, a call that Churchill himself eventually took up with vigour. An example of the uphill struggle they contended with to convince those in authority can be seen in the words Fisher used in a note to a colleague. He complained that Satan 'disguised as an angel of light' would not succeed in persuading the Admiralty or the navy that submarines would before long represent a serious threat to the fleet in the Mediterranean and the English Channel. As early as 1904, while still Commander-in-Chief at Portsmouth, he wrote to a colleague with remarkable foresight:

Our paucity of submarines ... [is] the most serious thing at present affecting the British Empire. That sounds big, but it is true. It is astounding to me, perfectly astounding, how the very best amongst us fail to realise the vast impending revolution in naval warfare and naval strategy that the submarine will accomplish! (I have written a paper on this but it is so violent I am keeping it!) Here, at Portsmouth, just to take a single instance, is the battleship *Empress of India* engaged on manoeuvres and knowing of the proximity of submarines, the Flagship of the Second Admiral of the Home Fleet, nine miles beyond the Nab Light (out in the open) so self-confident of safety and so oblivious to the possibilities of modern warfare that the Admiral is smoking his cigarette, the Captain is calmly seeing defaulters on the half-deck, no one caring an iota for what is going on, and suddenly they see a [dummy] Whitehead torpedo miss their stern by a few feet! And how fired?

From a submarine of the 'pre-Adamite' period [referring to early experiments with submarines], small, slow, badly fitted, with no periscope at all, and yet this submarine followed that battleship for a solid two hours under water, coming up gingerly about a mile off every now and then like a beaver! Just to take a fresh compass bearing on her prey and then down again. Remember that this is done (and I want specially to emphasise the point) with a Lieutenant in command of the boat out in her for the first time in his life on his own account, and half the crew never out before either.

27

Why, it is wonderful! And so what results may we expect when bigger and faster boats and periscopes more powerful than the naked eye (such as the latest pattern one I saw the other day) and with experienced officers and crews and with nests of these submarines acting together? I have not disguised my opinion in season and out of season as to the essential, immediate, vital, pressing, urgent (I cannot think of any more adjectives) necessity for more submarines at once – at the very least twenty-five in addition to those now ordered and building and a hundred more as soon as practicable, or we shall be caught with our breeches down, just as the Russians have been! And then, my dear friend, you have the astounding audacity to say to me: 'I presume you only think they [submarines] can act on the defensive!!' Why, my dear fellow, not take the offensive? Good Lord! If our Admiral is worth his salt he will tow his submarines at 18-knot speed and put them into the hostile port (like ferrets after the rabbits) before war is officially declared. In all seriousness I don't think it is even faintly realised the immense, impending revolution which [submarines] will effect as offensive weapons of war. When you calmly sit down and work out what will happen in the narrow waters of the Channel and the Mediterranean . . . how totally the submarines will alter the effect of Gibraltar, Port Said, Limnos and Malta, it makes one's hair stand on end.

Someone in the higher echelons, however, began to take notice, and soon Fisher was given the chance to develop his ideas and bring fresh impetus to the development of submarines in Britain. He was appointed First Sea Lord in 1904, and in his first set of estimates produced for the House of

Commons for 1905–6 he made particular reference to the hot potato of just how many submarines Britain needed to expand on the primitive boats of the existing complement which were so limited in capability and so dangerous to their crews:

> These boats have been constantly at work during the last two years, subject to manoeuvres of very great severity, but on all occasions they have proved themselves very reliable. You may classify a submarine as a daylight torpedo boat of moderate speed and very considerable radius of action. Certain areas in wartime, by the use of surface torpedo craft by night and submarines by day, might be practically denied to large ships. There is one other immediate and very important function of the submarine, and that is the defence of our ports, harbours and coast. It is quite clear that the use of the submarine extends the range of the defence far beyond the range of the guns of the forts defending the harbour. These vessels will not only defend the ports but link up the defences, and the possession of a sufficient number of them would greatly reduce the anxiety of any Admiral entrusted with the defence of our coasts.

Fisher was given the go-ahead to push on with a major expansion programme of what became known as 'Fisher's toys', and clearly the ideas of those around him were similarly expansive in terms of improving the boats in every respect and of turning the emphasis towards an attacking force as well as a defensive one. The British submarine design team was already working towards that aim. They were well aware by then that the Germans, from a late start, had ambitions to get well in front of both the British and the

French. Britain could certainly have been ahead of them all had it not been for a sluggish start through the apprehension of those in power.

Even so, in 1908 there were rumours in the newspapers of some dramatic developments in submarine construction in the UK, nurtured and encouraged by Fisher. Reports centred on a totally new design for what became the D-class, which turned out to be revolutionary in construction. *D1* was completed in time for trials in 1908, although another 18 months would pass before its predecessor, the C-class, went out of production. There were two significant technical developments in the design of the D-class. It was the first British submarine to have diesel engines built by Vickers, albeit invented by the German Rudolph Diesel. This would prove far more reliable and eliminated one of the major causes of danger to crew from petrol engine fumes. The other innovation was that *D1* became the first British submarine to have wireless. But the most important factor in the development of *D1* was that overnight the British fleet had an ocean-going submarine. The D-class would have a range of more than 2,500 miles, and could do a steady 14 knots on the surface at full speed and up to 10 knots submerged. She was the first British submarine with twin propellers, and her ballast tanks were not inside the hull but fitted on the outside as 'saddle tanks'.

She carried two 18-inch bow torpedo tubes like the C-class and an additional 18-inch tube in the stern. She was manned by three officers and twenty-four ratings and, for the first time in the short history of British submarines, the crew could stand up at full height (unless they were especially tall) without bashing their heads. One final addition was the facility for the fitting of a 2-pounder gun, eventually introduced as standard on *D4*.

The point was not lost on media observers – and presumably German spies – when *D1* emerged from the cocoon of secrecy that had surrounded the launch. On Merseyside, the *Liverpool Daily Post* had a special interest in shipping matters through the Cammell Laird yard at Birkenhead, which, along with Vickers at Barrow and Scotts at Greenock and Chatham, was one of the leading submarine producers in the UK. The newspaper welcomed the D-class as evidence that 'before long we shall have more than one submarine flotilla capable of crossing the North Sea for work hundreds of miles from their harbours . . . a fleet we have been building up so steadily will be available for not only direct home defence but to strike a blow in enemy waters'.

The statistics for submarine production in Britain during Fisher's term at the Admiralty demonstrate both the speed of that progression and the sudden change of direction from defensive to offensive capability. In the first decade of the new century, 62 A-, B- and C-class boats were built. The D-class boats had begun to come on stream in 1908. Eight were launched between 1908 and 1912. Then, the focus shifted again to the even bigger and better ocean-going vessels, the 700-tonne E-class, the first of which was launched in November 1912. She was 54 metres long, with a surface displacement of 652 tonnes (795 tonnes submerged), and carried 3 officers and 28 ratings. The earliest were powered by gasoline engines but, starting with *E7*, twin Vickers diesels became standard, with electric motors driving two shafts for 1,600 horsepower.

Admiral Fisher was by then no longer at the helm. He retired in 1910 at the age of 70 and received a peerage. A year later, Winston Churchill himself took up the reins in office as First Lord of the Admiralty. His respect and recognition of Fisher's experience are apparent from the voluminous exchange of letters between them, and on the very day of his appointment to the Admiralty, Churchill wrote: 'I want to see you very much . . . you have but to indicate your convenience and I will await you at the Admiralty.'

Although wider issues of the fleet remained paramount, Fisher's belief in submarines clearly made an impression on Churchill. His move to the Admiralty coincided with a situation that we now know was to be replayed almost to the letter in the late 1930s, with Churchill warning of Germany's naval expansion and of the possibilities of war. Fresh from the Spithead Review of the fleet, at which he went aboard a submarine, he declared at a meeting of the Committee of Imperial Defence on 11 July 1912:

The whole character of the German fleet shows that it is designed for aggressive and offensive action of the largest possible character in the North Sea and North Atlantic. The structure of German battleships shows clearly that they are intended for attack and for fleet action. They are not a cruiser fleet designed to protect colonies and commerce all over the world. When you go to the smaller types of vessels, the same principle can be traced. If there ever was a vessel in the world whose services to the defensive will be great, and which is a characteristic weapon for the defence, it is the submarine. But the German development of that vessel, from all the information we can obtain, shows that it is intended to turn even this weapon of defence into one of offence. They are building not the smaller classes which will be useful for the defence of their somewhat limited coastline, but the large classes which would be capable of sudden operations at a great distance from their base across the sea. So I think I am justified in saying that the German fleet, whatever may be said about it, exists for the purpose of fighting a great battle in the North Sea, both with battleships and with all ancillary vessels, against some other great naval power which is not referred to by them.

The Admiralty was soon slapping 'urgent' stickers on all their orders, and submarine production went into overdrive: no fewer than 57 E-class submarines were ordered for delivery between 1912 and June 1916. This was a time of great confusion, and by the end of the war the Royal Navy's submarine range would extend across 20 different designs and classes. The largest, designed to operate with the fleet, was more than 100 metres in length, with a submerged displacement of almost 2,500 tonnes. She carried eight torpedo tubes and a crew of five officers and forty-five ratings. She would not be produced until 1917, three years after the first test of war and real offensive action for submarine flotillas of participating navies arrived on 4 August 1914. Great Britain declared war on Germany, and the weapons, machinery and ships for the first true mechanical conflict were moved to the start lines of the most appalling and devastating battles the world had ever seen. Britain began the First World War with many more submarines than Germany but that situation was very quickly reversed. Germany stepped up production to a phenomenal rate, and when the totals were analysed from the 54 months of the war it would be seen that U-boats outnumbered the British submarine fleet by more than two to one. Furthermore, the majority of the British vessels in 1914 were the smaller types originally designed and intended for coastal defence. In addition to 55 boats of A-, B- and C-classes remaining in operation, there were 8 D-class and 15 of the new E-class submarines available in the autumn of 1914.

E-craft were being launched by the week – a very necessary target if the British were to keep within shouting distance of Germany's massive production schedule. Additional types – F-, G- and H-classes – were scheduled to begin rolling out of the production pens in 1915, but they represented a mere trickle compared with the crash programme mounted by the Germans from 1914 through to the last hours of the war. Everyone that saw action of any kind had a story to tell, usually dramatic and often with tragic consequences, followed with avid interest by a fascinated public. Space does not permit more than a summary in these pages of those heroic adventures of the men who went to war in these ridiculously dangerous machines (usually much loved by their crews), but recollections of some of their most famous exploits will demonstrate the courage of the men involved.

Submarines were to be engaged in vast arenas of sea warfare, and until well into the conflict too a great reliance was to fall on the skills and courage of the crews of the smaller boats. Although the British navy was far greater in both experience and numbers, the newly equipped German fleet about which Winston Churchill had been warning was lean, hungry and thoroughly modern. It was roughly half the size of the Royal Navy's but was more concentrated in what would become key areas of operation, with the Kaiser's expressed intention of using its U-boats to upset the British resolve by annihilating her shipping, starving her people of food and bringing the country to its knees. As the boats rolled off the production lines in increasing numbers, a creeping fear verging on madness developed, which centred on the 'new weapons' as the warring nations scrambled to outdo each other, seemingly oblivious to the appalling cost in human life. In the progression of it, whether it was gas in the trenches or U-boats blasting innocent merchant shipping and passenger liners out of the water, the capacity for inhumanity suddenly seemed limitless.

Curiously enough, however, the first Allied submarine to be lost was half a world away. In 1912, Australia had ordered two E-class submarines from Britain, code-named *AE1* and *AE2*. After an 83-day journey from Portsmouth, they arrived in tandem at Sydney harbour at dawn on 24 May 1914, and the British officers and crew remained on hand to train crews of the Australian navy. The British officers and about half the original crews of the two boats were still aboard with locally recruited men when Britain entered the war. On that same day, the Australian colonial government offered a force of 20,000 men to join the European Allies in any destination determined by the home government. That force would, in due course, become embroiled in the disaster at Gallipoli, but in the meantime the two Australian submarines were destined for a more immediate role closer to home. At that time, the islands of New Britain and New Ireland, which lay north-east of New Guinea, were in the hands of Germany, as part of the Bismarck Archipelago.

In liaison with the British War Office, the Australian government immediately dispatched a task force to capture the islands, whose waters were patrolled by five German cruisers. While Australian troops landed at Rabaul, the main town on New Britain, *AE1* and *AE2* joined Australian destroyers patrolling the waters around the islands. Although there were some heavy exchanges for the land forces, naval activity was uneventful. The Australian ships continued their patrols, and on 19 September HMS *Parramatta* lost contact with *AE1* after her British captain, Lieutenant-Commander T.E. Besant, reported in at 14.30 that he was heading towards

Blanche Bay, New Britain. That was the last contact with *AE1*, and the boat was never seen again. When she failed to return to base, a search was made but no clue as to her whereabouts was discovered, not even the usual telltale oil slick. It was assumed that she had accidentally struck some of the treacherous coral that abounded in the area and had sunk with all hands drowned as the boat flooded.

AE2, commanded by Lieutenant-Commander H.G.D. Stoker, also scoured the area of *AE1*'s likely route but found nothing. His boat would soon be called to service, along with Australian forces, in the Dardanelles, but in the meantime attention on both sides in the war was focused on the vital shipping lanes of the North Sea.

Heligoland Bight was the key to Germany's ability to sally forth, so German commanders sealed the route towards the Baltic Sea with a protective ring of U-boats, and laid mines and set coastal defence traps. In fact, the Royal Navy stood off, preferring instead to concentrate to a greater degree on the entrances and exits to the North Sea while sending small flotillas, with submarines, to patrol the eastern waters around the British Isles and to probe Germany's coastline to gain intelligence. The submarines included C-, D- and E-boats, and the first-time experience of going to war in craft with, as yet, still unsophisticated communications soon became apparent. Boats went out of wireless range and, in place, intelligence messages were sent back by homing pigeon, which were usually kept in the forward peak of the boats. When they were released, the pigeons faced a journey of perhaps 140 to 150 miles back to their owners' home lofts, where the messages were retrieved.

Usually, important messages were sent in triplicate, i.e. using three pigeons, but even this method did not always guarantee success. In *C12*, Lieutenant-Commander Keble

White was mystified by the fact that his pigeons were reluctant to leave the boat. Only then did he discover, according to his report of operations, that 'unfortunately, the OC Pigeons was very fond of animals . . . he had fed them too well and one and all in succession were loath to leave their happy surroundings'.

Closer to home, in the early months of the war, the Royal Navy was clearly concerned about marauding U-boats, as were the crews of ships, large and small. Later intelligence would show that there was good reason: on the day after Britain entered the war, ten U-boats were sent out to hunt down Royal Navy vessels in the North Sea. Three of them prepared to attack Royal Navy fleet manoeuvres close to the Orkneys on 8 August, and one of them, *U15*, was spotted and rammed by the cruiser HMS *Birmingham*. She sank with all hands. *U13* was also lost, cause unknown, and the U-boat flotilla retreated.

A month later, however, *U21* became the first submarine since the *Huntley* to sink an enemy battleship, audaciously close to the Firth of Forth. The U-boat torpedoed HMS *Pathfinder*, patrolling off St Abb's Head. The ship's magazine blew and she sank immediately with 250 men lost. Later in the month, a single German submarine, *U9*, under the command of Lieutenant Otto Weddigen, came upon three ancient cruisers, *Aboukir*, *Hogue* and *Cressy*. He stalked them, picked them off one by one, and within an hour had sunk the three warships, totalling 36,000 tonnes. They were sent to the bottom with 1,300 officers and men. The British nation was naturally appalled by this news and demanded retaliation in kind.

Britain's own account was opened by Lieutenant-Commander Max Horton in *E9*. In what was the first public mention of an illustrious name in British submarine history,

Horton claimed an old German cruiser, the *Hela*, on the approaches to Heligoland. He followed this up with a direct hit on the German destroyer *S116* in the North Sea in mid-September 1914. The euphoria of these first submarine successes was to be short-lived, however. A reversal quickly followed, and another 'first' in the history of submarine warfare was to be notched up: the first submarine to be sunk by one of its own kind. The victim was the British *E3*, which was sighted cruising on the surface in the Heligoland Bight by *U27* captain Lieutenant Bernhard Wegener. As he closed towards *E3*, he could see six of the crew on the bridge. At 275 metres Wegener fired a torpedo. It sliced *E3* in two and she sank within minutes. The German commander spotted four men on the surface but, according to his report, refused to move closer, fearing other British submarines in the vicinity. When he did eventually move *U27* towards the location of the sinking, no survivors were found. In the weeks and months that followed, the British 8th Flotilla operating off the east coast suffered five further losses, although the German fleet was sufficiently harassed to pull back and revert its exercising manoeuvres into the comparative safety of the Baltic Sea.

They were to be pursued by a small flotilla of British submarines, which initially consisted of three boats: *E1*, under the command of Lieutenant-Commander Laurence, *E9*, commanded by Lieutenant-Commander Horton, and *E11*, under Lieutenant-Commander Martin Nasmith. The first two successfully negotiated the heavily defended route into the Baltic on 18 October 1914. By the time Nasmith arrived, the alert had been raised and he could not get through the German anti-submarine and coastal defences. But the British would not give up.

As well as giving trouble to the German fleet in the Baltic, the submarines had an equally important task of interrupting shipments of iron ore from Sweden to Germany. This was eventually achieved, although, in terms of attacks on ships, successes were initially few, partly because the British submarines had been placed under inefficient Russian control, some of whose bases had not even been told of their impending arrival. But soon two submarines cut loose from the Russians and began to make names for themselves. The German propaganda machine complained bitterly of the 'underhand and criminal methods of the British pirate submarines' in the Baltic. They specifically named Max Horton, in *E9*, and portrayed him as a modern buccaneer. By then the two British E-boats had been joined by three others when *E8*, *E18* and *E19* successfully negotiated the minefields and defences into the Baltic. A fourth, *E13*, had run aground in Danish territorial waters and was eventually bought and salvaged by the Danish government.

Four of the smaller C-boats were also moved into the Baltic, but by an unorthodox route. They were shipped out via the Berents Sea to Archangel, and stripped of their batteries and other removable parts. They were then transported over land and down river to Petrograd, where they were restored to normality and sent into the Baltic to join the five E-boats. They were all to distinguish themselves in a successful Baltic campaign, sinking numerous enemy vessels, although it came to an unfortunate end. *E18* was lost with all hands, for reasons unknown, after having successfully torpedoed a German destroyer in May 1915. *C32* was severely damaged in an encounter with German ships and was deliberately run aground and scuttled by her crew in the Gulf of Riga. All remaining seven British submarines in the Baltic flotilla remained in operation until the Russian Revolution, when the Bolsheviks concluded a separate peace agreement with Germany at Brest-Litovsk in 1917.

One of the clauses for that agreement called on the new Russian administration to enforce a surrender of all British submarines under its control. The British submariners thus found themselves marooned in no man's land. Lieutenant-Commander Francis Cromie, senior officer in the Baltic flotilla, refused to accept the instruction and moved the remaining boats to Helsinki in Finland. As German troops headed for a landing 70 miles down the coast, London gave the order to scuttle the submarines if it became necessary, so as to render them useless to the enemy. One by one, the seven boats were taken out to sea and sunk by their own crews. The men themselves had been promised safe passage to Petrograd, although some were subsequently interned. Cromie himself remained in Russia as naval attaché at the British embassy, where he worked on in an attempt to aid the Allied cause. He would survive little more than a year. On 31 August 1918 he stood alone on the steps of the embassy attempting to hold back a mob intent on storming and looting the building. He was shot and trampled to death; in the aftermath of all that had happened, his courage and contribution to that vital Baltic campaign was somewhat overlooked.

The Baltic was, of course, just one of several heroic naval campaigns joined by British submarines in the First World War, and perhaps the most famous – and catastrophic – of all was being simultaneously played out in the Dardanelles. This was the place that would supposedly open the door to an Allied advance on the Gallipoli Peninsula. Instead, it was to become an appalling graveyard of men and machines.

CHAPTER THREE

Dash and Daring in the Dardanelles

The Dardanelles became a focus of attention as early as October 1914 when Turkey threw in its lot with Germany and in return received German military advisers, weapons and two brand-new ships, the *Breslau*, a light cruiser, and a magnificent battle cruiser of 22,600 tonnes, the *Goeben*. The two ships were stabled at Constantinople (Istanbul), and just to demonstrate whose side they were on the Turks occasionally unleashed their new big guns and sent them forth to bombard Russian Black Sea ports before scampering back into the safe home waters of the Sea of Marmara.

Constantinople, on the northern coast of the Marmara, was well away from the southern access to the sea, reached via the Dardanelles strait, which for centuries had provided the Turks with a natural defence to their capital city. It had become a focal point of history in that no attacking enemy craft had successfully negotiated the Dardanelles for a hundred years, although many had tried. It provided an easily defended passage, 40 miles long, running south out of the Marmara at the Gallipoli Peninsula into the Aegean Sea and on to the Mediterranean. Conversely, the Marmara was also a lifeline on which the Turks relied for shipments of many crucial supplies, including coal for their industries, railways and cities. The geographical hazards of the Dardanelles provided the infrastructure for a superb defensive position. Although several miles from shore to shore at its widest points, the Dardanelles produced a natural rat-run 12 miles upstream from the Aegean. Known as the Narrows opposite the town of Çanakkale, the passage reached a dogleg hazard reducing to just over a mile in width. It was there that Alexander moved his armies by a bridge of boats in 334 BC and where it was swum in legend by Leander and in fact by Byron.

At that point, too, unpredictable currents were at their worst as salt and fresh water converged in layers to make life difficult for even the most adept submarine commander. The strait's rocky banks were also strewn with forts and gun placements accommodating around 150 guns ranging from 6 to 14 inches in calibre. There were shore-mounted torpedo launchers, mobile howitzers, floating and fixed minefields and huge anti-submarine nets. The Allies intended to maintain a blockade of the Dardanelles, and in December 1914, well before the infamous invasion of the Gallipoli Peninsula was even conceived, the French and the British had a large flotilla of ships of all kinds settled in the wide harbour of Moudros on the Greek island of Limnos. Among them were six submarines, including three small British B-class boats: *B9*, *B10* and *B11*. In the last, Lieutenant Norman Holbrook kept on taking a look at the Dardanelles, and on the morning of 13 December 1914 he threw caution to the wind and decided to have a go at a hit-and-run raid. He warned his chaps that what he was about to do might mean they would be lunching with the fishes and then made a dash into the strait as fast as the little craft could carry them for around 12 miles. He sailed through minefields at Sari Siglar Bay and there came upon the Turkish battleship *Messudieh* at anchor. What happened next is described in the citation for Britain's highest honour, the Victoria Cross, awarded to Holbrook the following week:

> For most conspicuous bravery on 13 December, when in command, he entered the Dardanelles and, notwithstanding the very difficult current, dived his vessel under five rows of mines and torpedoed the Turkish battleship *Messudieh*, which was guarding the minefield. Lieutenant Holbrook succeeded in bringing the *B11* safely back, although assailed by gunfire and torpedo boats, having been submerged on occasion for nine hours.

It was, of course, the newness of such operations as much as anything that made Holbrook's actions worthy of such a high honour. He and all who followed into the Dardanelles were trailblazers of extraordinary skill and courage, driving those early boats into perilous situations while devoid of any form of technological aid. Furthermore, Holbrook's success prompted the naval commanders at Moudros to request a presence of the larger E-boats, convinced they would make a good impression. On 14 January 1915 the French submarine *Saphir* attempted a second run but she was lost with all hands just beyond the Narrows. In London, meanwhile, a more grandiose plan was emerging aimed at taking Turkey out of the war and freeing up the Dardanelles to take the pressure off Russian forces in the Caucasus and cause a diversion for the Germans from the main event, the war in France.

The plan, devised by British Munitions Minister David Lloyd George in conjunction with Winston Churchill, General Kitchener and Admiral Sackville H. Garden, was initially seen as a navy-led operation, with the big guns blasting the shore batteries ahead of landings by a combined force of British, Australian, New Zealand, Gurkha and French Foreign Legion troops. The opening salvos were fired in February, when the ships from the Allied flotilla shelled the shore approaches at the mouth of the Dardanelles.

The Turks fell into disarray and were running, until three ageing British ships sailed straight into an unnoticed minefield and were sunk. The Allied naval commanders ordered an immediate halt to the bombardment and pulled the ships back into the Aegean for fear of losing more. It was then resolved to invade the region by land through Gallipoli, and what was called the Mediterranean Expeditionary Force was assembled in Egypt under Sir Ian Hamilton. The Anglo-Australian–New Zealand force was later enlarged with Gurkhas, while French and Foreign Legion troops were to attack on other fronts. As the Allied forces began their landings on difficult approaches with high hopes of taking the Gallipoli Peninsula, there were 60,000 Turkish troops lining the high and rocky outcrops, picking them off like a fairground shoot. From the outset, the British-led operation seemed doomed and ill prepared, relying, for example, on tourist maps for their invasion plans. History would show that it was a foolhardy and poorly managed undertaking that ultimately cost 505,000 casualties from the two sides and ended only when the invading Allied forces called a halt and withdrew. While nothing can detract from the courage of the fighting forces, the Gallipoli disaster somewhat over-shadowed remarkable work by British and Australian submariners.

The submariners' contribution to the effort was one of the few highlights, if such they can be termed, in the unfolding tragedy, although again not without cost. Their mission was to break through the Dardanelles, get into the Sea of Marmara and attack the Turkish ships and shoreline instal-lations. In theory, Constantinople itself was the ultimate target of the invasion plan, but in practice it never seemed a serious proposition. The E-boats had begun arriving ready to take up the challenge in March, ahead of the planned invasion of Allied ground forces scheduled for 25 April. They included Australia's only remaining submarine, *AE2*, sister of *AE1*, which was, it will be recalled, the first submarine lost in the war. *AE2* came in ahead of the Australian troops, who would form a large part of the 410,000 men under the British flag called into service during the nine-month campaign. Exactly half of them would be cut down, casualties of both conflict and conditions.

The first to try to run the gauntlet of the Dardanelles was *E15*, under the command of Lieutenant-Commander Theodore Brodie, twin brother of C.G. Brodie, who was captain of *C11* when she was accidentally run down by the ss *Eddystone* in 1909 and sunk. At dawn on 17 April 1915, Brodie prepared for the journey towards the Marmara. He made good progress and passed the 12-mile mark before he was forced to dive deeper to get beneath a minefield. As he did so, *E15* was caught by the infamous swirling current, which turned her in a half-circle and carried her towards the shore where she ran aground with her conning tower exposed. Brodie discovered he was directly below the guns of Fort Dardnus, which opened fire immediately. The captain blew his tanks and ordered full astern, trying in vain to jolt the vessel free. He decided to take a look at the surroundings to envisage an escape route for his crew. As he opened the hatch in the tower, a shell fired from an approaching Turkish torpedo boat slammed against the hull and killed him. A second shell hit the battery compartment and the crew had no alternative but to surrender.

The incident was witnessed by an aircraft of the RN Air Service based at Moudros, and with the boat still aground and capable of being salvaged, her secret papers, relating to operations and communications, being read and the boat returned to use with a German crew. *B6* under Lieutenant R.E. Birch was sent into the strait to torpedo *E15*. He was met with a veritable hail of heavy gunfire and, although he managed to fire the two torpedoes, both missed their target and Birch was forced to retreat. Over the next forty-eight hours, two destroyers and then two battleships attempted to reach the stricken submarine and destroy her with shellfire. All four were met with fierce and accurate fire from the shore batteries and had to retreat. Finally, in what really was a last-ditch effort, two 17-metre steam picket boats, each equipped with side-mounted torpedo launchers, set off under cover of darkness and finally came within range. One of them was picked up in the glare of the searchlights at the last moment and took a direct hit. The second fired her torpedoes and then dashed towards the companion boat to pick up survivors. As the boat cautiously made her way back along the coastline, a massive explosion confirmed that the task was completed.

The forced destruction of *E15* in no way dampened the enthusiasm of the submariners to try to force the Dardanelles. The next boat to make the attempt was Australia's *AE2*, which began the journey through the strait in the early hours of 25 April,* the same day that ANZAC troops landed on the beaches at Gallipoli. Lieutenant-Commander Hew Stoker, the Irish-born captain of *AE2*, took her steadily on the surface under a moonless sky until, suddenly, his boat was swept by searchlights. The shellfire that quickly followed forced him to dive, and as he did so he ran straight into a minefield. The wires holding the floating mines scraped noisily and uncomfortably across her hull, and it was nothing short of a miracle that one or more did not detonate. As he emerged from the minefield, Stoker went to periscope depth and as he approached the Narrows he spotted a destroyer, which had clearly recognised the disturbance in the calm waters and was bearing down on *AE2* to ram her. Stoker dived and in the avoiding action ran aground beneath a fort and was fired on immediately.

Fortunately, the submarine was so close to the walls of the fort that the troops could not depress the guns enough to hit their target, giving Stoker the chance to jerk the vessel free after about eight minutes. He then sailed on through the final part of the passage towards the Sea of Marmara, and it became clear that now a large number of surface craft were looking for him. *AE2* had also suffered some severe damage, and a combination of both factors forced Stoker to keep his boat on the bottom for 13 hours by which time there was barely enough air to sustain life. Finally, however, he was able to get on the move, and at 7.30 a.m. on 26 April the jubilant Stoker reported by signal to an equally jubilant headquarters staff that *AE2* had entered the Sea of Marmara. In spite of the somewhat fragile state of his boat and without a gun, Hew Stoker and his crew immediately began to cause havoc.

---

* Thereafter to be known as ANZAC Day.

Virtually overnight, enemy shipping was curtailed substantially. Lieutenant-Commander Edward Courtney Boyle was dispatched in *E14* to join Stoker. He, too, successfully negotiated the Dardanelles, to enter the Marmara on 29 April and rendezvous with Stoker in Atarki Bay to discuss a plan of action. They agreed to meet up again the following day off Karaburun Point. As he approached that meeting place, Stoker discovered a Turkish torpedo boat, the *Sultan Hissar*, ahead of him. He dived to let her pass but as he did so *AE2* suddenly went out of control, perhaps as she hit a denser layer of water, and she surfaced unintentionally in spite of Stoker's attempt to keep her down. The *Sultan Hissar*, close at hand, fired a torpedo, which missed, but subsequent shellfire penetrated the pressure hull in three places. Stoker himself later described the dramatic scene.

We were caught! We could no longer dive and our defence was gone. It but remained to avoid useless sacrifice of life. All hands were ordered on deck and overboard. The holes in the hull were all above water, and therefore not in themselves sufficient to sink the boat, though preventing all possibility of diving. While the crew scrambled up on deck, an officer remained with me below to take the necessary steps for sinking. The third officer, on bridge, watched the rising water to give warning in time for our escape. A shout from him . . . and we clambered up, but through the conning tower windows I saw there was still a minute to spare. I jumped down again and had a last look round, for, you see, I was fond of *AE2*. What a sight . . . food, clothing, flotsam and jetsam of the weirdest sorts floating up on the fast-entering water in the place which we had been so proud to keep neat and clean. An anxious shout from above: 'Hurry, sir, she's going down!'

In the wardroom my eye was caught by my private dispatch case which contained, I remembered, some money. That was bound to be useful. I ran and picked it up, and darted up the conning tower. As I reached the bridge the water was about two feet from the top of the conning tower; besides this only a small portion of the stern was out of water. On it were clustered the last half-dozen of the crew; the remainder were overboard. Curious incidents impress one at such times. As those last six men took the water, the neat dive of one of the engine room ratings will remain pictured in my mind for ever. Perhaps a minute passed and then, slowly and gracefully, like the lady she was, without sound or sigh, without causing an eddy or a ripple, *AE2* slid away on her last and longest dive.

Stoker, his two British fellow officers and twenty-nine ratings, half British and half Australian, were rescued from the Marmara by the torpedo boat and were taken to Constantinople and captivity as prisoners of war.* Boyle remained in the Marmara until 15 May. On his return, he discovered that news of his exploits had been received with glowing accolades in London, and three days later he learned that:

The King has been graciously pleased to approve the grant of the Victoria Cross to Commander Edward Courtney Boyle, for the most conspicuous bravery, in command of submarine, when he dived his vessel under

* *AE2* lay forgotten, her story largely unknown to the Australian public. In 1998 the Australian ambassador in Ankara, David Evans, suggested a search mission to underwater explorer Selçuk Kolay, director of the Rahmi Koç Museum in Istanbul, and the wreck was subsequently found.

enemy minefields and entered the Sea of Marmara on 27 April 1915. In spite of great navigational difficulties from strong currents, of the continual neighbourhood of hostile patrols, and of the hourly danger of attack from the enemy, he continued to operate in the narrow waters of the Straits and succeeded in sinking two Turkish gunboats and one large military transport.

There were yet other VCs to be won in this sequence of events in the Dardanelles. *E14* was replaced in the Marmara by *E11*, captained by Lieutenant-Commander Martin Nasmith, whose exploits were to become the stuff of even greater legend. He began the first of three passages through the Dardanelles on the night of 18 May 1915. Sixteen hours later, *E11* emerged safely into the Sea of Marmara, and almost immediately Nasmith began in the manner that was to make him famous. First, he seized a Turkish vessel and strapped her to the landside of his submarine to serve as a disguise as she passed shore observers. By 23 May *E11* had sunk a Turkish gunboat and several smaller craft, and on that day a Turkish transport ship, the *Nagara*, which was heading for the Dardanelles, came into Nasmith's sights. He surfaced quite close to the transport, close enough to hold a conversation with two men taking the air on deck. One was a Bavarian doctor, the other Raymond Gram Swing, a writer from the *Chicago Daily News*.* As *E11* drew closer, Nasmith appeared in the conning tower, wearing a white sweater, and hailed the ship, cupping his hands around his mouth.

'Who are you?' he shouted.

Turkish sailors panicked and started to jump into the sea,

---

* Later to become a well-known radio broadcaster during the Second World War.

while the American called back: 'I'm Swing of the *Chicago Daily News.*'

'Glad to meet you, Mr Swing,' shouted Nasmith, 'but I mean what ship is that?'

'The Turkish transport *Nagara.*'

'Well, I'm going to sink you.'

'Can we get off?' Swing asked.

'Yes,' said Nasmith, 'but you'd better be damned quick about it!'

Lifeboats were being lowered to the water as the two men spoke, but the panicking sailors dropped them unevenly so that the first two partially submerged on reaching the water. Nasmith and Swing more or less supervised the release of the remaining lifeboats, and, when all crew and passengers were safely aboard, a boarding party from *E11* took explosives aboard the Turkish ship. As Nasmith's *E11* sailed away, the *Nagara* blew up in a sheet of flame. She had been carrying ammunition.

Nasmith sailed on, this time heading for the Golden Horn, the harbour of Constantinople itself. Then, as the ancient city came into view, he began to plot the deliverance of his metal to the heart of the Turkish Empire. As he neared the harbour that no one in the city suspected could ever be attacked from the sea, *E11*'s first torpedo missed, then turned a complete circle and he had to dodge it as it boomeranged back towards him. It then doubled back and went on to make a very loud bang as it hit and blew up a wharf. His second delivery sank a Turkish gunboat.

The effect on the Turks was electric. Government officials in the city were in panic, believing they were under attack from a group of submarines. Troops embarking on ships bound for Gallipoli were disembarked and sent ashore. Traders began boarding up their shops, and citizens ran for cover.

During the course of the following week, Nasmith sank ships and small boats on the approaches to the Golden Horn, often simply by putting boarding parties with explosive charges on board the target vessels rather than using up his valuable stock of torpedoes. It also became known later that he had altered the settings on his torpedoes so that if any one of them missed the target, they would not sink to the bottom, but could be recovered and reused. Nasmith himself would swim out to the floating torpedo and undertake the difficult and dangerous task of defusing the charges before the torpedoes were brought back on board.

E11 was public enemy number one for the Turks, who were convinced that she was not operating alone and that a number of enemy submarines were in the Marmara. Nasmith also cheekily topped up his own supplies from craft his men boarded, and they kept going for almost three weeks before heading back to base. The journey through the Dardanelles was again packed with incident, including the collection of a mine that became lodged around the casing. When he cleared the minefield, Nasmith went full speed astern and managed to free the mine from his boat and returned safely to base on 6 June.

Back in London, it was announced:

The King has been Graciously pleased to approve the grant of the Victoria Cross to Lieutenant-Commander Martin Eric Nasmith, for the most conspicuous bravery in command of one of His Majesty's Submarines while operating in the Sea of Marmara. In the face of great danger he succeeded in destroying one large Turkish gunboat, one ammunition ship and three store-ships, in addition to driving one store-ship ashore. When he had safely passed the most difficult part of his homeward journey he returned again to torpedo a Turkish transport.

Meanwhile, Boyle in *E14* returned to the Marmara to keep up the pressure and was joined eight days later by Lieutenant-Commander Ken Bruce in *E12*. The latter discovered that in the meantime the Germans had strung a heavy-duty steel mesh across the Narrows, and his boat became stuck fast as he attempted to break through it. Full astern, full ahead: three times Bruce made the manoeuvre. On his last attempt, with the electric motors in danger of burning out, he crashed through and sailed on into the Marmara, where he remained for a week before his motors required attention and he had to withdraw. Nasmith came back to join Boyle, and literally within minutes of entering the Marmara he had sunk a transport. Next day he sank another transport and then while on the surface shot up a column of Turkish troops passing along a coast road, with his brand-new 12-pounder gun. His greatest triumph came just before dawn on 8 August, when Nasmith found the Turkish battleship *Harridin Barbarossa* in his sights. He stalked the ship for 20 minutes before firing a single torpedo. It scored a direct hit, followed soon afterwards by a massive explosion when the magazine went up. The battleship sank within minutes.

Nasmith and Boyle continued their patrols, sinking ships and bombarding troops on the coast road well into the autumn. They were joined in September by Lieutenant-Commander Archie Cochrane, 33-year-old captain of *E7*, making his second tour of the Marmara. But bad luck dogged Cochrane from the outset. First, he discovered that a second net had been positioned in the Narrows and, as he tried to break through, part of the metal entwined around his propeller. He was forced to make some erratic underwater manoeuvres which lasted two hours but found it impossible to move forward through the net. He decided to lie doggo with the boat still in the net until after dark. As things stood, every time he made a move the marker buoys on the surface, attached to the net for the safety of Turkish shipping, also moved, giving warning to the patrol boats now lining up on the surface to take a pot shot at *E7*.

Later on, a depth mine floated down and exploded close by. The submarine rocked violently, but there was no evident damage. Cochrane decided to burn all confidential papers, just in case. He made another attempt to free the boat without success and remained on the bottom for a further eight hours. A second mine exploded soon after 6.30 p.m. The whole boat shuddered, light fittings shook and shattered and other equipment was tipped from its housing. In the hope that the explosion had also damaged the net, he made one final, vain attempt to nose forward. It was then that he decided to save the crew from certain death, *E7* having been submerged for over 13 hours and with virtually no air left.

He asked for full astern and managed to surface promptly in the midst of an array of enemy craft waiting to shell him. Amid a hail of gunfire, Lieutenant John Scaife scrambled on deck to surrender the crew. As the firing died when the opposition realised what was happening, two motorboats manned by German submarine crews came alongside and took the men off. Cochrane himself was the last to leave, and as the rescue boats cleared the stricken submarine a time-fuse explosion set by Cochrane before he left blew up, and *E7* returned quickly to the bottom. Cochrane joined Hew Stoker in the prisoner-of-war camp at Yozgat. They made two escape attempts, the second with 24 other officers. Cochrane and seven others stole a motorboat and successfully made it across to Cyprus.* The rest were recaptured.

Back in the Marmara, Martin Nasmith was taking the war more directly into the Turks' front garden, eventually launching a one-man commando-style operation which, as we will see, became a model for a future generation in the Second World War and beyond for the men who later formed the Special Boat Service. Nasmith had taken to regular shelling of a viaduct where the main railway to Asia Minor ran along the coast in the Gulf of Ismit. The line was damaged but still operative. Nasmith and First Lieutenant Guy D'Oyly-Hughes came up with a plan. The latter would go ashore himself and blow it up. They built a wooden platform, large enough to bear a substantial demolition charge but light enough to be pushed by one man. *E11* took D'Oyly-Hughes as close as possible to the viaduct.

The intrepid saboteur, with a torch, whistle and revolver, manhandled his charge to the beach and carried the load towards the target. He arrived to discover a repair gang working under arc lights on damage inflicted by the *E11* gun earlier in the day, so he hauled the charge 135 metres down the track to a culvert and stuffed the explosive inside. The crack of the fuse gun echoed in the night, attracting the attention of the Turks at the viaduct. D'Oyly-Hughes dashed for the beach and started swimming along the coast in the direction of *E11*. As gunfire began to rain down from the cliffs, the conning tower of *E11* loomed up and the exhausted D'Oyly-Hughes was pulled aboard.

Nasmith's patrol lasted 47 days, a record equalled by no

---

* Cochrane became MP for East Fife after retirement from the navy in 1922. Later knighted, he became Governor of Burma in 1936, although he returned to naval service in the Second World War, commanding an auxiliary cruiser in the Atlantic convoy operations. Hew Stoker was eventually freed and became an actor and playwright.

other commander in the First World War. During that time, the crew of *E11* sank 11 steamers, 5 large sailing vessels and 30 small sailing vessels. By then, the need for such daring assaults was diminishing rapidly as the land battles around Gallipoli were firmly entrenched in a hopeless stalemate from which there seemed no respite from the daily sacrifice of human life. That one battle zone had engaged more than a million men from the two sides, half of whom became casualties.

Early in December 1915 the Allies finally decided to call a halt and to withdraw. The final act was to evacuate 90,000 men, 4,500 animals, 1,700 vehicles and 200 guns, which began after dark on 18 December. With the main Allied flotilla fully committed to this mammoth task, in which speed was of the essence, the submarines were to provide some side action to entertain the Turks and Germans. Nasmith continued his campaign in the Marmara and at the mouth of the strait before finally calling it a day two days before Christmas, when he crashed through the anti-submarine nets at the Narrows for the last time, homeward bound.

During the run of the Dardanelles campaign, 13 Allied submarines had completed 27 successful passages through the strait. Seven were sunk, but the scorecard was somewhat uneven. The Turks lost 2 battleships, a destroyer, 5 gunboats, 11 transports, 44 steamers and 148 sailing boats. The effect on the Turkish supply lines was catastrophic, and for the rest of the war the blockade on the Dardanelles was kept up.

It was not until the very last stages that some unfinished business was attended to when the two German-built ships *Breslau* and *Goeben* ventured down the Dardanelles and into the Aegean on 19 January 1918. They ran straight into an Allied minefield. The *Breslau* was sunk immediately. The

Goeben was severely damaged but managed to limp back towards the Narrows. To be absolutely sure she did not re-emerge, she was bombarded by Royal Navy aircraft, which scored 16 direct hits, but the cruiser was still not sunk. *E14*, now captained by Lieutenant-Commander Geoffrey White, was dispatched into the strait to make a torpedo attack. The story of his journey was to be told in the *London Gazette* in May 1919:

On 21 January 1918 the German battle cruiser *Goeben*, which had been mined while attempting a raid against Mundros, ran aground off Nagara Point in the Dardanelles. Repeated air attacks failed to achieve any noticeable results and at dusk on 27 January HM submarine *E14* [formerly Boyle's boat when he won his VC] under the command of Lieutenant-Commander G.S. White left Imbros in the desperate hope of torpedoing her. Despite being caught in the anti-submarine nets, White succeeded in bringing *E14* up to Nagara only to find the *Goeben* had [been towed away] during the night. There was nothing White could do except to reverse course and start back down the Straits. When off Chanak he sighted and fired at a large merchantman, but the torpedo exploded prematurely and *E14* was badly damaged. For two hours the submarine continued her dived passage towards the open sea but finally she became so flooded as to be uncontrollable. White gave the order to surface in the hope of making a final dash clear, but *E14* was hit by gunfire from the shore batteries. With no hope of escape White altered course towards the shore to give his crew a chance of safety, but was himself killed by shellfire shortly before *E14* sank.

Lieutenant-Commander White, who had two sons and a daughter he had never seen, was posthumously awarded the Victoria Cross, received by his widow at Buckingham Palace on 2 July, her late husband's birthday. His submarine, *E14*, also had the distinction of being awarded the VC twice. That four of the five VCs awarded to members of the submarine service during the First World War resulted from operations in the Dardanelles could in no way be seen as a slight against activity elsewhere. The campaign against the Turks, where swashbuckling commanders captured the headlines, has to some extent overshadowed the operations of the British submarine collective as a whole, going about their business in the coastal waters of the United Kingdom and the Atlantic, where the pressure on the British fleet was immense.

While examples of great heroism and often tragic consequences abounded during the 54 months of war, the overall picture emerges from the statistics. Only then does the sheer scale of the production of submarines by both sides and the ultimate consequences become apparent. Operating with the fleet or simply roaming in search of German targets became an absolute priority, as indeed did the manufacture of an ever-increasing number of submarines. On 9 January 1915 the Kaiser gave notice to the world of Germany's intended unrestricted submarine warfare, to become effective at the end of the month.

British yards were already under severe pressure, which was not helped by the faint-hearted attitude of the Americans, who were reluctant to get involved almost until the last. Twenty of the new H-class submarines, for example, were ordered from the Bethlehem Corporation of America at the outbreak of the war, but because of concern over America's neutrality the first ten were completed at the Vickers yard in Montreal. The remainder were not delivered until America entered the war, by which time they were barely needed. In fact, 36 H-class boats were built in the remaining three years of the war along with 3 F-class and 14 G-class. Other, newer models introduced from 1915 onwards were J-, K-, L- and M-classes, which included experimental boats that had particular design features, such as the use of steam turbines powered by two oil-fired boilers in the case of the K-boats. The figures tell their own story.

In all, 203 submarines were launched under the British War Emergency Programme between 1914 and 1918, although many would not actually be commissioned before the war ended; some were even scrapped before they were completed (see Chapter Four). The British lost 59 submarines through enemy action, accident or friendly fire during the war years; Germany's losses of U-boats in the same period amounted to 209 sunk by enemy or accident; 176 others were still in service at the end of the war, and German yards were filled with boats under repair or still under construction. The cost was crippling to national economies.

These were the stark realities that confronted the British government as the prospects of an early victory quickly disappeared from view. The descent into sheer bloody murder on the high seas really began on 4 February 1915, when Germany declared that the international waters around the coasts of Great Britain and Ireland would henceforth become a war zone. All shipping sailing under the British flag would be sunk on sight, and the Germans said they could not guarantee the safety of ships from neutral countries because of the difficulty of identifying flags at a distance or in fog. They also made much of a totally false accusation that the British were running up neutral flags when the occasion demanded.

On 7 May the threat became a reality. *U20*, under Lieutenant-Commander Walther Schweiger, was – according to the German version of events – heading home at the end of a week-long patrol off the south coast of Ireland, having sunk a miserable two steamers and one sailing boat. Schweiger was travelling west from Waterford at 1.20 p.m. when he saw a very large passenger liner steaming into view, sailing eastwards. The liner came closer and closer, until the jubilant Schweiger could hardly contain himself: she was an unmissable target, and at 2.09 Schweiger gave the order: Fire.

From a range of less than 730 metres, there was no chance of avoidance, no chance of a miss, no chance of escape for hundreds of innocent souls – men, women and children – on board. The torpedo struck amidships. Within 20 minutes the great liner lurched beneath the waves in a great mass of white foam. Schweiger had sunk the pride of Cunard, the *Lusitania*, a magnificent liner of 31,500 tonnes, and in doing so 1,198 passengers perished. Around the world, the reaction was one of stunned disbelief, but not in Germany. Naval chief Admiral von Tirpitz received hundreds of telegrams congratulating him. An article in an influential German newspaper summed up the 'national pride' with the comment that 'the news will be received by the German people with unanimous satisfaction since it proves to England and the whole of the world that Germany is quite in earnest in regard to her submarine warfare'.

Despite the fact that 124 Americans were among the passengers who died, near 'riotous scenes' were reported in New York's German clubs and restaurants, which declared a celebration for 'Der Tag'. Elsewhere, of course, the monstrous crime was universally condemned, and few believed that it was a coincidence that Schweiger just happened upon the *Lusitania* but, more likely, had been lying in wait. That view was reinforced when it became known that the German ambassador to the United States had published a warning to those intending to embark on the *Lusitania* days before she sailed.

The deadlocked war of attrition in the trenches and Germany's home-front crisis of shortages of food and supplies through the blockade being waged by the British fleet turned the Germans towards a merciless campaign on the high seas in which submarines were to spearhead a blockade of the British Isles. In spite of the international protests in the wake of the *Lusitania*, Germany began to focus U-boat attention increasingly on unarmed merchant shipping in addition, of course, to any British fleet ships they might come upon. In spite of the assurances given to America, in August 1915 *U24* torpedoed and sank the small White Star liner *Arabic* and in early 1916 the French steamer *Sussex*, with the loss of American lives.

The Battle of Jutland, waged on 31 May and 1 June 1916 between the British Grand Fleet and the German High Seas Fleet, resolved nothing. British losses in both ships and human lives were greater than Germany's. Even so, her capital ships returned to home ports and did not venture to give battle again during the war. Nevertheless, during the remainder of the war, German cruisers managed to run the blockade that the British had established from the outset and, with large numbers of new U-boats coming off the production lines, naval commanders again resorted to unrestricted submarine warfare, convinced that they could starve the British into submission.

The attacks of German submarines on British shipping in the North Sea and the Atlantic brought staggering losses which the British navy seemed powerless to halt. In the autumn of 1916, British and Allied shipping sunk by the Germans reached 300,000 tonnes a month, double the totals of the summer. Even this figure was minuscule in comparison with the figures soon being racked up. By March 1917 losses passed half a million tonnes and in April an incredible 850,000 tonnes, amounting to 350 ships lost in that month alone. It became clear, after the war, that German naval command thought it had done enough to bring Britain to her knees. Certainly, the desperation of the Allies over these casualties can be seen from the figures released by the Admiralty at the end of the war. The total tonnage of Allied ships sunk by German submarines, surface craft and mines was nearly 13 million tonnes, but more than 40 per cent of that total occurred in a single year, 1917.

Britain, however, was not done for. At last the Admiralty began to shake itself out of the downward spiral. Talk of Britain not being able to continue the fight was banished. The pages of British submariners' and naval logs are filled with their own heroic encounters at this stage of the war, but it is clear that, although dozens of new boats were on order, the Germans were still outpacing the Allies in their production of U-boats. Britain was building them flat out and, with America's entry into the war, new submarines became available. The system of convoying fleets of merchant ships was introduced, with warships on guard, seaplanes for spotting submarines and depth bombs or charges for destroying them. In the late summer, the tide was turning.

By the beginning of 1918 the Allies began to regain the momentum, and a daring operation being planned in the spring of that year finally helped curtail the U-boat campaign. Many of the U-boats that caused so much damage in the Atlantic were based at Bruges, in Belgium. Their safe haven was easily and strongly defended, allowing them to come and go with comparative ease. Their hideaway was 8 miles from the open sea and accessed through two canals, one via Ostend and the other Zeebrugge. A joint operation was planned utilising air, land and sea units to block the canals and force the U-boats to use the more dangerous northerly route where the British could get at them.

It was planned to sail old ships to the canal entrances and sink them, a task that the Royal Navy undertook with relish. A crucial side element to the main operation was handed to the 6th Submarine Flotilla. It entailed blowing up a viaduct connecting the Zeebrugge mole to the mainland to stop troop reinforcements being brought to the scene at the time of the raid. Two older-type submarines were nominated for duty, *C1* and *C3*. Six tonnes of explosives were packed into the bows, and it was planned to ram the submarines under the viaduct using an automatic pilot. In theory, the crew would make a quick getaway in a motor skiff a mile from the target, and they would hopefully be well clear when the time-fuse blew the whole lot to kingdom come. Only unmarried volunteers were accepted, and the crew was stripped to a bare minimum of two officers and four ratings.

Lieutenant Aubrey Newbold was already captain of *C1*, while Lieutenant Richard Sandford, who had just reached his twenty-sixth birthday, took command of *C3*. The task force moved out after dark on 22 April, with the two submarines towed by destroyers towards a rendezvous point 5 miles from the viaduct. *C1* never made it, having been delayed en route, and Sandford took *C3* into attack alone, discarding the use of the autopilot to guarantee success. As Sandford neared the viaduct, German gun placements were firing all around, and star shells bursting directly overhead brought fake daylight for the gunners to take a range and fire. Sandford held a steady course and made it to the target, ramming the bow of the submarine into the side of the masonry. Overhead, there were howls of laughter as German troops mistakenly believed a British submarine had become stuck. Even so, as Sandford led his five crew members out after setting the time-fuse, the Germans opened fire. Their little motor skiff was badly shot up and the engine was useless. So they had to row. As they pushed off, two of them were hit, then Sandford himself took two bullets. Four of the six were wounded, but they managed to keep rowing until they were rescued by a picket boat, driven by Sandford's brother, from their destroyer. As they clambered aboard, the satisfying sound of a terrific explosion from the place they had just left confirmed that the job was done – and, indeed, the viaduct was missing a very large chunk in the middle of the run.

All who took part in the operation received medals, and Sandford was among eight officers involved who were awarded Victoria Crosses. His citation read:

> He eagerly undertook this hazardous enterprise, although well aware (as were all his crew) that if the means of rescue failed and he or any of his crew were in the water at the moment of the explosion, they could be killed outright by the force of such explosion. Yet Lieutenant Sandford disdained to use the gyro steering, which would have enabled him and his crew to abandon the submarine at a safe distance, and preferred to make sure, as far as humanly possible, of the accomplishment of his duty.

There were many heroes that night, but in Sandford's case the story ended in ironic tragedy. He died four months later in a Yorkshire hospital having contracted typhoid fever.

CHAPTER FOUR

The Unlucky K-Boats: An Appalling Toll

The end of the First World War saw Britain with more submarines than she now wanted. The Royal Navy's own stock of boats in service, under repair or awaiting commissioning when the war ended, was in excess of 200 craft, including the surviving but obsolete A-, B- and C-classes. Then, under the terms of the armistice that ended the war, all ships in Germany's possession would be surrendered, and the size of any future German navy kept within strict limits and monitored. The Treaty of Versailles under which these stipulations were made also called for Germany to be barred from keeping, buying or building any new submarines.

The Germans were forced to surrender to the Allies the bulk of their ships, comprising 10 battleships, 17 cruisers, 50 torpedo boats and 176 submarines. Most of the fleet, with the exception of the submarines, was interned at Scapa Flow in November 1918, with German officers and crews still aboard. In reprisal for what they considered to be ridiculously harsh surrender terms, the crews began scuttling their own ships on 21 June 1919. All operational U-boats were delivered into the hands of the Royal Navy, temporarily giving the British the largest submarine fleet in the world. The British naval architects and scientists spent months poring over the German craft to purloin any technology or ideas that had not yet occurred to themselves. Most of the U-boats would in due course be scrapped, along with dozens of Britain's own stock of submarines. Around 200 damaged or unfinished U-boats were also destroyed where they lay in the German shipyards. It seemed an appalling waste, but in reality it was chicken feed when set against the cost of the war itself to all the belligerents, amounting in total to about $186 billion. Casualties in the land forces amounted to more than 37 million, with almost 10 million deaths among the civilian populations caused indirectly by the war. Famously talked of as the war to end all wars, which would bring permanent world peace, quite the reverse would result. The treaty provided the root cause of an even greater conflict – that, and a maniac called Adolph Hitler.

From the British standpoint, the only salvation was that the nation had not fallen to defeat at sea at the hands of the U-boat commanders, although it had been a very closely run thing. Not unnaturally, perhaps, the British made it a priority task to dispose of the German submarine fleet in double-quick time, and for the most part that would eventually mean a journey straight to the bottom. In the corridors of power, thoughts were already turning to the future. Having come through the devastating experience of having so much of their fleet and the nation's merchant ships wiped out, the British naval chiefs went through a heart-searching reappraisal of the needs of the Royal Navy and came to conclusions that set the clock back 20 years. In attending a Washington conference of the five naval powers

– the others being France, the United States, Italy and Japan – in 1921, the British representatives shocked everyone by proposing a total worldwide ban on submarines.

Their case was to be presented in an argument strung around the morality of underwater warfare and the threats that it posed to all seafaring nations. The proposal received no support from the other four nations and, in any event, it was virtually unenforceable on an international basis, so the status quo remained. Meanwhile, the British government embarked on a major culling programme, scrapping and selling literally dozens of submarines, many of which had seen little service and some not even commissioned. Of the early boats, 10 out of 13 As, 9 of 11 Bs, 27 of 38 Cs and 3 of the 9 Ds remained in service. All were scrapped. The others still in service in 1920 were:

E-class These boats had seen terrific service during the war years but were all destined for the knacker's yard. Twenty-seven had been sunk in enemy action, mined, scuttled or lost for reasons unknown. The remaining 30 were all scrapped by 1924.

F-class Only three were built; all were used for training and then scrapped.

G-class Designed initially as an overseas patrol boat, with powerful engines and long endurance submerged, the G-class also had the distinction of being the first to carry a 21-inch torpedo as well as two 18-inch tubes on both bow and beam. Fourteen were built, and four were lost during the war, including *G7*, the last submarine lost to enemy action, sunk in the North Sea on 1 November 1918. The remaining ten were to be sold or scrapped.

H-class Forty-three were built between 1914 and 1918; this was another workhorse of the period. Eight were lost, eighteen were scrapped or sold in the 1920s and the remainder were kept in service for several years hence, some still active in the Second World War.

J-class Seven launched, one lost and the remainder transferred to Australia in 1919.

L-class Another major production schedule produced this class from midway through the war. The design was based on an elongated E-class; 34 were ordered, although only 27 were commissioned. They were of variable designs to provide boats for basic torpedo armament, as minelayers and later all carried a 4-inch gun mounted on the superstructure; three were lost (two accidentally) during the war and another sank with all forty hands in 1924. The rest remained in service until the 1930s, when most were sold, although a handful were still in service at the beginning of the Second World War.

R-class Ten were launched in 1918, but few were commissioned before the war's end. They were notable for their very attractive streamlined hull design, which produced a fast underwater speed capability. They were designed specifically as attack boats and had a huge firepower of six 18-inch torpedo tubes. Since most of them were launched when the need for attack boats had virtually passed, they saw little in the way of active service and were all scrapped in 1923. Two more, known as the second R-class, with various amendments, were built in 1930.

In addition, there were other experimental boats, including the V-class, which was noted for her increased hull strength achieved by external framing between the inner and outer hulls, thus allowing the submarine to dive to 45 metres, as opposed to the norm of 30 metres. Four were built and were taken out of service in 1919. In pursuit of the ultimate diving machine, the *N1*, also known as *Nautilus*, was built over a four-year period at Vickers, went through various changes of mind and cost £203,850. She was, at 79 metres in length, twice the size of any existing submarine and designed to have a diving depth of 60 metres. The boat was regarded as a failure and never saw service of any description other than for training purposes and as a depot ship.

Omitted from the above list is the K-class, which went into production at the start of 1916 and of which twenty-one were built, although two were converted and appeared in the later M-class collection. The K-boat was experimental in a number of ways and requires a more detailed explanation, although not just because of her innovative features. The boat was distinctly unlucky, and a succession of disasters that ensued arose without any help whatsoever from the enemy.

The K-class was a rushed project in both design and build. Naval intelligence reported that Germany was in the process of launching a U-boat that was huge in size and would travel at more than 20 knots on the surface. The Admiralty said they had to have something similar to protect the Grand Fleet. The words used were 'bigger, better and immediately'. Unfortunately, there was nothing at all on the stocks that could produce such a swift boat of any size. The diesel engines then in use were only just good enough for existing, smaller classes and would never propel a boat of the proportions envisaged at any speed. There was an air of panic as Sir Eustace Tennyson d'Eyncourt, RN Director of Construction, took the bold decision to use steam engines, but in truth there was no other power package that would suit. Sceptics would point out that steam power and submarines had never yet been merged successfully, but the Director of Construction had little option.

Out of this emergency came the K-class, a giant of a boat then almost three times larger than any submarine in the British fleet. It was 103 metres in length, with a surface displacement of 1,850 tonnes and 2,450 submerged. She carried a crew of 55 and was driven by a pair of massive steam turbines powered by oil-fired boilers which could produce a speed of 23 knots on the surface and 10 knots dived from 4 electric motors. The K, costing an astronomical £310,000 apiece (compared with £130,000 for a destroyer), was specifically designed to operate with the fleet and looked in appearance more like a destroyer than a submarine. There were eight 18-inch torpedo tubes on the bow and beam.

Steam power had a number of drawbacks. The boilers had to be shut down on the command of 'Dive!' The funnels were then retracted into their housings and covered by watertight shutters. Four mushroom-shaped ventilators that took heat from the boiler room were also retracted and sealed. The whole process of shutting down the boilers, starting the electric motors and sealing the half-dozen or so places where funnels and ventilators had been could take up to five minutes, as opposed to the thirty seconds a conventional submarine needed to perform the dive routine. Thus, there were a number of very evident flaws to the K-class, but she met the two key criteria of being large and fast.

It was perhaps a prophetic omen that the first of the class to be accepted into service almost changed the course of history in a serious way. The future King George VI, then a youthful naval officer in the Grand Fleet, was having a personal demonstration run in the vessel and was at the side of her captain, Commander Ernest Leir, as he spoke in fulsome terms about the submarine's capacity, speed and diving ability. With that, *K3* went into an uncontrolled dive, without being asked to do so, and ended up bow down on the muddy bottom in 40 metres of water off Portsmouth. However, since the boat itself was over 100 metres long, the shiny new bronze propellers were shimmering in the sunlight above the water. It took 20 minutes of delicate manoeuvres before Commander Leir managed to extricate his boat from the mud and return the future king to safety.

K3 continued to play up, and a few months later, while on patrol in the North Sea, again buried her nose during an encounter with unexpectedly heavy seas. Water swept down the funnel and put out the boiler fires, leaving Leir without power to control her. He limped home on the small auxiliary diesel engine with the boiler room flooded. Among other incidents in those early days, sister craft *K2* was rocked by an explosion in the engine room just after she had submerged. Her skipper, Lieutenant-Commander Noel Laurence, escaped what could have been a far more serious incident by bringing her quickly back to the surface as the crew was ordered to firefighting stations, only to discover that fire-extinguishers had inadvertently not been fitted. They had to collect water in iron buckets to put out the fire, and luckily there were no serious injuries.

K6 also hit problems during her diving trials. Having submerged during tests at Devonport, the boat simply refused to return to the surface after the ballast tanks had been blown. The fifty men on board, including dockyard workers, were trapped for two hours before the trouble was traced to a fault in the compressed-air system. Next, *K4* ran aground at Walney Island during surface trials, and then *K11* suffered generator failure when she, too, shipped water through the funnel intakes during trials on heavy seas. By now, some dockyard workers were refusing to go down in the K-boats until rigorous checks had been carried out. Even this did not halt the succession of incidents, and the next was to be fatal. On 29 January 1917 *K13* was to prove its number was unlucky for some.

Her skipper, Commander Godfrey Herbert, was in the process of final acceptance procedures, and 10 days earlier he had notched up 23.5 knots over a measured mile to go into the naval history books as the world's fastest submarine. On the morning of the dive trials, he set off from base on the Clyde heading eventually for the calmer and less busy waters of Gare Loch. He had a full crew of 53 and an unusually large number of civilian passengers – 14 managers and employees of the shipbuilders, Fairfields, along with 11 civilians and Admiralty personnel and Commander Francis Goodhart, captain of the newly commissioned *K14*, which was soon to go through a similar trials process. In all, there were 82 people on board as the submarine made her way to Gare Loch. There were two mishaps en route. First, *K13* was caught in traffic and ran aground. As Herbert manoeuvred the boat back, she swivelled completely so that he had to travel backwards until he reached a suitable place to point her in the right direction. Later on, a short test dive was carried out and ominously the boiler room sprang a leak. It was not considered serious enough to halt the trials, and they carried on with the journey.

They stopped for lunch at 1.15, for which the VIPs adjourned to the accompanying small ship *Corner*, and two hours later *K13* continued on her way towards Gare Loch, minus two civilians who must have had some sort of premonition, because they said they did not wish to

continue. Eventually, *K13* reached Gare Loch and
Commander Herbert prepared for the first dive with a
check of instruments. One was said to be 'flickering',
but Engineer-Lieutenant Arthur Lane reckoned it was
nothing more serious than a bad connection and pressed
on. The importance of this instrument was perhaps under-
rated, because it showed whether the boiler room ventilators were completely closed before the dive commenced,
and that may well have had a bearing on what happened
next.

Chief Petty Officer Oscar Moth received the order to trim
her for 6 metres, a fairly shallow dive but any depth in a
submarine is dangerous if something goes wrong. And something seriously wrong was about to bring fear and tragedy to
all those on board. Barely had the boat reached the depth
when Lane buzzed the captain and told him through the
voice-pipe: 'The boiler room is flooding, sir. Surface. Surface.' Herbert gave orders to blow Nos. 2 and 3 tanks to take
her up. The VIPs looked on with alarm as the crew dashed
into action and compressed air was blown into the for'ard
ballast tanks. Herbert asked for a report and Coxswain
Moth, watching the depth gauges, gave the first indication of
serious trouble: 'Not responding, sir.' Seconds later, he
reported: 'Out of control, sinking fast.'

Herbert snapped out his instructions to close all watertight
doors, drop for'ard keel and blow all tanks, but all his efforts
were to no avail. *K13* was going down, and there was nothing
he could do to stop her. She dropped with a bump. As the
captain picked up the voice-pipe to give the order to stop
engines, water spurted out, which meant the engine room
must have been totally flooded. Then flames erupted on the
control switchboard, which the men beat out with their bare
hands. Electrical circuits started to blow, and choking fumes

and smoke began to fill the compartment. Herbert was already wondering how much of the boat was flooded and how many crew he had already lost when a knocking was heard on the rear bulkhead of the control room. The captain ordered the watertight doors to be opened with caution, and two seriously traumatised civilians fell through the doorway and informed him that all compartments beyond the torpedo room amidships were flooded. At least 30 men were already feared drowned. Herbert made a last desperate attempt to reach Lane on the telephone system but the line was dead. The question now was how long would it be before the rest of the boat was flooded? He knew very well that at 17 metres the pressure of the sea was 25lbs per square inch, and the bulkheads were designed to withstand only 15lbs per square inch.

Herbert and his officers racked their brains for a solution. The boat was immovable, the flooding was becoming more serious by the second and there was no means of contacting the surface. Hopes of signalling two other submarines known to be in the loch that day were also shattered when the underwater transmitting device was found to be inoperable because of fire damage. In short, Herbert concluded, there were only two options – that someone on the surface would realise they were in trouble and launch a rescue mission or those still alive faced a slow and torturous death.

He ordered an immediate head-count of survivors. The news was already grim: 31 of the 80 on board were dead. Professor Percy Hillhouse, Fairfields' senior naval architect, was called on to make some calculations: how long would the air last? His estimate was equally grim. He reckoned that the air would not sustain human life for more than eight hours, and it was possible that the weakest among them may begin dying even before that. Everyone on board was ordered to sit quietly and to avoid unnecessary movement to conserve oxygen. There was no panic; just a calm resignation of their plight.

Almost an hour had passed before the first signs of concern began to emerge on the surface. One of the submarines also in the loch had picked up a noise and had seen air bubbles surfacing. The captain signalled the senior naval officer, Clyde, to report a possible accident, and called for immediate investigation. However, in spite of the K-boats' accident-prone reputation, their response was, to say the least, tardy. It was six hours before a rescue mission was mounted.

The gunboat *Gossamer* and salvage vessels *Tay* and *Thrush* were dispatched to the scene. Meanwhile, Lieutenant Ken Michell, captain of *B10*, who had reported the possibility of trouble, had gone to the spot where he estimated *K13* had dived. After a good deal of searching, he discovered telltale patches of oil and a stream of air bubbles rising continuously from the depths. He remained at the spot and launched a dinghy for his men to keep watch until the rescue boats arrived. Darkness was already beginning to close in, and the incoming mission would have had great difficulty in locating *K13*'s position.

Below them in the stricken vessel, it seemed a certainty that death would overtake any possible rescue attempts as the time ticked perilously towards the deadline calculated by Professor Hillhouse. Apart from the increasing foulness of the air, no drinkable water was left either, the tanks having been contaminated by the flooding. It was also freezing cold, now that the power had gone off. A little food was available, but few wanted it, troubled as they were by the thought of impending demise. Sheets of paper were distributed for those who wanted to write letters to their families. Some even wrote their wills.

On the surface, the rescue mission, such as it was, made slow progress towards the spot where *K13* lay, and even when they eventually arrived there would be no well-equipped team of trained rescuers ready to swing into operation. No such organisation existed within the Royal Navy, in spite of 16 years of experience and many boards of inquiry resulting from past submarine disasters. It still came down to the ingenuity of the men who answered the call, utilising whatever equipment they happened to have with them at the time. It was a hit-and-miss affair in every sense, amply demonstrated by the fact that when *Gossamer* finally reached the spot where *K13* lay well after midnight, it was discovered that although they had a diving suit on board, not a man in the crew had been trained to use it. When finally a man was found who could go down, he was pulled back almost immediately because the suit was so old that it let in water and he almost drowned. *Thrush* arrived half an hour later and that ship had neither a diver nor a suit on board.

Two hours passed before a diver was located and made his descent into the murky, freezing waters of the loch. He found the submarine almost immediately and tapped out a message on the hull to announce his arrival. The reply from inside the submarine was barely audible, but seemed to say: 'All well before engine room bulkhead.' This, relayed back to the surface, gave a somewhat false impression of conditions. Hillhouse's deadline for survival was already passed, but for those working on top there seemed no immediate cause for concern. Herbert, realising that the poisonous air would very soon begin claiming lives, was concerned that the salvage people would attempt to raise the boat first, rather than get assistance to those on board. He reckoned that by then they would simply be raising a coffin containing 80 bodies and said as much in a private discussion in his cabin with Commander Goodhart.

Between them, the two experienced commanders, who knew the dangers better than anyone on the surface, worked out a plan. They somehow had to get word to the rescuers and suggest ways of ensuring immediate assistance, and impress on them the absolute urgency of the situation. They agreed that if they put a man into the conning tower, and then opened the hatch, there was just a chance that he could escape and get to the surface. It was a highly dangerous operation, but possibly the only chance for the survival of those on board. Goodhart himself insisted he should make the escape bid since it was the captain who traditionally remained with his crew. Herbert, however, would assist in launching him on his way.

In fact, when it came to the point of releasing Goodhart, both men were sucked out of the conning tower. Goodhart never made it. He hit his head, was knocked unconscious and drowned. Ironically, it was Herbert himself who was swept to the surface . . . alive. He was spotted immediately and picked up, and although weak and close to drowning he wasted no time in helping to direct the rescue. He frantically tried to hurry the operation along, but as the hours passed his despair over the fate of his men was evident. Attempt after attempt failed to get the necessary air hoses connected; when they finally did make a connection, the pipes were found to be frozen. From inside the submarine, the frantic message was tapped out for the divers: 'Give us air . . . give us air.'

The pipes were finally cleared 35 hours after *K13* had gone down, and Herbert was convinced that few could have survived. However, the vital air supplies were now operating and, next, a large hose was taken down through which water and food was fed. Using the air supply hose, the forward main ballast tanks were blown again, raising the bows of the boat closer to the surface. Heavy-duty wire ropes were looped under the bows to hold the boat in position, and a hole was cut through both hulls with oxyacetylene equipment. When the breakthrough came, the remaining 47 on board were brought out – 57 hours after the boat sank and miraculously all alive. Soon afterwards, the wires holding the boat in position came adrift and she crashed to the bottom again. *K13* was raised six weeks later. A later court of inquiry heard that an inspection revealed that the ventilator doors were open and the instruments showed it. Engineer-Lieutenant Arthur Lane was blamed. He and one of his men, John Steel, had tried to escape through the engine room hatch as the boat was sinking but had drowned. Lane's body was found two months later. Steel's was never recovered. The boat was salvaged and was later re-commissioned as *K22*.

Not by any means was that the end of the troubles that were to befall the K-class boats, and the unlucky *K13*, in her new guise as *K22*, would once again be badly damaged during chaotic scenes in one of the most horrific accidents in naval history. On 1 February 1918 two submarine flotillas, the 12th and 13th, made up entirely of K-class boats, nine in all, were operating as originally intended with the fleet. They were assigned to what was known as Operation EC1, a huge exercise off May Island in the Firth of Forth involving the 5th Battle Squadron and a force from Scapa Flow. The Battle Squadron consisted of 5 battle cruisers, 3 battleships, 14 light cruisers, several flotillas of destroyers and the 2 K-boat flotillas. The 12th Flotilla consisted of *K3*, *K4*, *K6* and *K7* and was led by Captain Charles Little in the cruiser *Fearless*. The 13th Flotilla was made up of *K11*, *K12*, *K14*, *K17* and

K22 and was led by Captain Ernest Leir in the destroyer *Ithuriel*. They all sailed from Rosyth with darkness closing in.

As they approached the estuary, the 13th Flotilla was sailing in line when a group of minesweepers crossed over their path ahead of them, and two of the boats took immediate avoiding action. *K11* and *K17* both went to port and only just missed a collision; *K14* swung around in a wide arc and was rammed by *K22* (the salvaged *K13*). Both submarines were damaged, and as she battled to stay afloat with flooding problems *K22* was hit squarely by the destroyer *Inflexible*. Her starboard ballast tank was ripped apart and thus *K22* was foundering and needed to be taken under tow.

Leir in *Ithuriel* became aware of the mishap and led the remains of his flotilla back towards the scene to launch a rescue operation. He was now steaming in the opposite direction to the oncoming fleet, travelling in excess of 21 knots, and an even worse situation developed. The battle cruiser *Australia* missed *K12* by inches, but *Fearless* could not avoid ramming *K17*. The submarine began sinking instantly and had vanished within seven minutes.

Miraculously, all 57 crew managed to escape – at least, they thought they had. They were splashing about in the water waiting to be rescued. Tragically, however, three destroyers steaming towards them were unaware of their presence and ran over them. Only nine survived, one of whom died later. Worse was to come. In the chaotic state of the fleet, ships and submarines alike were desperately attempting to regain their stations, and there were several near misses and much scraping of metal before the final tragedy of this appalling mess: *K6* rammed *K4*, which was virtually cut in two. *K4* sank instantly, and her entire crew of 55 went down with her. None survived.

Naturally, then, the 'K' prefix became universally known in the service as standing for 'killer'. The title was well deserved and continued to attract these unfortunate and tragic incidents long after the war. The converted K-class boats were re-designated M-class and were given revolutionary features that were to make them more like submersible battleships. They were to be armed with a 60-tonne 12-inch gun, which had a much greater range than any torpedo but could be fired only from a depth of 6 metres, hardly a concealed position, and reloading had to be carried out on the surface. Although the plan to convert four K-boats, *18*, *19*, *20* and *21*, into the M-class range was approved in 1916, none was ready in time for war service and only three were complete. They became *M1*, *M2* and *M3* but were immediately rendered obsolete by the Washington Disarmament Treaty, which limited the size of submarine-mounted guns to 8.5 inches. Two were converted to minelayers and the third became the first-ever submersible aircraft carrier.

But the change of prefix did not rid the boats of the jinx of the K-class. While submerged, *M1* sank after a collision with a Swedish coaster, SS *Vidar*, off Start Point on 12 November 1925 with the loss of her crew of 68. The wreck was found in 1999 by a sport diver 35 miles southeast of Plymouth. *M2*, meanwhile, had a hangar fitted with a gantry to lift a light seaplane aboard (see photograph). She went down mysteriously just 2½ miles off Portland on 26 January 1932. She was seen to nose-dive at an angle of about 45 degrees by a passing cargo steamer whose captain did not know anything about submarines and did not realise the significance of such a dive. Only when newspapers carried the reports of '*M2* Missing' did he come forward, but by then the 67 crew and two RAF airmen had already perished. Before long, the submariners who knew of the

K-class story were pointing out that *M2* was commissioned exactly 13 years earlier.

Numerous attempts to raise and salvage the boat were made by the navy, but they finally had to abandon her to the sea. Two theories for her demise were considered: that the plane hangar developed a leak and caused severe flooding or that, when the submarine nose-dived, acid escaped from the batteries and the crew were gassed. Once more, public appeals were launched to assist the young families of the men who died. In September 1970 *M2* claimed her seventieth victim when a 30-year-old skin-diver, Frank Thorne, from Taunton, Somerset, was diving around the wreck and did not return. It is believed he became trapped in the aircraft hangar.

Only *M3* saved the reputation of the class, operating as a minelayer prior to being scrapped in 1932. She was the only one of the K- and M-boats that escaped incident in the period from first launch in 1916 to final withdrawal from service in 1932. Sixteen were involved in major accidents, and eight finished up on the bottom of the sea, giant coffins for the dozens of crew members who lost their lives in this awkward monstrosity. In those 16 years of relatively undemanding operations, over 300 men lost their lives in K-class or converted K-class boats – not one of them to enemy action.

Slightly more successful in terms of Britain's apparent determination from 1915 to build the world's largest submarine was the *X1*. She emerged from those discussions midway through the war about designing bigger and better boats than Germany possessed. Whether Britain had really succeeded in doing that was debatable, but what it did achieve – eventually – was the creation of a cruiser submarine of 3,600 tonnes submerged. It was in no uncertain terms a true submersible cruiser, which could travel at 18.5 knots on the surface, was 110 metres in length, and carried four 5.2-inch guns in twin turrets. She was completed in 1925 and successfully passed a rigorous trials procedure. The trouble was, now, that since the idea was conceived in 1915, world power play had changed. There was no role for her in the British fleet, and the major danger was that she might be copied by potentially hostile nations. And so the world's greatest living submarine had a troubled life spent mostly in dockyards; she never made a significant journey and the colossus was finally scrapped in 1937.

For most submariners, the demise of such massive boats was no bad thing. In the wake of the K-boat disasters, other peacetime tragedies all too frequently punctuated the first quarter-century of the submarine service. For many years, life beneath the waves provided no attraction for either officers or ratings, who had joined the navy to sail the seas – not under them. For a while forced recruitment became necessary as fears about sheer reduction of life expectancy for submariners became a quite vocal issue. The British experience, more so than that of any other nation apart from Germany, was sufficient to put the fear of God into a good number of ratings in both surface and underwater vessels. There had been so many casualties lost in boats from which there was often no hope of escape or survival. Captain Ronald Mills, who went into the navy from Dartmouth at the age of 17, found himself in submarines in the early 1920s, and, like so many others, it had been a case of you, you and you, two paces forward:

I had actually put in to specialise in naval navigation, but there was a bit of a drive then for getting on to submarines and I was conscripted. That was the long and short of it. I had no choice in the matter. I wasn't very pleased rather naturally, but after I had been in for my first three years I appreciated the extra pay that I was getting and I was thinking of getting married and one thing and another and I thought I had better stay on. So I did – I stayed on another 20 years.

Throughout the inter-war years Britain continued to press for the abolition of the submarine or, at the very least, restrictions on the numbers built. But that did not stop the Admiralty from commissioning new designs and some fairly revolutionary work in research and development of new technology. In spite of the Admiralty's initial reluctance over the continued deployment of submariners, Britain soon led the world, technically if not in numbers. Admiralty funding for new safety and detection methods also went ahead in leaps and bounds.

One of the most outstanding discoveries was a device known as ASDIC, named after the initials of the committee that sponsored the work. The machine was devised for locating submerged submarines and was far more sophisticated than the existing listening device, the hydrophone. It would principally be fitted at the bottom of a destroyer and, moving slowly through a wide arc, the ASDIC could transmit and receive signals. When the sound waves struck a submarine, they bounced back, and the echoing 'ping' – famously heard on so many films about submarines – was picked up by the receiver. The elapsed time between sending out the signal and hearing the answering 'ping' told the ASDIC operator how far away the submarine was. The destroyer could then accurately move in for a depth-charge attack. However, ASDIC, the forerunner of sonar, was put to good use by submariners against surface targets and eventually took over from the hydrophone, which was unable to measure with any accuracy the speed, course or distance of an enemy vessel.

In the meantime, the latest designs of faster boats more closely related to the hunter-killer theory of submarine warfare came on stream in succession from the late 1920s to the end of the Second World War. The O- (the first class of submarines to be given names rather than numbers), P-, S- and T-classes contained modifications and experimental techniques which the naval architects were keen to establish. Extensive trials as each new model progressed focused increasingly on speed, range, reliability of engines, extended diving depth and increased firepower. O- and P-boats, which came into being from 1929 to 1932, were used for a new vista, opening up for submariners a tour of duty on the China station, based at Hong Kong, from where extensive patrols were carried out around the Far East.

Next on the production line came the S-boats, built between 1931 and 1943. These were initially intended for use in Northern European and Mediterranean waters but were eventually used almost entirely in the Far East, based on the Hong Kong station. They were moderately large boats, ranging in size between 1,300 and 1,700 tonnes surface displacement. They set new standards in manoeuvrability and had a very fast diving speed, although early models were prone to some teething problems, including leaks. They also provided for a large number of torpedoes carried, allowing a large salvo to be fired at a particularly important target. The second S-group, completed between 1933 and 1938, included boats with a welded hull, which increased diving depths to 105 metres, 15 metres deeper than riveted-hull boats; this proved a godsend when depth charges came into use in the Second World War.

By the turn of the 1930s, the new developments and smart new boats, few though they were, became something of a honeypot attraction for adventurers and thrill-seekers – young men who liked a challenge, were slightly rebellious against the heavy hand of authority and who sought perhaps a more relaxed area of operations than that imposed in the famously strict discipline of the Royal Navy. Many would write home about the joys of service in the Far East, a lifestyle that was such a contrast to the austerity of the 1920s and the Depression in the early 1930s. Commander Philip Francis recalls his early service in what was to become a long career, predominantly in submarines:

I went into the navy because my father thought it was a good thing. He worked in the City of London, and he realised that perhaps it was better to get away from London and in those days we did what we were told to do. I went to Dartmouth in 1922 when I was 13, shortly after the move from Osborne. I always remember arriving at Dartmouth. We were marched up to the front of Dartmouth and we were shown what was written on the front of the college and it is quoting Samuel Pepys: 'It is upon the navy under the good providence of God that the whole wealth and prosperity of this country largely depends.' Well, that was certainly the case then.

I eventually became a submariner partly because you got five bob a day extra. You also got more responsibility when you were young. You could be captain of a submarine at the age of 23 or something like that, which we rather fancied, and a lot of my friends went into submarines and I rather think that had something to do with it. I had a great friend who was my brother-in-law and we both discussed it. We did our courses and everything together. We were based at HMS *Dolphin* [the shore base at Gosport]. I was a junior officer and then went out to China to join *Otus*. There were 12 submarines out there, O-, P- and R-boats, and I was torpedo officer. We were based in Hong Kong and in the summer, when it got too hot, we went way up in the north. That was in the days when the country was run by the warlords. They didn't have any organised government, and each warlord ran his little area in his own way – he demanded his dues from the locals and as long as they paid him he didn't want to fight. Our job during this time was very much anti-pirate operations. The pirates were quite active. They used to attack the coastal shipping, and on one occasion David Leuth, who eventually became First Sea Lord, was captured by the pirates and we had to pay vast compensation to get him back.

We lived on depot ships, and Hong Kong was wonderful during those days. I was much better off as a sub-lieutenant in Hong Kong that I was really for the rest of my life. Everything was very cheap. I had a polo pony; I had a speedboat; a Chinese servant. I was a jockey, raced in Hong Kong a lot, and the social life was pretty hectic. Quite enough girls. We used to go duck shooting and snipe shooting and there were lots of games you could play. I did two spells on the China station and then I sailed back to England from Hong Kong and that took a year, 1933–4.

We had decided to have this boat built and sail it back to England. Five of us, all submariners, put down £500 each. We had been there for three years and were

The classic successful attack seen through the periscope of a conventional British submarine of the type used throughout the Second World War and beyond. It was the kind of warfare that a senior Naval figure earlier in the century described as 'underhand, underwater and damned un-English'.

One of the earliest British-built submersibles, *Resurgam*, designed and built by a young man of the cloth, the Reverend George Garrett. It sank off North Wales on its way to trials in December 1879.

Holland 1, the first Royal Navy submarine, designed in America by John Holland but built at Barrow-in-Furness in 1901 at a cost of £35,000. Five of its class were built; they were primitive vessels with an equally primitive periscope.

Inventor John Holland in one of his early submarines.

The way they were... the crew of submarine *E14* whose commander, Lieutenant Commander Geoffrey White was posthumously awarded the Victoria Cross in January, 1918.

Another hero of the First World War was Lieutenant Commander Martin Nasmith, commander of *E11*, who was also awarded the Victoria Cross.

A great welcome home to Britain for the crew of *E11* whose daring exploits along the Dardanelles were followed avidly by an enthralled British public, prior to what became the disaster of Gallipoli.

During the First World War bigger and more powerful submarines were built to match the German U-boats. Among them was the M class, one of which, *M2* (above and below), was converted into a submersible aircraft carrier. The wings folded back to allow the plane to be pushed into a hangar. *M1* (bottom) meanwhile was mounted with a massive 12-inch gun. Both were lost with all hands.

Thetis, a proud new member of the T class, seen (left) being launched, fell victim to tragedy. She sank with 103 men on board, including crew and local VIPs, during trials. Incredibly, her stern was raised (below) and rescue vessels managed to put men on the hull before she sank again, with great loss of life. Bottom, the submarine was beached and later reappeared under a new name, *Thunderbolt*.

X1, the largest conventional submarine ever built by the Royal Navy, 110 metres in length, carrying four 5.2-inch guns in twin turrets, commissioned between the wars but scrapped because of an unreliable engine.

Blowing the tanks ... how a submarine exhales prior to diving, with air leaving the main ballast tanks.

A rare photograph of the mine-laying submarine, *Seal*, captured by the Germans after the boat was seriously damaged by depth charges and air attacks, with many crew seriously injured or suffering effects of a long spell submerged. The shell holes are clearly visible.

Officers and men of Second World War T class boat, *Truant*, commanded by Lieutenant Commander Hugh Haggard DSO, DSC, returning home after a two-and-a-half year spell in the Mediterranean and the Far East, the Jolly Roger flag denoting a long list of successes.

Lieutenant Commander Malcolm Wanklyn, commander of one of the most successful submarines in British history, who was awarded the Victoria Cross shortly before his boat *Upholder* was lost with all hands in April 1942 after being depth charged and sunk by an Italian torpedo boat.

Lieutenant Commander Norman 'Bill' Jewell on the bridge of *Seraph*, another of the most famous Second World War boats from which he launched the body of a man bearing false papers regarding the Allies' planned invasion of Europe, a story that became known as The Man Who Never Was.

Heavy metal ... preparing torpedoes in the bowels of *Telemachus* (above) which sank the Japanese submarine *I-166* off Penang, in July 1944, and after the war spent ten years with the fourth submarine squadron in Sydney, Australia.
Below: embarking torpedoes into *Spiteful* from a depot ship prior to patrols in 1943.

entitled to three months' leave. The journey of a lifetime was on navy half-pay. The boat cost £800 and we had a lot of money to fit her out and store her up. From Hong Kong, we headed on to Japan, then across to Canada, to Vancouver and the west coast of America, to Los Angeles. There we were given a tour of the Hollywood studios and met Fred Astaire and Ginger Rogers. We were then towed through the Panama Canal by a Fyffe's banana boat and onwards to England.

Commander William King has rather contrasting memories. He also came out of Dartmouth, which, he said, 'was run like a Japanese prisoner-of-war camp and I hated it'. He entered the navy as a cadet at 17 in the battleship HMS *Resolution*. At one point in his training, he went to sea in a submarine and decided that he never wanted to go in one again, but the Royal Navy had other ideas:

At the end of the commission you came home and did the courses, gunnery and so on, and eventually went to sea as a sub-lieutenant. I did not want to specialise, but when it came to my time there were no volunteers for submarines, and the Admiralty said, You, you and you, right turn, quick march. Not one of us wanted to go into submarines. That was 1931, and I was to remain in submarines for the next 15 years. We did quite a long course and then I left to join HMS *Orpheus* on the China station, which by all accounts was going to be quite a pleasant interlude. I remained for two and a half years, and to a large extent it was actually great fun because there was tremendous variety. Hong Kong was not a great population then, rather like a Victorian town, and one also got the chance to go off into the hinterland of China. Then the fleet would go north, which had a lovely Mediterranean-type climate in the summer. Our patrols also covered Manchuria, Borneo, Singapore and the Philippines.

The military purpose was quite simply to represent the Great British Empire, to balance the rising power of the imperialistic ambitions of Japan and to keep an eye on the Chinese warlords. It was just a case of showing the flag. Things were a bit nervous. One of the submarines had been sunk just before we got there.* We were based on a marvellous depot ship, HMS *Medway*.

We lived in the submarine, and very uncomfortable it was too. We had no air-conditioning at all, and at the end of one patrol for two weeks we wrote a report saying that submarines could not be expected to patrol in those waters without air-conditioning. *Orpheus* was a hell boat in those conditions in 1932. We complained then but nothing happened, nor would it – in fact, to switch forward ten years, I was commanding a submarine in the Malacca Strait in the Malay Peninsula without air-conditioning, and 50 per cent of my crew went sick. It was a situation that was soon to confront many submariners.

And so a curious and barely believable state of affairs was already emerging as the likes of Francis and King, quoted

---

* On 9 June 1931 *Poseidon* was in collision with a cargo ship, the *Yuta*, en route from Shanghai, which cut a V-shaped wound in the submarine's saddle tanks. The order to abandon ship was immediate, but she sank so quickly that 26 men went down with her. Among the survivors was father-of-three Tom Morris, who tragically was in *M2* when she was lost with all hands during routine exercises off Portland Bill a year later. He had been a month away from discharge after completing 12 years' service.

above, returned from their respective postings in the Far East to find themselves in preparation for something that wasn't supposed ever to happen again – another war. Both would soon find themselves on stand-by to take command of new submarines that were soon to be rolling off the slipways of Britain's shipyards where, within very recent memory, millions of pounds' worth of earlier models had ended their days as scrap!

CHAPTER FIVE

Close Enough to Touch: The Submarine They Couldn't Save

Britain's on–off love affair with submarines continued to be punctuated by the reluctance of the Admiralty to commit to a large fleet of submersibles. Successive influential naval figures made no secret of their desire to maintain restrictions on their numbers by the international community well into the 1930s. But it was already too late for that, even if there had been support from former allies – which there wasn't! Britain, fresh from such social problems as the General Strike, had built only eight O-class and six P-class boats since the mid-1920s, most of which would see service in the Far East. America, Japan, France and even Russia all possessed more submarines than Britain – and soon, anyhow, there was a new fear that would change the complexion of everything.

Hitler's rise to supreme power in Germany signalled the start, once again, of a fresh appraisal. The Nazis began by repudiating the Treaty of Versailles and in March 1935 demanded renegotiation of the permitted level of their armed forces. Britain's appeasement of Hitler in these times through the creation of the Anglo-German Naval Agreement allowed him to begin rebuilding the German navy, supposedly to be kept within 35 per cent of the tonnage of the British Royal Navy. The single exception to this was in the dispensation for a new U-boat force, under the command of Admiral Karl Dönitz, which was allowed a tonnage 45 per cent of Britain's. The figures were both meaningless and unenforceable. Hitler made it clear that he would no longer be hidebound by a 20-year-old treaty and was already on the way to creating a new navy, although his plans for it were still far from complete when the Second World War broke out. Dönitz wanted a 300-strong U-boat force, but not even a quarter of that ambition had been achieved by 1939. However, the Germans were soon to make up for lost time.

With Winston Churchill once again warning of the dangers of the German arms build-up, along with the ambitious tendencies of the Japanese, the Admiralty began to re-examine the needs of its own submarine fleet. In the mid-1930s this comprised in the main part of boats that derived from the First World War, plus 20 or so O-, P- and S-class boats. There were also three Porpoise-class boats, large 1,560-tonners designed as minelayers. That there had been no enthusiasm from the British government, as ever strapped for cash, or the Admiralty to rebuild its submarine force would become woefully evident at the outbreak of the Second World War.

In the early 1930s the S-class led the production lines. It continued on through the decade and into the war years, eventually consisting of three groups ranging in size from a surface displacement of between 735 and 870 tonnes. It was a medium-range boat with a crew of 36 and intended for use in Northern European and Mediterranean waters. It was known to be highly manoeuvrable, could crash-dive fast and was a popular boat with crew members. The S-boats were also heavily armed. The first two groups came with six 21-inch torpedo tubes. Group three, built between 1940 and 1945, came with an additional torpedo tube, at the stern, and also had a greater depth capacity. They were to be sent to the Far East and the Pacific. In all, 62 S-class boats were built between 1931 and 1945 and provided outstanding service.

Soon after Hitler tore up the Treaty of Versailles, the Admiralty began a new building programme, now adding the T-class, another highly versatile boat, which had a surface displacement of 1,325 tonnes and a crew of 57. The design was under constant review, and the class underwent various modifications and improvements, especially with the advent of improved technology in engines and construction. More than fifty were to be built in the ten years to the end of the war, although by the 1937 estimates seven T-class had been due for completion in 1939 and four in 1940. In fact, only three had been commissioned at the onset of the war.

The third major component of the British submarine fleet in the Second World War would be the smaller U-class, which went into production in 1938, although when war broke out none had been commissioned. Originally designed to replace the H-class, the U-boat had a surface displacement of up to 759 tonnes and a crew of 31. Another highly commendable boat, she was badly needed. At the onset of war, the emergency building programme, which had produced so many submarines in 1914–18, was once again invoked, and the day after hostilities began seven T-class and twelve U-class were ordered for double-quick delivery. Every shipyard in Britain was once again put on round-the-clock production.

As we will see, there were to be some spectacularly famous

exploits in the years ahead from each of those three classes. But the launching of the T-class in the weeks before the outbreak of war brought with it a particularly disastrous accident.

The third of the T-boats scheduled for commissioning was HMS *Thetis*, which was built by Cammell Laird. After her launch in 1938, she was to undergo final acceptance trials in the late spring of 1939. Her captain, Lieutenant-Commander Guy Bolus, had stood by her during her fitting out and, with a crew of five other officers and forty-eight ratings, left the yard at Merseyside for trial runs in the Clyde estuary during May. There were a few problems to be ironed out, which was not unusual with a new boat, and *Thetis* returned to Cammell Laird for adjustments. The diving trial was postponed until 1 June in Liverpool Bay.

Thetis was to sail from Birkenhead soon after 9 a.m. that day with an unusually large number of people on board. In addition to the crew, there were officers from the flotilla *Thetis* was to join when she was fully commissioned, civilian observers from the Admiralty, 26 employees of Cammell Laird, five from other shipbuilding firms who would be building T-class boats, two members of staff from City Caterers of Liverpool, who were supplying the luncheon, and a Mersey pilot: 103 men in all. The weather was fine, the sea was calm with only a touch of an easterly wind. Everyone on board was looking forward to an interesting trip, and for the non-sailors it was an adventure to be enjoyed with perhaps a touch of apprehension. The older among them might have remembered the *K13* disaster, which set off in such similar circumstances, but of course there had been many submarine trials since then, with traditional trips and a good lunch for shipyards' workers and civilians at the time of the commissioning trials.

Accompanying *Thetis* during the initial stages of the trial was the *Grebecock*, a two-year-old steam tug manned by a crew of seven and laid on by Cammell Laird as part of their contract with the navy. On board was a navy observer and submariner, Lieutenant Dick Coltart, whose task it was to keep a general watch and to warn any ships that might sail into the diving area. The *Grebecock* was also to stand by to take off any passengers from *Thetis* who might wish to disembark after lunch, before the diving trials actually began. This point was reached soon after 1.30 p.m. around 40 miles from Liverpool and 15 miles from Great Ormes Head at Llandudno.

As *Grebecock* came in closer to collect the passengers, it became apparent that everyone planned to stay aboard. The captain appeared above and hailed through a megaphone: 'I shall not be disembarking anybody. Take station on my port quarter. The diving course will be 310 degrees.' Ten minutes later, Lieutenant-Commander Bolus made a formal signal stating that he was diving for three hours. He then left the bridge, the conning tower hatch was closed and he stepped down into the control room. At 2 p.m. precisely, he gave the order to dive, but *Thetis* stubbornly refused to go down.

Arthur Mawson, the engineer on *Grebecock*, would recall:

It was certainly not a straightforward dive. We could see she was blowing her tanks. She went down a touch but was kind of hovering. She would submerge one end and come up again, submerging the other end and coming up again. Then after quite a while she just disappeared below the surface, very quickly. Our captain actually said out loud: 'My God, she's gone down quick.' And he turned to Lieutenant Coltart and said: 'She's gone funny, hasn't she, sir?'

Dick Coltart had no way of knowing, nor was he able to do much about it anyhow. There was no radio contact with the submarine. He told the tug skipper to shift forward and try to hold position close to where *Thetis* had dived. Why had *Thetis* vanished so quickly? What was happening inside the submarine can be learned from the testimony given at a subsequent inquiry and investigations. After announcing his intention to begin diving trials, Lieutenant-Commander Bolus had a problem getting the submarine to submerge below 6 metres. His first lieutenant, Harold Chapman, who had the trim calculations on which the dive depended, undertaken by Admiralty overseers, said loudly, 'It just doesn't make sense,' and turning to Bolus posed the question, 'I wonder if numbers five and six torpedo tubes are full?'

One of the Admiralty people said: 'I don't think they should be.'

Chapman looked at the paperwork and said: 'Well, according to the trim statement, they should be.'

A check was ordered to ensure that *Thetis* had taken on all the water necessary to complete the dive. Crucial to this were the bow torpedo tubes, according to the trim statement, where the bottom two of six should each have contained 100 gallons. With the aid of five crew members, torpedo officer Lieutenant Frederick Woods began an examination of the tubes. They were tested by checking a valve on the inner door of the tube. The first four were dry and, because of the vertical location of the tube numbering, he then checked number six. The valve showed a spray of water, but the tube did not appear to be full, holding just enough water to be 'slopping about'. When he came to check number five tube, which should have been full, the preliminary check, which should also have provided a spray of water from the valve, brought no reaction and he assumed it must have been empty. What Woods did not know was that the number five valve was blocked by paint and was defective when he decided to open the tube door to check to see if it was dry.

The crew also had difficulty in moving the lever for an inspection of the tube, until suddenly it moved forward with a jerk to the fully open position. A spurt of water came out, followed by a loud crash as the tube's rear door burst open and a torrent of water gushed into the torpedo area at enormous speed.

'My God, we're flooding,' Woods shouted, and gave instructions to his colleagues to inform the control room and tell them to blow the tanks. But within a minute the water was reaching the level of the bottom of the watertight door leading to the torpedo stowage compartment. It was obvious from the rush of air through the submarine that the torpedo tube was now open to the sea, and the captain ordered all watertight doors closed. As he did so, the submarine went into a dive. Woods ordered the men out and tried to fasten the watertight door leading to the stowage compartment, a process that entailed tightening 18 butterfly nuts.

One of them fell off, making it impossible to secure the door properly. At that very moment, the lights in the compartment blew. The water continued to rise and the captain now faced a critical decision. If it reached the next compartment that housed the batteries, there would be a reaction of chlorine gas that would poison all on board. He ordered the men to close the watertight door from the stowage compartment, controlled by a single wheel in the centre, regardless of whether the others had evacuated the stowage area.

Leading stoker Walter Arnold was among those alongside Woods as they emerged from the forward compartment. He would testify at a later inquiry that with the boat sliding down at an angle, it needed three men on the door to close it, and as the last two men made their escape from the stowage area, the water was just about to lap over the door and into the next compartment. Had it done, said Arnold, 'it would have gone over the batteries and, of course, chlorine, and that would have meant curtains for the lot of us'.

The submarine glided downwards so that her bow stuck firm in the mud and gradually settled to a less compelling angle. The submarine's two forward compartments were now totally flooded but were sealed from the remainder of the boat. There was no panic, said Arnold, and everyone believed that the situation would soon be resolved.

On the surface the time passed slowly, with Dick Coltart and the crew of *Grebecock* staring at the sea waiting for a sign. The quarter-hours dragged by like hours and, although there was no real indication of anything untoward, an air of anticipation and apprehension was apparent on board the *Grebecock*. Four o'clock came and went and not a sign of *Thetis* emerged. Lieutenant Coltart was becoming anxious but told the tug skipper that it was possible the boat could have surfaced elsewhere.

The look on his face, according to Arthur Mawson, told another story, and as the end approached of the three-hour period of diving that Bolus had specified, Coltart felt he could wait no longer to raise the alarm. He decided to send a wireless signal to the submarine base at Fork Blockhouse, which would have to be routed through various stations. He made a carefully worded signal, which did not indicate alarm but would hopefully instigate reaction at the receiving end. It said simply: 'What was duration of *Thetis* dive? Coltart.'

The passage of the signal to Gosport was to take an inordinately long time. The signal was received at Seaforth wireless station at 4.56 p.m. It went to Liverpool at 5.05 and to London at 5.19. At 5.38 the message was received at

Gosport post office, but here it was delayed further. The telegraph boy's bicycle had a puncture and the message was not delivered to Fort Blockhouse until 6.15 p.m. By then, Fort Blockhouse was already trying to make contact. The signals officers had been calling *Thetis* since before five o'clock asking for confirmation of surfacing at the prearranged time of 5 p.m. None came.

The duty staff officer was informed, and he instructed that attempts to contact *Thetis* should continue at ten-minute intervals. Coltart's signal from *Grebecock* finally arrived and had the desired effect. Concern turned to worry, and within three minutes the ship nearest to the area was located. The destroyer *Brazen*, steaming in the Irish Sea, was ordered to divert towards Liverpool Bay and carry out a search for the submarine. The RAF was also called for assistance, and at 7.40 p.m. a flight of four Ansons from Glasgow joined the hunt as dusk began to close in.

It was almost dark when the aircraft arrived over Liverpool Bay, but they continued routinely trailing up and down their given search coordinates, with the co-pilot of each aircraft peering through the bomb hatches of the aircraft. There were a few false-alarm sightings, and although they continued the search for as long as they were able the Ansons found no trace of *Thetis*. By then, six of the Royal Navy's fastest destroyers had been dispatched from Portland, leaving at 9.40 p.m., while a salvage vessel, the *Vigilant*, left Liverpool soon after, but it was now more than seven and a half hours since the submarine submerged. At just before 11 p.m. the RAF updated its report on the search. They had drawn a complete blank, and observers on *Brazen* had spotted nothing either, and nor had they picked up any signals on the ASDIC monitors. At first light, just before 5 a.m. the search resumed, and *Brazen* moved to a new area, to the south and west of where the *Grebecock* had attempted to hold position.

Unknown to them, the tug had a short anchor, which had failed to hold the vessel firm, and she had drifted miles from her original spot. *Brazen* gradually took a wider arc, and almost three hours later observers spotted what appeared in the distance to be a red marker buoy; the destroyer headed towards it. As she drew closer, an incredible sight brought the crew of the ship on deck to view it – 5.5 metres of the stern of the 83.5-metre-long *Thetis* protruding from the sea. She lay at an angle, nose down in 45 metres of water 15 miles off the North Wales coast. Still trapped inside were 103 men. The question was: could they be rescued? In theory, the task did not look an especially onerous one, even though the air in the submarine was already running out.

In practice, a rescue was to prove virtually impossible. Inside *Thetis*, Bolus held a mini-conference with his officers and decided that it would be necessary for a volunteer equipped with Davis Submerged Escape Apparatus (DSEA) to get into the flooded compartments through the forward escape chamber, close the door to tube five and open two drain valves. This would entail the dangerous task of withstanding 32 kilogrammes of pressure for 15 minutes or so. Woods and two others stepped forward, but each in turn found the pressure too great and were unable to enter the flooded compartment.

Bolus next decided to try to lift the boat's stern by pumping out the ballast and oil in a makeshift mêlée of pipes. Meanwhile, conditions in the boat were getting desperate. In normal circumstances, there would have been enough air to last up to forty hours. With a third of the floor space sealed off, and twice the normal number of people on board, the air quality diminished rapidly, and many were feeling the effects, with light-headedness, sickness, general exhaustion and serious struggling for breath. The civilians among them were especially in a dire state.

The only remaining solution was to attempt to leave the craft for the surface through the rear escape chamber, which was estimated to be only 7.5 metres below the surface. Even then, only four men could be evacuated every half-hour – the length of time to flood and empty the escape chamber – and the only real hope of everyone surviving was to get an air line into the boat. Bolus decided that two men must try to get to the surface, hopefully find help and explain exactly what was needed. Captain Joe Oram, the officer commanding the 5th Flotilla, and Lieutenant Woods were selected. Oram would carry a message sealed in a waterproof container tied to his wrist in case he drowned in the attempt. Coincidentally, as they made their way successfully into the rear escape chamber, *Brazen* had arrived at the scene. She signalled her presence by sending down two light depth charges. A muffled cheer went up inside the boat, and Oram and Woods successfully made their escape to the surface. Both popped up to the surface within seconds.

They were picked up by a rowing boat from *Brazen*, and when all was explained to the captain it became clear that the ship did not have the equipment to send down an air line. Back in the submarine, Bolus decided to attempt to make another escape attempt, this time sending up four men – two civilians and two crew. They were fitted up with the DSEA and reminded of the drill, that when the chamber flooded and the water went over their heads, they were to breathe normally using their breathing bags and then push the escape hatch open. Stoker Arnold, who was among those helping the four to escape, would say:

The chamber flooded up but nothing happened. We

gave them plenty of time to escape and still nothing happened. We drained the compartment down again, and three of them were dead and the other one was in a very bad way. We had to get the bodies out then, which took us about two hours because we were in such a low state. They were taken below and the survivor, a young apprentice from Cammell Laird, sat down on the deck, but I don't think he lasted long after that.

At the time, the reason for the escape attempt going so badly wrong was never established, although it was thought the men had panicked as water flooded the escape chamber. Stoker Arnold was then asked if he would attempt an escape with another crewman, Frank Shaw. They both agreed, went through the same procedure, and within seconds of the escape hatch being pushed open were shooting towards the surface 'like corks'. The time was then 10 a.m. 19 hours since *Thetis* had dived, and on the surface a would-be rescue operation was proving to be totally ineffective, while back on Merseyside worried relatives and wives of shipyard workers had gathered at Cammell Laird and were demanding to know what had happened. At that point, it seemed that since four men had already escaped, other survivors would soon begin appearing on the surface and the families were told that a major rescue operation was under way.

To some extent, that was true. *Brazen* had now been joined by the salvage vessel *Vigilant* from Liverpool, the Llandudno lifeboat, six destroyers, five tugs, and another salvage vessel anchored in a circle around the spot where *Thetis* lay, all close enough to touch the stranded submarine but pinning their hopes on a mass escape in the manner in which Arnold and Shaw had just arrived at the surface. In fact, nothing more happened from below, and nothing more was heard apart from banging on the hull when a diver finally went down to survey the scene.

The first diver, inexperienced in that work, could do nothing. Others were sent for and oxyacetylene cutting gear and air compressors were on the way from Liverpool. Soon after one o'clock, a nine-centimetre wire rope was hooked round the stern, and the salvage boats would try to drag or hold *Thetis* while attempts were made to open a manhole cover on the stern of the boat.

Eventually, the wreck-master from *Vigilant* climbed on to the protruding stern himself in an attempt to loosen the outer plate. He struggled with the bolts for an hour and was on the point of opening the hatch when the boat lurched violently and he had to be pulled clear. There now seemed only one final hope available: to cut a hole in the side with the oxyacetylene gear. To carry out this operation successfully, *Thetis* had to be raised slightly to keep the planned hole above the water line.

At 3.10 p.m. on 2 June, as *Vigilant* made an effort to achieve this, the wire rope snapped and *Thetis* plunged back to the bottom, taking with her the 99 men still on board. Even this might not have ruled out the possibility of more survivors if an air line could have been brought to the boat, as it was with *K13*. But given the limited equipment and skilled rescue operatives on the surface, any of the remaining possibility seemed beyond them. The following day, the Admiralty concluded that the hope of there being any survivors was now so remote than any further rescue attempts were pointless and issued a statement saying: 'It is regretted that hope of saving lives in *Thetis* must be abandoned.'

It would be three months before *Thetis* was brought back into the daylight. In fact, it was on the very day that Prime Minister Neville Chamberlain declared that Britain was at war with Germany – 3 September 1939 – that the salvage team towed her to a deserted Welsh beach, where naval inspectors went through the boat to find the cause of the disaster. An eventual tribunal, which heard evidence from forty-nine witnesses, including the four survivors, found six contributing factors: the rear door of a torpedo tube was opened when the other end was inexplicably open to the sea; the test cock on the rear door was blocked with paint; the crew failed to close a watertight door properly; the crew failed to pump water from the flooded compartment; there was no effective assistance from the surface; and the crew failed to save themselves by the Davis Submerged Escape Apparatus. The findings did nothing to satisfy many of the relatives, widows and orphans of those who went down in *Thetis* or the trade unions representing the shipyard workers.

A claim on behalf of the relatives was lodged, and in the first instance the resulting court case went in their favour. The decision was reversed on appeal, and the case finally ended up in the House of Lords six and a half years later. In the meantime, with the mayhem of war intervening, along with millions of military and civilian casualties, some of the imperative nature of the tragedy had faded. The five Law Lords upheld the appeal and rejected the claim for damages. They concluded that after a long investigation, it was necessary to prove liability against one of the parties sued. It was their opinion that no such proof existed.

Thetis was the last submarine to be sunk in the inter-war period. In the twenty-one years between the two wars, fourteen submarines had sunk, six of them with the loss of all hands.

At 11 a.m. on the day *Thetis* was beached in North Wales, submarines at sea received the signal: 'Commence hostilities with Germany forthwith.' Four minutes later, *Spearfish*, commanded by Lieutenant J.H. Eaden, was sent a torpedo by a German U-boat in the North Sea. It missed, but submarines had established the first confrontation with the enemy. Before the day was out, Germany repeated the horror of its First World War attack on the *Lusitania* when *U30* torpedoed and sank the passenger ship *Athenia*, which was en route to the United States.

In the early months of the war, there would be many such encounters, a number of them costly and tragic, in the back yard of the northern and eastern regions of the British Isles, and a number of submarines that were in that front line would not remain long in the war.* On 10 September the first British casualty occurred, but it was due to error rather than enemy skill. An old O-class, *Oxley*, which was originally built for the Royal Australian Navy in 1926 and returned to British service in the 1930s, had been refitted to be held in reserve just before the war began. *Oxley* set off on her first major patrol off the coast of Norway. In heavy seas, at night and in poor visibility, she was spotted in the distance by one of her companion submarines, *Triton*.† She failed to make the correct recognition signal. As a result, she was unfortunately mistaken for a U-boat and torpedoed and became the first submarine loss of the Second World War.

Of the 54 crew, only her captain, Lieutenant-Commander H.G. Bowerman, and one other survived. But such a misfortune, coming only a week after *Thetis* had been brought to

---

* *Spearfish* was attacked again later that month in the Kattegat. She was repaired at Newcastle upon Tyne, came back to torpedo and severely damage the pocket battleship *Lutzow* on 11 April 1940, then sank two fishing vessels on 20 May, but was herself torpedoed and sunk by *U34* off Norway on 1 August 1940. The sole survivor was taken prisoner.

† *Triton* herself was lost with all hands while on patrol in the Adriatic on 6 December 1940. She had been attacking MV *Olympia* but nothing more was heard from the boat.

the surface, would not be relayed in full to the British public. Churchill, now back at the Admiralty, decreed that the loss of *Oxley* should be attributed to an accidental explosion. It was not until the 1950s that the truth was revealed. Also put on the secret list were details of a similar occurrence on 14 September 1939 when *Sturgeon* fired three torpedoes at her own sister ship, *Swordfish*. Fortunately, they missed. Both mishaps were due in part to the close patrol distances between the stations assigned to submarines employed off Norway. They were barely 4 miles apart, so as to give the most effective cover against German shipping trying to break through. The situation was eased somewhat when the RAF was able to put up longer-range patrol aircraft and the distance between submarine patrol locations was increased from 4 to 16 miles. The interaction of aircraft and submarines in itself presented new problems, in that submarines from the air look much the same, whether British or German, especially in wintry weather. Several submarine commanders complained in those early days. Captain Ronald Mills in *Tetrarch* was among them:

I had withdrawn from the coast to charge batteries at about six o'clock one evening and we saw a flight of aircraft east-bound up at about 5,000 feet. I recognised them as Blenheims so we fired off our recognition grenades and then to my horror I saw them peel off out of the sky and come diving straight down on me. I crash-dived as fast as we could and then bombs exploded when we had got down to about 70 feet. They were all round my stern and they were close enough to lift the engine room hatch and do a certain amount of damage. Later on that night there was a signal from the Admiralty to enquire if any of our submarines was in a certain position at a given time, to which I replied, in explicit terms, 'Yes, that was me. Good attack. Close miss.' I was subsequently reprimanded for this signal because they thought it was rather condescending to the RAF who had meanwhile claimed a kill. I had to go over to Coastal Command and apologise to them. The 64,000-dollar question was why they had not recognised me. They said they thought I was firing at them, but still the codes of colour grenades are clearly laid down every day. They should have recognised us as a friendly submarine, but they didn't. In fact, in those days we had so many attacks made on us by friendly aircraft that it became a habit that submarines, when making their arrival signals, would say, 'Expect to arrive in such and such a time, friendly aircraft permitting.'

So the first two or three months of operations had not gone especially well, and Churchill decided to act. On 9 January 1940 he appointed the First World War hero of Baltic fame, Vice-Admiral Sir Max Horton, to take over the expanding submarine force. But if Horton had any notion of a repeat performance of his own Baltic campaign in 1914, when he was accused of being a pirate by the Germans, he would have to put it on hold. The first three days at his desk brought only bad news of successive British losses:

Seahorse: sunk by German 1st Minesweeping Flotilla in Heligoland Bight. Crew of 39 lost.

Undine: Scuttled by her crew after being depth-charged by German minesweepers *M1201*, *M1204* and *M1207* in Heligoland Bight. The crew became prisoners of war.

Starfish: Depth-charged and sunk by German minesweeper *M7* in Heligoland Bight. The crew survived to become prisoners of war.

CHAPTER SIX

The Terror of Depth Charges, Mines and Attacks from the Air

As in the First World War, Heligoland Bight and Skagerrak had already become the hunting grounds of the British submarines as their German opponents began unrestricted submarine warfare. German shipping leaving home ports offered the most vital targets. There was also a great fear that the British Expeditionary Force being shipped across the Channel would be a natural target for both U-boats and Luftwaffe. The German navy had, since early December, also been laying vast minefields and travelling ever closer to the British war channels.

The British submarine response in New Year 1940 fell on Max Horton's shoulders. Both he and First Lord Winston Churchill were concerned with two particular aspects. One was the possibility of a German invasion of Scandinavian countries, which would virtually tie up the approaches to enemy waters. The second was the unhindered supply of iron ore, which was being turned into ships and aircraft, coming down into Germany from northern Sweden – exactly the same problem that first emerged in the First World War. The ore was being transshipped through the ice-free port of Narvik in northern Norway, still a neutral country. These two situations, which had been worrying the British military planners since the turn of the year, merged into one problem on 9 April when Germany invaded Denmark.

On the same day, the British War Cabinet pronounced that British submarines could and would henceforth sink transport ships in the region on sight, and two days later it extended that order to cover any ship sighted within 10 miles of the Norwegian coast. The fact that Max Horton had committed virtually his entire force to the Norwegian campaign a week earlier showed good foresight on his part. Although the British force would stay well away from the Baltic, where Horton had made his name, he dispatched every available submarine to join those already on patrol to cover all the German exits from Heligoland Bight, Skagerrak and the Kattegat.

The Skagerrak strait, between the southern coast of Norway and the Jutland peninsula of Denmark, was a vital seaway. Together with the Kattegat strait, it connects the North Sea with the Baltic Sea. About 150 miles long and from 75 to 90 miles wide, the Skagerrak is shallow near Jutland but deepens near the Norwegian coast. The strait is subject to violent storms. During the First World War the naval Battle of Jutland was fought in the Skagerrak, and Germany had the advantage of natural hazards.

These treacherous waters, then, were the scene of Max Horton's arc of submarines at the beginning of 1940. These were supplemented by others whose crews had the specific task of laying 50 mines apiece on each trip, and in the first half of the year there was probably not a single home-based submarine commander who did not see service there. Several would never return. The extent of their activity is demonstrated by the amount of shipping sunk by the submarine service in the month between 8 April and 4 May: close on 35 assorted vessels, of almost 90,000 tonnes, with the loss of 4 British submarines. It was an exciting, hair-raising, harrowing time, especially for the less experienced submariners, largely because it was the first time in history that efficient depth charges were to be used in abundance – in addition to the normal hazard of mines.

Depth charges first came into use during the First World War. The early forms of the weapon consisted of large cylinders containing TNT, which were rolled or catapulted from the stern of a ship. In the intervening years, depth charges and machinery for launching them had improved dramatically, and experimental work on new designs was ongoing and came into use in the early stages of the Second World War. The use of a new and more powerful explosive called Torpex, a mixture of RDX, TNT and aluminium, substantially reduced the size of depth charges. The casings were also streamlined to make them sink faster and thus more difficult to avoid. To have literally dozens of these sinking towards your boat and exploding all around as the commander looked worryingly at his depth gauge was one of the most frightening experiences imaginable.

With memories of the *Thetis* tragedy still fresh, the thoughts of young sailors – and a good many older ones for that matter – might often turn to whether or not their particular boat could withstand bombardment beneath the sea. Indeed, there were to be a number of curiously associated incidents that harked back to *Thetis* in those early months. The first involved Captain Ronald Mills, an experienced submariner who had just finished a term in China and returned to take command of a new T-class boat, the *Tetrarch*, which was in the process of completion at Barrow. On arrival in August 1939, he discovered that he had been seconded to lead a naval team working with a Liverpool salvage company on *Thetis* and subsequently took part in a detailed reconstruction of events. The experience was soon to come in very useful, as he explained:

It enabled me to discuss very freely with the medical officers who came up to make an examination of the *Thetis* the possible length of time that those fellows would have remained conscious, and the fact was borne clearly on my mind that under certain pressures inside a submarine, your expectation of active life after about 24 hours in foul air is very small.

This fact was impressed on me so that when it came to the crunch, I definitely used it. The opportunity came rather more quickly than I had ever imagined, in the spring of 1940. I had left Portsmouth intending to join the 3rd Flotilla up in Rosyth, but when I got halfway up the North Sea I was ordered to go over to the south coast of Norway into the Norwegian campaign, and join a patrol line that was across the Skagerrak. Allowing for the time to get across the North Sea and creep my way up to my position, I didn't get there until 22 April and I was charging my batteries on the surface that night when we heard a loud hydrophone effect approaching. I could make out about four or five enemy minesweepers or trawlers, and so I had to dive even though we hadn't finished charging the batteries, and they bumbled around me all day.

I couldn't come up to the surface as I wanted to do and at six o'clock that night I [rose to periscope depth and] sighted a convoy crossing from east to west across to Norway consisting of three destroyers escorting a very large merchant ship. I closed at full speed, and at the end of ten minutes I fired two torpedoes on a fairly broad track, and two minutes later I put up my periscope to see what had happened. The enemy had sort of turned away and now coming down the track of my torpedoes were three German destroyers in line abreast. I crash-dived to 300 feet which was supposed to be our maximum depth, and two minutes later I heard the hydrophone effect of destroyers coming overhead and a loud series of bangs as they discharged their depth charges. This went on for about half an hour. They dropped 30 depth charges very close to me; everything rattled and shook. I was glad to think that they were exploding in shallower water than I was.

Nothing much happened for the next hour or so until at eight o'clock that evening we heard the destroyers moving away and the hydrophone effect of reciprocating engines showing us that the trawler flotilla or minesweeper flotilla had taken over the hunt. I tried the normal thing, to get away on one motor, but that brought a volley of depth charges. I had a conference with my engineer officer, and it was very much in my mind how long we could remain where we were if they stayed over us, given that pressure was building inside the boat. My memory turned to my conversation with the doctors over *Thetis*, and it struck me that we had less than 24 hours to live.

So I decided that the most important thing was to get

rid of the pressure by taking the risk of surfacing among the hunting vessels. I came up to the surface very gradually, lashed the conning tower hatch before I knocked off the clips, and I got the signalman who was following me up the ladder to take a firm grip of my legs because I said when the hatch opens we'll be blown out like a cork from a bottle. Eventually, we surfaced and I opened the conning tower hatch and I went sailing up into the air, the signalman still holding my legs, and clutched on to the for'ard periscope to stop me from going overboard.

However, after about a minute this cloud of vapour that had carried us upwards dispersed loudly and I had to get back on to the deck of the bridge. I ordered gun action, and the gun's crew opened the hatch and went to the gun. I looked round me and the nearest enemy vessel was about 1,500 yards away. It was the middle of the night. The awkward thing about a submarine using its gun is that it is on the for'ard side of the bridge and you have to close the enemy to use your gun, so I got the engines started, closed towards them and fired off a few rounds, although I don't think we got any hits. We then got their searchlights on us, and I saw there was another ship fairly close by, so I gave the engines a couple of minutes to clear the atmosphere and then, when the nearest vessel got within 500 yards of me, I crash-dived back to 300 feet. Actually, we went down in a very steep dive to 400 feet before I could check up and then I did a rather spectacular surface.

I was trying to control the ship from diving 20 degrees bow down and I steadied her up at 400 feet, over-corrected and came shooting up to the surface again. I don't know what the enemy were doing, but we did break surface and before I could get the hydroplane* to hard-dive again, back we went to 350 feet. We had stopped all motors, as I thought, but they still seemed to keep contact on me and dropped depth charges about every five minutes or so. Eventually, we found that a very small motor up in the for'ard end of the submarine had been accidentally left running, and as soon as I stopped this all attacks finished. They didn't get on to me again although they were cruising around me.

We had had by that time about a hundred depth charges.

I said the answer was to remain stopped and hope that they will go away. I called trim at 350 feet, and my engineer and I stayed in the control room for the rest of the night and the next day anxiously watching the bubble on the hydroplane unit, and if the bubble started to go forward it meant the bow was coming up and vice versa. I got a man with a couple of buckets of water to come into the control room and as the bubble tended to go forward so he walked through the submarine to the for'ard end until the bubble came to central and he came back again when the bubble went the other way and so on. This proved very satisfactory, and we held trim stopped for a period of 12 hours.

We started to build up a pressure in the boat and the air was getting foul again; the battery had gone down to about as low as you can go. The voltage had gone down below 2 volts a cell, so I brought the ship up gradually to periscope depth and then ran my air compressors (which won't run below periscope depth) and switched on the

* The horizontal vane on the hull of a submarine for controlling her vertical motion.

115

air humidifier. I ran all available fans for ten minutes and I also authorised an extra rum ration. This was about 11.30 on the day following our first counter-attack. I managed to keep the ship under control on auxiliary drive, which is the slowest you can go, and at 11.30 that night I reckoned it was dark enough to surface. To my surprise I saw what had seemed to be land was fully illuminated – whereas the cities of Norway were all blacked out. I assumed I had come up about a couple of miles up the coast of Sweden, which meant that I had drifted, by means of sub-surface current, some 50 miles from the initial attack.

Anyhow, that was the end of that dive. I came up and stayed in the lee of the Swedish coast until I had recharged the batteries, reported my position, because I had been out of touch with the Admiralty for almost two days, and then I had orders to find my way home again. That was the end of the first patrol.

In fact, Mills modestly overlooked the fact that *Tetrarch* took the record for staying submerged for the longest known period to that point of 43 hours while under heavy counter-attack by depth charges. When he finally came up for air, his crew were literally falling as if drunk. But he did confess:

Being under depth-charge attack is fairly alarming and sounds as though one is in a 15-inch turret standing between the guns when the guns go off. It's a sort of thunderous noise, a very alarming noise. We were very lucky that we were not badly hurt, but when I got back to Rosyth I had immediate docking to see what damage there might have been and the whole of my pressure hull was rippled all the way along. The crew reacted very well. They all remained absolutely still throughout, apart from putting on extra clothes. I had told them to get what clothing they could because it was going to be cold and it was – bloody cold.

The effects of successive long spells under water, accompanied by depth-charge attacks, could have untoward effects, especially when the charges were poured into the sea by a posse of marauding destroyers, angry because the submarine had just fatally damaged one of Germany's brand-new cruisers – which is exactly what happened to Admiral C.H. Hutchinson. He was at the time a lieutenant-commander of another of the early T-boats, *Truant*. He had carried out a number of successful patrols in the North Sea during the Norwegian campaign. He'd already sunk an enemy ship of 2,400 tonnes on 24 March 1940 and two weeks later, during almost continuous patrols, he, along with other boats, was to provide protection and diversion for what proved to be the ill-fated Allied landings of troops at Narvik to counter the German invasion. He recalls what happened as he approached his patrol position:

The sea was flat calm, but visibility was negligible due to fog. In the early part of the night I could hear ships' propellers on my hydrophones. They appeared to be all round me, and quite obviously this was part of the invasion fleet. But instruments in those days were not accurate enough to be able to keep me safely on the surface without almost certain collision with ships that were obviously very close and invisible. This was very frustrating. I tried going in various directions on the surface to try to get a clearer picture of what was around. I dived and tried to get some sort of picture by ASDICs or hydrophones. None of this worked out, and I was unable to find an exact target. Daylight came and the fog began to clear, but nothing came into view until about seven o'clock that evening. My attention was drawn to some propeller noises, very faint, to the north.

These gradually got louder, and eventually I could see through the periscope a German cruiser coming towards me, screened by at least three or four escorts, small destroyers. I went down to 60 feet to get a burst of speed so as to get inside the screen and ahead of the oncoming cruiser. After I had eased down the speed and it was safe to raise the periscope without showing a lot of feather, I found that I was in an ideal position to be able to fire. Down periscope, and in about two minutes' time, raised it, hoping that I would be able to give the order to fire fairly quickly.

To my disgust I saw that the cruiser and her escorts had altered course about 70 degrees to the eastwards, placing me in a most unfavourable position. She was rapidly running away from me. It was a case of now or never. I fired a large salvo of torpedoes set shallower to catch the escorts and the middle torpedoes a bit deeper to catch the cruiser, and then again the last torpedoes shallower to catch the escort that appeared by now to be astern of the cruiser. I raised my periscope to take a look and could see nothing but a very enlarged after-part of a destroyer which was right on top of us. In fact, I was staring at a fat cook at the galley door.

Unbeknown to Hutchinson at the time, he had torpedoed the German cruiser *Karlsruhe*, which was homeward bound from Oslo. The Germans were naturally furious. The cruiser was abandoned by her crew and was so badly damaged that Berlin ordered that she should be scuttled immediately. While two destroyers went about picking up survivors, the other two escorts were given orders to hunt down the submarine and blast it out of the water with depth charges. As Hutchinson rightly surmised:

Retribution was bound to follow. And sure enough, it did. The first two explosions were very violent indeed. Everything appeared to jump around. Anything that was loose in the control room, such as a logbook, leaped off its table. Various pipes began to hiss compressed air. Leaks began appearing, and the stern began to get heavy and our depth increased. I tried to pump water out from a tank aft, but quickly stopped because it would have acted as a certain marker to those on the surface. Our Sperry compass was going round in circles, as was the magnetic compass, with the explosions shaking up the metal of the ship's hull and making the magnetic needle finding it difficult to make up its mind exactly where north was. However, that didn't matter.

The thing was to shake off whoever was at the top plastering eggs on us. Here, I think I must point out that submarine training up to that point had never given us any experience of depth-charging. I had only once heard a depth charge in my life until this occasion, and that was at the safe distance of about 5 miles away. So in a way we were facing a weapon that was new to us. The attacks on us went on and on, some getting perilously close. By now we were down to about 350 feet, which was a great depth then, and I'm quite sure this saved us and that the depth charges were exploding well above us. *Truant* was riding at a nasty angle with bow up, stern down, due to the leaks aft around the propeller glands and various other places.

However, we did manage to keep control, and after about two hours – going round in circles because we had no compass – I deemed it safe to see if we could come up and have a look through the periscope. Just before we got to periscope depth, another set of explosions occurred and down I went again with a good deal of banging going on all around. I stayed down for another hour or so, and when we came back up there was nothing in sight. So we limped home for repairs. When we got back to Rosyth we were given a great welcome . . . the battle cruiser *Renown*, with a shell hole through her fo'c'sle, was anchored off Rosyth and her crew lined the decks and gave us a great cheer.

It was on Hutchinson's next patrol that the significance of depth-charging began to hit home. He had been given the task of transporting and landing a commando unit who were to go behind enemy lines on the Norwegian coast to cause mayhem. They included the swashbuckling Lord Lovat and his piper, who were both later to become prominent in the exploits of the newly founded British commando units. Hutchinson remembers:

My orders were to cross the North Sea and go about 90 miles up the Hardanger Fjord, which was well and truly under German control, taking with me this bunch of military bravadoes and land them at the head of the fjord. They came aboard with such weapons as plastic explosives, cheese wire for silencing sentries, ghastly looking knives and generally looking like a gang of cut-throats. But I must say I admired them. They were as keen as mustard to get going, but they had probably never volunteered to dive in a submarine, and certainly would not have expected the experience of being depth-charged. Unfortunately, we were – and torpedoed as well. A great red flash, huge explosions and then this terrific shaking. We dived deep, and I began to investigate the damage. We had taken on quite a bit of water; the batteries were also damaged, and one in particular was in a parlous state with several cells broken. Chlorine gas was apparent, so we really had no alternative but to turn back and once again limp home on a wing and a prayer.

It was on the way back to Rosyth that I realised my nerve had partly gone. Before that patrol I had been given fairly powerful drugs because of my inability to sleep but, of course, I could not take them while at sea. Regrettably, I made the decision that although I could be accused of letting the side down, I did not think it was fair to take on a wartime crew in my condition. I imparted the news to my first lieutenant and well remember the look of horror on his face. So I made a signal that I was returning to base and that the commanding officer needed a relief. I could barely face my crew, but back at Rosyth I was hauled off to hospital and that finished my time with *Truant*.

One of Hutchinson's good friends, Lieutenant-Commander Rupert Lonsdale, also met a barrage of enemy fire as his boat, *Seal*, entered the Skagerrak during this period of great activity and high drama for the British submarine force. For Lonsdale, it would also mean the end of his war service, the indignity of having to surrender his boat, followed by five years in a German prison camp and a court martial when he returned home.

Rupert Lonsdale, who was recognised as a fine, compassionate leader of men and a skilled submariner, had already been awarded a mention in dispatches for his part in an Atlantic convoy protection operation. On 4 May 1940 he was given the task of laying mines in the Kattegat, for which his boat, *Seal*, was fully adept. She was one of six specialised minelaying submarines launched in the 1930s with a surface displacement of 1,560 tonnes. They were named the Porpoise class.* All vessels of the class had balloon tanks in the forward superstructure to balance the buoyancy of the mines aft and to prevent the submarine diving stern first.

Having taken on a cargo of 50 mines at Immingham, Lonsdale was given an area deep into the enemy-controlled waters of the Kattegat to spread them. On the journey over, he was attacked twice from the air, the first of which is believed to have come from friendly fire. *Seal* continued to dodge the fire, and with great bravado Lonsdale eventually steamed into position, where he laid his 50 mines, according to instructions, in a record time of 45 minutes, then turned to go home. It was to his great credit that their positioning ensured success, and the mines he laid were in due course deemed responsible for sinking four ships. He was on the return journey when he ran into assorted surface and airborne attacks and then, ironically, one of his hydroplanes caught on a German mine-mooring wire and the boat rocked

* Four of the remaining Porpoise-class minelayers did not survive the war, all lost without survivors and listed as 'cause unknown': *Grampus* in the Mediterranean in June 1940; *Narwhal* off Norway in August 1940; *Cachalot* in October 1941, no further details known; and *Porpoise* in the Malacca Strait in January 1945 – the last British submarine to be sunk in the war. The only survivor of the Porpoise class was *Rorqual*, which remained in service until April 1946.

and shuddered and sprang leaks everywhere after the massive explosion that followed.

Seal went stern first to the bottom with serious flooding, and for the next 23 hours sat in 39 metres of water, stubbornly refusing to budge. With enemy activity above, Lonsdale and his men waited quietly for ten hours before making their first attempt to surface, which failed. He made three separate attempts and in a last-ditch effort released the 11-tonne drop keel, a device that once disposed of would prevent the submarine from diving again. Even that did not work.

The batteries were running low and barely producing any light, the atmosphere was foul, carbon dioxide poisoning was beginning to affect the crew and the point came when – like the men on *Thetis* – they were simply incapable of operating the Davis Submerged Escape Apparatus through fear of flooding the entire submarine.

As their plight became increasingly desperate, someone said, 'All we can do is pray', and, realising the possibility of imminent death, that is exactly what they did. Lonsdale held a prayer meeting in the control room and summoned up what remained of his badly impaired respiratory functions to recite loud and clear the Lord's Prayer and a couple of others he made up himself.

That seemed to give the men enough impetus to give it one last try. Lonsdale had the idea that if he could get enough men up into the bow, which was considerably higher in the water than the stern, while at the same time blowing tanks and using the last remaining power to run the motors, it might just be enough to free the boat. The men clawed their way through the forward compartments to get as near to the bow as they possibly could and, sure enough, *Seal* began to tilt back to the surface, where she was immediately bombed and machine-gunned by a German Arado seaplane. The damage was already serious enough to immobilise *Seal*, and Lonsdale's hopes of being able to limp into Swedish waters were now dashed. Furthermore, some members of the crew were in a dire condition. The situation stumbled from bad to worse when a second aircraft appeared over the horizon, saw the Arado buzzing around the British submarine and hurried over to join in the fun.

Rupert Lonsdale quickly destroyed confidential papers while his officers wrecked all the craft's sensitive equipment, and then put up the white flag to save his men, several of whom were badly wounded. The seaplane landed and the submarine commander personally swam over to it and surrendered his submarine to the aircraft captain, Lieutenant Schmidt. Lonsdale and his men were made prisoners of war and remained in captivity throughout. *Seal* was towed to Kiel docks, where she was re-commissioned as a U-boat, largely for propaganda purposes, and was eventually scuttled in 1945. In prison camp, Rupert Lonsdale won a second mention in dispatches for his work with prisoners of war, but on his return home he had to face the compulsory court martial, as does any captain who loses his ship. He was acquitted with honour and his sword was returned to him by the president of the court. Outside, a group of his men cheered as he came out. He remained in the service for two more years before he retired from the navy and trained to become a priest.*

Meanwhile, Hitler's blitzkrieg across Europe had ended any possibility of stepping up the momentum of the Norwegian

---

* He became vicar of Morden-with-Almer, Dorset, in 1951, and his later ministries included two in Africa and one in the Canary Islands before his retirement in 1970. Rupert Lonsdale died in 1998, aged 93.

campaign. At the time, the Allied force that was attempting to boot the Germans out of Norway actually had the invaders on the run, and on this occasion defeat was snatched from the jaws of victory. The Royal Navy was forced to set up a shoreline barrage on German positions while all Allied troops were pulled out through Narvik. Pressing needs in France, and more precisely the evacuation of the British Expeditionary Force gathering at Dunkirk, meant that Denmark and Norway had to be abandoned to Nazi occupation. By June 1940 the greater part of mainland Europe was similarly under the jackboot of Nazism, and Britain stood alone in the fight, with only her dominions to call on.

The Allied withdrawal from Norway in the first week of June 1940, coupled with the German advance across Europe, had a dramatic effect on submarine warfare, and indeed the whole outlook of the war. While Britain ordered the retreat of 36,000 Allied troops from Norway, 338,226 men of the British Expeditionary Force were to be rescued from Dunkirk in the heroic sea lift. The Nazi war machine pounded forward, and French Premier Marshal Henri Pétain asked Hitler for an armistice to save France from the blitzkrieg that quashed the Low Countries. The terms of the German occupation of France gave the Nazis control of much of the French coastline while Pétain set up a capital at Vichy in the unoccupied south-east.

As Winston Churchill took over as Prime Minister, he warned that the Battle of Britain was about to begin. It would do so, officially, on 8 August, and the Royal Air Force famously came to the fore. The Battle of Britain was also a costly period for the submarine service. Minelayers and patrols were strung out in operations as far north as the important and well-protected Norwegian port of Trondheim, all the way down the North Sea off the east coast of the British Isles into the English Channel and, soon, were extending their activities towards the French Channel and Bay of Biscay ports. Ever longer patrols were necessary to contribute to the relentless watch for any signs of an invasion, while at the same time pursuing effective attacks on the enemy fleet.

In addition, the convoys of supply ships coming in from North America and the British colonial nations all needed protection, a task that fell predominantly to surface escorts but with considerable submarine involvement. Already under pressure for both manpower and boats, Britain's submarine flotillas suffered further heavy casualties in the month prior to the beginning of the Battle of Britain when the prospect of a German invasion seemed a certainty. Boats still operating off Norway were particularly vulnerable because of the long hours of daylight, thus reducing the possibilities for battery-charging, surface recovery or rescue after attacks. This, coupled with increasing numbers of U-boats, anti-submarine sea craft and air attacks, meant that Max Horton was forced to order a temporary withdrawal of patrols from the danger zones off the coast of Norway, such as Trondheim.

He did, however, continue to make his boats available for covert and special operations, such as landing agents, saboteurs and resistance organisers and transporting equipment. *Seawolf*, under Lieutenant-Commander J.W. Studholme, for example, landed Norwegian naval officers for an intelligence mission on Ullers Island on 4 July and returned five days later to collect them. It was an early example of many such operations to the Norwegian coast and later in virtually every theatre of the war. As we will discover from first-hand accounts, submarines were used to deliver into enemy-held territory agents, saboteurs and members of the various newly formed units such as the Special Boat Service, the SAS and the Special Operations Executive as well as general intelligence operatives. Submarine commanders also provided a great service in picking up literally dozens of foreign nationals fleeing the German-occupied countries in a variety of small craft that might otherwise never have made it across the tortuous waters of the North Sea.

The risks were great, and they were only to worsen as the war progressed and this type of activity increased. By necessity, the submarine commanders would have to go perilously close to the coast, often well within range of shore batteries. The simple task of unloading groups of saboteurs into their canoes, in which they would paddle ashore, for example, could entail staying on the surface for a quarter of an hour or more in U-boat-infested waters, or in the direct line of fire of surface ships or the frequent patrols of anti-submarine aircraft. It was the last component of the Germans' defences that was now beginning to make serious inroads into the British submarine force. In quick succession in that month of July, a number of boats were either sunk or scuttled by their crews because of damage from a new weapon: the air-dropped depth-charge bomb.

On 5 July Lieutenant-Commander Peter Buckley in *Shark* had been surprised by the arrival of an anti-submarine seaplane while on the surface on the western approaches to Skagerrak. He ordered a crash dive, but too late to stop a depth-bomb attack. A spray of machine-gun fire bounced off the bow as he dived, and the boat was barely 6 metres down when the first bomb hit it, followed by four or five more. Buckley went as deep as he dared but the damage was considerable and the boat listed at a 35-degree angle. He called for reports from his officers, and it was soon clear that *Shark* was in serious trouble and that he had to get her back to the surface. The Sperry compass was wrecked, the steering had failed, water was pouring in aft and the starboard main motor was out of action.

With the dive continuing uncontrollably, Buckley had to gamble on using remaining high-pressure air in an attempt to get *Shark* back on the surface and take their chances. The alternative offered no prospect of survival. The confidential books and secret charts were made ready for destruction, ammunition was prepared ready for use with the submarine's 3-inch gun and the Lewis gun on the bridge, and all rifles were handed out to the crew. Buckley brought the boat to the surface at an incredible angle and the guns were manned immediately. Within a short time, they were spotted from the air and the bombing resumed. The first attack came in low and exploded on the starboard side, washing two men overboard. Buckley and his crew would not give up. They fought back, firing their guns on the attacking aircraft until all but three of *Shark*'s crew had been wounded. Buckley himself was badly hurt yet ignored calls for surrender signalled by light from one of the seaplanes. At one time there were nine or ten German aircraft circling. Finally, after holding out for five long hours, Buckley ordered the surviving members of his crew to abandon ship. In his eventual report, he explained that it was the arrival of four Messerschmitt Me 109s that made it impossible for his men to continue:

> They continued to rake the bridge with machine-gun and cannon fire. Their fire was devastating, and it was obvious to me that the end was now in sight, although everyone stuck to their posts in magnificent manner until wounded or killed. Having many wounded or dead, I reluctantly decided to capitulate. Nearly all our casualties had been sustained during the attacks by the

Messerschmitts, and at the finish the bridge was a shambles of wounded men, blood and empty cartridge cases.

After we had been stopped for about 30 minutes, one of the small seaplanes landed close astern of us. Its two airmen eventually came aboard. Shortly afterwards, their plane broke adrift and keeled over and sank. They explained they had been hit in one of the floats during the action, but I think it was probably due to a bad landing but they didn't care to admit it. The pilot was very nervous and was particularly loath to remove his finger from the trigger of his Luger.

Four trawlers were on their way to accept the men into custody as prisoners of war. An hour or so later, a larger seaplane landed and Buckley and another of the badly wounded were evacuated. As the plane took off, he could see *Shark* listing badly and deep in the water. The men settled down to wait for the trawlers, which arrived four hours later. One of them attempted to take the stricken submarine under tow, but even as they tried to get a line to her, *Shark* made her own last stand and defied capture. She reared up and sank, damaging the stern of the trawler as she went.*

Then came a curious revelation from the Germans in their communiqué about the success of their anti-submarine air patrols. They mentioned that two submarines had been attacked that day: one was badly damaged and the other sunk. Of the other S-class boats on patrol off Norway at the time, *Salmon* had failed to respond to signals, the last one of which ordered her to return to base at Rosyth. *Salmon* was

---

* Peter Buckley was hospitalised for three weeks before joining the others in a prisoner-of-war camp. He returned to active service after the war, retiring in 1965 with the rank of rear-admiral.

one of the most famous of all submarines in the early stages of the war. She had the distinction of sinking the first German U-boat, *U36*, of the war on 4 December 1939. She halted the German liner *Bremen* on 12 December but was forced to submerge when attacked by a flying boat. She torpedoed the cruisers *Nürnberg* and *Leipzig* as they covered a destroyer minelaying operation off the Tyne the following day, and sank *U54* in the North Sea on 12 April 1940. On 9 July 1940 she failed to return home and was declared lost with all 41 hands. Later it was discovered she had been following a route through a fresh minefield, laid only two days before.

On 22 July the minelayer *Narwhal*, sister ship of *Seal* in the Porpoise-class, left the Humber to lay mines in the southern approaches to Trondheim. No further contact was made, and she was assumed lost with all 59 hands after the Germans confirmed a hit in the area in which she had been operating. On the same day one of the three large River-class submarines, built in the mid-1930s at a cost of £500,000 each as successors to the K-class as fleet submarines, also failed to respond to signals. The *Thames*, under Lieutenant-Commander W. 'Dunks' Dunkerley, had left Dundee for patrol and did not return, assumed lost with all 61 hands.

Before the end of the month, another of the S-boats, *Spearfish*, also went missing. She also had a history, having torpedoed and severely damaged the pocket battleship *Lutzow* off the Skaw (now Skagen, on the northern tip of Denmark), on 11 April 1940, putting her out of action for a year, and then sank two trawlers on 20 May 1940. On 1 August her sinking was confirmed by German communiqués, having been torpedoed by *U34* off Norway. Miraculously, one crew member survived the explosion. Able Seaman William Pester, a recent recruit to submarine life, was apparently sucked through an aft hatch, which was blown open. He was picked up on the surface and taken prisoner.

Fate also extended a hand to Chief Stoker G.W. Oliver, on one of the First World War-vintage boats, the tiny *H49*, whose captain, Lieutenant Dick Coltart, then 27 years old, had taken up his first command. On the one and only patrol he would lead, setting out from Harwich, he signalled that he was attacking six merchant ships 9 miles off Texel, Holland, and thereafter apparently brought his boat to the surface in misty conditions. He was unfortunately to arrive not far from a group of four German anti-submarine trawlers who immediately pursued him as Coltart ordered a crash dive.

Five groups of three depth charges were dropped over the spot where he submerged, and soon an oil slick appeared followed by an air-bubble patch. Three further depth charges were dropped and *H49* was lost – with only one survivor: Stoker Oliver. He would later explain that when the depth charges began exploding around *H49*, the Davis Submerged Escape Apparatus sets were handed out to the crew. But there were not enough to go round, and Oliver volunteered to go without. As Lieutenant Coltart made repeated efforts to surface without success, Oliver, only partially conscious, became aware of a circular light above him in the engine room. The hatch had blown open and he found himself being drawn inexorably towards it and onwards to the surface, where he emerged half-conscious to be picked up by the Germans. None of his 22 colleagues survived.

There were noteworthy aspects of the loss of *H49*. Dick Coltart had succeeded Lieutenant Mike Langley as captain of *H49* when Langley was given command of the more modern S-class *Swordfish*. But Langley himself survived only three weeks longer than his former crew. His new boat was bound for duty off Brest, to report any concentrations of enemy shipping. But *Swordfish* never reached her station. She struck a mine off St Catherine's Point, Isle of Wight, and broke in two – a fact confirmed when the wreck was discovered by divers in 1983. Coincidentally, Coltart's *H49* was also found by divers the following year.

Dick Coltart, it may be recalled, was also a witness to the *Thetis* disaster. He was the young naval observer on the tug that accompanied the T-boat towards her diving trials, and it was he who raised the alarm when she had not surfaced at the appointed time. Before the year was out, one more *Thetis* connection emerged. Captain John Stevens, then a lieutenant, was assigned to a new ship being commissioned at Birkenhead. Dartmouth-schooled and in the navy since boyhood, he had been in the submarine service for two years when war broke out. He initially served as torpedo officer on a brand-new T-class boat, *Triumph*, which was commissioned at the Vickers Armstrong yard at Barrow in April 1939, a month before *Thetis* began her final trials. *Triumph* was also bound for the North Sea patrols, and Stevens took the role of torpedo and gunnery officer and correspondence.

We were sent to patrol off the Norwegian coast with the rest. We were watching, reporting and attacking German warships, if any. The squadron we were attached to moved to Rosyth from Dundee, and we were expecting to have Christmas in harbour when suddenly, on Christmas Eve 1940, we had a hail over the loudspeakers from the depot ship telling us to get ready for sea straight away. We shot off within the hour to the North Sea. Some intelligence had apparently come out that there was a new German minefield through which was swept a channel for their own ships and we might find a good target.

It was about 100 miles off the German coast. We arrived at our position and took up the usual routine of being dived by day and on the surface at night, charging our batteries. We had a rudimentary form of Christmas dinner after we surfaced at our position, and on Boxing Day we were dived and again surfaced in the evening. I shall never forget the time . . . it was six minutes past eleven when there was an almighty crash. We'd struck a floating mine. It was an old-fashioned mine with a sinker and wire cable. Obviously, the wire had parted, and by the Geneva Convention such mines were supposed to be made safe if they broke adrift. This one wasn't, and it did a lot of damage. Up for'ard in the *Triumph*, we had eight torpedo tubes of which six were within the pressure hull and two were external tubes on top of the pressure hull. All of these were loaded with torpedoes, fully armed with primers and detonators, and a pistol. The pistol in those days resembled a fan, and when the torpedo was fired, this fan would spin round until a certain safety range had been run out so that it didn't blow up in front of you.

Of the torpedoes in those tubes after the explosion, the two external ones had vanished. Of the torpedo tubes within the pressure hull, three had their bow caps – the doors that keep the sea out – blown off; in one case the fan pistol was all there except that all the fan blades had been blown off. It was a very great tribute to the safety arrangements that are a bit irksome at times. But in this case, had they not been in place we would have been blown to kingdom come. The engines didn't stop and we went circling round, so we had to buckle to and get ourselves back to Rosyth for repair. We were very fortunate that there were no casualties. We made a signal about what had happened and limped slowly home. At first light, aircraft were sent to protect us on the journey back. We eventually took the *Triumph* to Chatham for repair, which took a year before she could go back into service.

In the meantime, Captain Stevens was moved to a shore base and then acted as British liaison officer on a French submarine before being moved to an ancient H-class submarine on anti-invasion patrols off the Dutch coast. After three months, he was told to report to Cammell Laird to stand by for the commissioning of what he only knew to be 'Job No. 568'. Stevens went on:

At Laird's shipyards in Birkenhead, I didn't know the identity of the ship, and I found she was another T-class, named *Thunderbolt*. It was only then that I discovered the history of this boat. She had been sunk with heavy loss of life on trials in her previous existence – as HMS *Thetis*. She had been salvaged, pumped out and put back into Cammell Laird, who were invited to restore her to her former glory. We left the shipbuilders and went into training, working out practices in the Clyde. Some of the men were, quite naturally, a little uncomfortable.

In our first operation, we went down to the Bay of Biscay and patrolled off the mouth of the Gironde, where there was a U-boat base. We had a certain amount of good fortune, because when we had been there about a week, an Italian submarine came in with a German naval trawler escort. We fired six torpedoes, one of which struck her, and she sank. There were about three survivors, those who were up on the conning tower. At the time, we were very elated because having been sunk as *Thetis* with a very great loss of life, we rather got the feeling then that not only did this submarine work, but we'd had a success.*

Stevens's activity in the Bay of Biscay was typical of what had transpired since the Norwegian campaign was reorganised to allow more submarines to be deployed around the French coast and on into the Mediterranean as well as additional duties on the Atlantic convoys in the desperate situations now arising in that particular arena.

---

* Captain Stevens later took up a new appointment, and *Thunderbolt* went on to a successful campaign in the Mediterranean, playing a key role in the attack on Palermo harbour under Operation Principal on 3 January 1943. Two months later, however, on 14 March 1943, *Thunderbolt* was depth-charged and sunk for the second time in her life – this time by the Italian anti-submarine boat *Cicogna*, off St Vito, north of Sicily. Only two of the crew survived.

CHAPTER SEVEN

U-Boat Wolf Packs and the Truth about Enigma

German control of many of the strategically important naval bases and aerodromes in their occupied territories meant that, at a stroke, they had buttoned up the coastlines fronting the whole of the French Atlantic Ocean, the Channel, the North Sea and the Baltic. This provided the Nazis with unparalleled supply routes to keep their combined military forces well manned, fuelled and equipped as well as providing safe coastal refuge for their capital ships and U-boats. Again repeating their tactics of the First World War, the Germans hoped to subdue the British by starving the nation of food and fresh equipment by targeting overseas lifelines on which Britain depended. Germany's main naval weapon in these attacks was to be the U-boat, and control of the Biscay ports provided the Germans with bases from which they could go out into the Atlantic without having to pass either through the Channel or around the north of the British Isles at the end of every patrol.

Almost a third of British imports came via long hauls from colonial ports, journeys that were lengthened by having to avoid normal shipping routes. The closure of the Suez Canal to the east, for example, meant a long detour, increasing the distance to Bombay from 6,000 to 11,000 miles. The Atlantic crossing, however, became the focus of German attacks, as Winston Churchill warned in April 1941:

> In order to win this war Hitler must either conquer this island by invasion or he must cut the ocean lifeline which joins us to the United States. Wonderful exertions have been made by our navy, and our air force . . . by the men who build and repair our immense fleet of merchant ships, by the men who load and unload them, and, need I say, by the officers and men of the merchant navy, who go out in all weathers and in the teeth of all dangers to fight for love of their native land and for a cause they comprehend and serve.

Convoys of between 40 and 60 ships would steam in columns with 2 miles between each column and a third of a mile between each ship. A twelve-column convoy would extend 5½ nautical miles in length and almost 2 miles deep. The escorts of surface ships, submarines and aircraft would accompany convoys at various stages en route. The benefits to the merchantmen of sailing in convoy could be seen almost immediately. In the first full two years of the war, 12,057 ships arrived at British ports in 900 convoys. Only 291 ships in those convoys had been lost to enemy action, just under 2 per cent of the total. But there was a chink in the lifeline, and it became known as the Atlantic gap.

In the early months of the war, naval escorts for outgoing convoys from the British Isles could go only 300 miles out to sea before having to turn back to escort incoming convoys. Escort destroyers could stay out safely for only seven days without refuelling, which meant three and a half days' cover for a convoy and three and a half days back. This was increased to 400 miles by October 1940 and to halfway across the Atlantic by April 1941. Since air cover for shipping could also be provided from the British Isles, from Canada and Iceland, the Atlantic space left open to the U-boats was reduced by May 1941 to a width of around 300 miles. Even so, it was a yawning chasm, and in any event it did not stop German submarines exploiting the targets wherever they might find them.

Under the guidance of Admiral Karl Dönitz, the U-boats gradually built their devastating coordinated attacks on British and neutral shipping, with the Nazis once again playing the 'unrestricted warfare' card, which meant they would hit anything and everything that came within their sights. This was amply demonstrated by the 1941 sinking of the *Arandora Star*, an independent ship of 15,000 tonnes carrying German and Italian refugees from Liverpool to Halifax, Nova Scotia. In August the Germans hit the Dutch liner *Volendam*, which was carrying 320 refugee children, off Malin Head, and only good fortune and an excellent rescue operation saved them. A month later, 200 adults and children on the *City of Benares*, sunk by a U-boat attack, were not so lucky.

In spite of running huge convoys protected by surface escorts and submarines, the Allies were soon losing thousands of tonnes of shipping every month. In response, the Admiralty ordered more British submarines across the Atlantic to Halifax, Nova Scotia, Canada's finest harbour, and one of the best in the world at that time. Its extensive docks received shipping from far and wide and, closer at hand, the West Indies and American ports. There were also shipbuilding yards, an oil refinery, a naval station and a naval dockyard that had accommodation for stores and warships. Some boats of the 2nd Flotilla based on the Clyde were sent to Halifax to reinforce the surface escorts of the Atlantic convoys and, in part, to act as decoys for the U-boats and German warships. John Stevens, in *Thunderbolt* (ex-*Thetis*), recalled:

> The mounting convoy losses in the Atlantic were causing grave concern. There was considerable apprehension about the possibility that the German big ships would come out and mow down the convoys, in addition to the U-boat threat, which was substantial. We were sent over to be based in Nova Scotia along with half a dozen other submarines to provide ocean escorts for Atlantic crossings. Contingency plans were laid whereby the commodore of the convoys would try to draw whatever German ships appeared so that they came within our sights, ready to be sunk. It was not a popular job. We ploughed along on the outside of the convoy. The weather was very unpleasant, and we went out from Canada to the south of Iceland and back again.

Although Dönitz laid the focus heavily on his U-boat force, which had dramatically doubled and then trebled in strength since war was declared, individual warships with their escorts were also a menace to Allied shipping. The names of Germany's big battleships, such as the *Bismarck* and the *Tirpitz*, became as well known to the British public as their own famous ships, and the Royal Navy declared it would hunt them down, as indeed it did in one of the largest operations against a single enemy ship, the *Bismarck*. In

May 1941 British warships chased, trapped and finally sank the pride of Germany in what was recognised as a brilliant manoeuvre about 620 miles off the coast of France. From then on, the largest German warships were seldom seen, and the pressure on the British fleet came from German submarines, whose capability was demonstrated by one single statistic: between July and December 1941 the German U-boat strength was raised from 65 to more than 230.

By then, U-boats were roaming around in packs. They were called wolf packs, known to the Germans as *Rudeltaktik*, and were created by Dönitz specifically to operate against the Allied convoys. With a pack of heavily armed submarines, he reckoned a 30- or 40-ship convoy would be a duck shoot, with sufficient distance between them for the U-boats to retreat quickly before they could be attacked by the escorts. He finally had enough U-boats and handy coastal bases to try his idea, and initially it was exceedingly costly to Britain and her Allies. The first recorded 'pack attack' was launched against convoy number HX72, which began with 21 ships from Halifax, Nova Scotia, on 9 September 1940. Additional ships coming up from South America joined a day later, and finally 42 ships formed into 9 columns and set off on their journey across the Atlantic. Escorts were the Royal Canadian Navy destroyer *Saguenay* and patrol vessel *French*. They were joined by the armed merchant cruiser HMS *Jervis Bay*, which was subsequently pulled out as the convoy reached 500 miles west of Ireland to escort an outward-bound convoy back to America. This left a gap of around 17 hours when the convoy was unescorted. Destroyers of Western Approaches Command were to pick up the convoy around 300 miles west of Ireland. On 20 September 1940 the convoy was spotted by U-boat commander Günther Prien in *U47*. He was already famous in Germany for the sinking of the British battleship HMS *Royal*

Oak at Scapa Flow in October 1939. *U47* had, a few days earlier, carried out an attack on convoy SC2 and since then had been reporting weather conditions for the Luftwaffe raids on Britain. Prien signalled that he had sighted a large convoy and Admiral Dönitz personally took command of what was to become the first pack raid in the Battle of the Atlantic.

He instructed *U47* to sail ahead of the convoy and to keep watch until reinforcements arrived. He then dispatched five other U-boats to form a 30-mile-wide patrol line which Dönitz calculated would meet the convoy the following day. As the Allied ships approached, Dönitz ordered the U-boats to close in and attack, and in his diary for 22 September 1940 he wrote:

> Five boats, which lay up to 380 miles away at the time of the first sighting, were able to attack this homeward-bound convoy as a result of the accurate shadowing reports: 13 ships were sunk. This success was due to early interception far to the west of the weakly escorted convoy, correct tactical procedure of the boats in shadowing and operating over wide areas, and favourable weather. The action of the past two days has shown the soundness of details, worked out before the war, concerning attacks on convoys and the use of radio when in contact with the enemy.

The British account of the attack on HX72 put the losses at 11 ships, totally 72,727 tonnes and carrying over 100,000 tonnes of supplies and 45,000 tonnes of fuel. HX72 was the first Allied convoy of the war to lose more than five ships. The British naval commanders leading the convoys were also astonished to discover that German submarines had now begun operating among convoys at night as surface vessels; because of their small silhouette they were extremely difficult to see in the dark. Against this form of attack, the ASDIC was of little use because the U-boats were already on the surface.

Thereafter, the packs would work to a distinct pattern, with the Atlantic carved into prearranged grids and using patrol lines to scout for convoys. Once the convoy was located, a single U-boat would shadow it to report direction and speed. In the early stages, Dönitz directed many of the operations himself. He had all reports relayed back to his own command and would give his instructions for the deployment of the remaining boats in the pack attack on a convoy. Sometimes he would go for the strategy of picking off the stragglers, of whom there were always several. On other occasions he might surround a particular section of the convoy, and the packs would attack more or less in unison, usually at night and on the surface. Almost 140 wolf packs would be formed during their most active period, between 1940 and 1943, operating together for around two or three weeks. The smallest group would consist of 3 or 4 boats, although larger groups – even as many as 20 in one pack – were not uncommon. For the convoys, it was a fearful encounter to pick them up one by one on the ASDIC, circling like sharks. For the British submarine crews it was that – and more. The long journey across the Atlantic put a severe strain on the diesel motors, and bridge personnel in particular had to take the strain in the face of terrifying Atlantic weather conditions.

Former Petty Officer John Monan was on the submarine *Taku* in February 1941, heading for Nova Scotia in a Force Ten gale, when the engines gave up in the middle of the Atlantic and they lost power in incredible seas that threatened to overturn the boat. And if that wasn't enough, Monan recalled:*

> As I passed through the control room I noticed one or two crosses on the chart. I learned afterwards from the other lieutenant officer, who I was relieving in the motor room, that the crosses were U-boats just waiting for suitable weather to attack us. Later, as I passed through the control room again, I glanced at the chart and found that one or two more crosses had been added. As I took over the watch in the motor room I could see into the stokers' mess and I noticed one or two of them praying. One leading stoker started to sing quietly 'When I Survey the Wondrous Cross'. It seemed to do the trick. Two ships came out to look for *Taku*. For a while it was considered that the only solution was to scuttle the boat and for the crew to be transferred. In fact, they eventually got a towline over to her by rocket, and brought her back to base in Scotland for repairs.

With so many submarines required for Atlantic duties, every available boat was pressed into service. Although 53 new submarines were on order for delivery in 1941, plus another 9 coming in from the USA under Lend-Lease and 3 which had been built in British yards for Turkey but now kept back, there would be tasks enough for all. Until the new boats were commissioned, more of the pre-1919 H- and L-boats were being used for frontline stations. They were ill equipped, technologically impotent and exceedingly uncomfortable for the crews.

* In an article for *Submariners' News*, the newsletter of the Submariners' Association.

Yet a training flotilla of H-class submarines, which Commander F.W. Lipscomb* pointed out 'should never have been in existence, let alone on operational patrols', took the brunt of an 18-boat force pulled in from all quarters to form what became known as an 'iron ring' around Brest. They were on station around the clock to harass German shipping coming out of the well-protected harbour in the lee of north-west France. It was a haven for the enemy's big guns and fuelling for U-boats attacking the Atlantic convoys. It meant long stays under water. Lipscomb described the blockade as 'an exceptional event in submarine history', although there was the precedent in the First World War when Britain threw a similar blockade around Zeebrugge.

Meanwhile, out in the Atlantic the U-boat wolf pack tactics presented considerable difficulties in tracking their movements and being precise about their locations. In 1941, however, an event occurred that, although not directly involving the British submarine service, was to have a profound effect on its future deployment, and indeed the outcome of the war.

For this reason, although something of a diversion to the main thrust of these chapters, the story that is now about to unfold is given full attention here. Elements of it remained classified for many years after the war, and in the meantime there were interjections from a US navy unit who performed a similar operation (much later in the war) resulting, finally, in a fictional story told in the Hollywood film *U571*, released in April 2000, which claimed the accolades for the Americans. Distortions and inaccuracies have thus occurred. David Balme, who was a young British officer at the centre of this tale, became so concerned about some of the acts attributed

---

* *The British Submarine*, published by Conway Maritime Press, 1975, p. 74.

to him, which were totally untrue, that he provided a permanent record of events in an interview for the Sound Archive of the Imperial War Museum. His account is a blow-by-blow recollection which, because so many other witnesses confirmed it, cannot be challenged.

Balme begins his story by recounting his early career, having gone to Dartmouth at the age of 13 in 1933. In 1938 he was patrolling off Palestine in a minesweeper and, after taking his sub-lieutenant's course, he joined HMS *Berwick*, a cruiser, in Birkenhead, where she had just been refitted, and headed straight out for very active service in the Mediterranean. The Greek campaign was opening up, and *Berwick* was part of a major fleet operation, ferrying thousands of British troops to their start lines. By Christmas 1940 *Berwiek*, along with a large British contingent, was assigned to escort a substantial convoy of supply ships coming up from Australia. They knew that heavy German ships were at sea, and sure enough a major battle developed. *Berwick* was severely damaged and ten crew killed in a head-to-head with the German cruiser *Hipper* while the convoy sailed on unhindered. *Berwick* limped back to Portsmouth and was destined for the repair yard for some months. David Balme then joined the destroyer HMS *Bulldog* in February 1941, the year of his twenty-first birthday. For the remainder of his story, let us defer to his own words:

In was the happiest ship and the best time I ever had in the navy. It was a small ship, with a magnificent captain. There were only about four officers, executive officers, an engineer and a doctor. We were a small team and we were all kept very busy and had a lot of responsibility. We were the lead ship of the 3rd Escort Group, escorting convoys from the UK. A convoy would consist of about 40 merchant ships, and they would come, some from Liverpool, some from the Clyde, where we were, and some would come up the east coast and join us. So we would start off and gradually, as we got to the north-west tip of Scotland and set off into the Atlantic, we would have collected a convoy of 40 ships. Our escort group consisted of three destroyers, three or four corvettes, a couple of armed trawlers and a rescue boat, with several doctors, an operating theatre and we had nets for people to climb up on board if their ship had gone down.

No escort vessel could afford to stop to pick up survivors if a ship was torpedoed, which is why the rescue boat came along behind. We used to take this convoy across to a position south of Iceland and then we would go into Iceland to refuel, and another escort group would come out of Iceland and take the convoy on for another few days. The second escort group would then pick up another convoy coming from America to the British Isles and they would stay with them for about four days.

That was the terrific use of having a base in Iceland: we could get the convoys well north into the Atlantic, as far as possible from the U-boat bases. Even so, every trip you made you lost some ships. You were attacked, you went into a counter-attack or you detailed other ships to go and counter-attack. Britain had her back to the wall with regard to the supplies coming across the Atlantic. We didn't know then how bad it really was, but what we did know was that we were losing ships all the time and we knew they were full of rich and valuable cargoes, everything from oil to aircraft. We could see all the aircraft on decks. I suppose when you had forty ships you lost two or three on two occasions, one didn't

realise how vital those extra ones were. We weren't really
in a position to think too much about that. It was only
later that we would learn how desperate it really was,
and that perhaps the whole bacon ration for a month
was in one ship or something.

And so we come to David Balme's description of a momen-
tous day in the history of the Second World War, 9 May
1941:

I'd had the morning watch that day, which is four
o'clock to eight o'clock, with the convoy of about 40
ships. I had a shower, ate breakfast and then I suppose
about eleven o'clock I'd go up to the bridge. That was
the time of day when we used to congregate on the
bridge. It was a sunny day, blue sky, always a bit of a sea
in the Atlantic but not especially rough. It must have
been just after noon when suddenly two ships were
torpedoed: two enormous explosions and columns of
water rose up between them.

We immediately turned the convoy 45 degrees away
from where we expected the U-boat to be and we, being
the leader of the escort group, were in the centre ahead
of the convoy. We went off to the expected area of the
U-boat and there were two corvettes on that side too.
The captain told the rest of the escort to stay with the
convoy, in case there were other U-boats about, and
instructed the convoy to keep moving. As we moved in,
one of the corvettes, the *Aubretia*, immediately got
contact with the U-boat and fired depth charges. We
were just about arriving on the scene when she fired her
second pattern of depth charges and it pushed the
U-boat to the surface.

It is the dream of all escort vessels to see the U-boat coming to the surface, then you really know you've got her. As she came up, *Bulldog* opened fire on the conning tower with every gun we had. The noise in that submarine must have been desperate as the shells and machine-gun fire rattled on the hull. There must have been absolute panic. They just came piling out. Some did try to man their guns but we were all so close we opened up the machine-guns and they were either killed or jumped overboard. Twenty or thirty I suppose were just swimming about in the water. But she didn't sink. Normally you'd expect the submarine crew to set the detonating charges as they came out and then down she goes – lost for ever – but she didn't. She stayed on the surface and there was no attempt by the crew to scuttle her. My captain realised that immediately and said, 'Right, we will board her.' We must have been only about 300 yards from her by then. So the pipe went up for the seaboat crew, a rowing boat on davits. The captain turned to me and said, 'Sub, you take the seaboat.' By the time I reached the deck, the chief gunner's mate was dishing out revolvers and webbing and lifejackets.

My crew of seven or eight seamen get into the seaboat, an extraordinary thing like a whaler pointed both ends and five people rowing three on one side and two on the other, and we lower away until the boat is just off the water. With a big sea running in the Atlantic, you roll backwards and forwards and when you get to about 6 feet, I shout, 'Out pins,' and the seamen in the bow and the stern pull out two pins from the gear which is holding the boat up. So now nothing is holding the boat in the air except for a slip, just like a bent finger, and a seaman stands by this slip, and as *Bulldog* goes into a trough the rowing boat is launched on the crest of a roller. It can be very nasty because it could break over you and swamp you. This time, we dropped beautifully and we started rowing.

Meanwhile, the *Aubretia* was rescuing all the survivors from the sea, and this was all done with extraordinary efficiency. The survivors were picked up almost instantaneously, and Commander Baker-Cresswell, my captain, shouted over through a Tannoy to the *Aubretia*, 'Get them down below, quickly.' They were bundled away so they couldn't see what was going on up top. Had one German seen us going on board that U-boat, he would have got the message back somehow to Germany.

We brought the whaler alongside the U-boat, whose number was *U110*, and my bowman jumped off and held the boat steady. I had to climb over the oarsmen before jumping on the U-boat. It was a terribly round and slippery thing. I took out my revolver, walked along the casing and climbed up a fixed ladder into the conning tower. There was, I am glad to say, nobody about, but surprisingly the hatch, a round hatch 2 feet in diameter, was closed. It made me wonder if there were still some men on board. As I descended into the boat, I waved my revolver around in case anybody was there, just to have a shot at him if he appeared. I climbed straight down into the control room and this was really the worst moment. I was an easy target, as I needed both hands for going down.

Still no sign of anyone, fortunately, and I went just up to each end through the watertight doors, which were swinging, to make sure there was no one about. Having established that the crew had abandoned ship, I shouted up to my signalman, Pollock, who was still on the upper conning tower with his semaphore flags. I told him, 'Signal *Bulldog*: all clear,' and I told the rest of my crew, 'Come down below.' They all came down, leaving the signalman up top for communicating to *Bulldog*. My instructions were to strip the submarine of everything – papers, equipment, everything that we could easily get out that day. I formed a chain, two people on deck, two people in the next conning tower and so on down the ladders, and we were going to pass everything up we could lay our hands on.

We started off with the books, of course, every book on every bookshelf, all the maps and charts, navigation manuals, steamship manuals, coding books, signalling books . . . everything. Then we had a calamity even before we had loaded a single item. Our whaler was caught by the heavy seas and was smashed up against the side of the U-boat. We semaphored *Bulldog* and the captain arranged for another of our destroyers, HMS *Broadway*, to send over a boat. *Broadway* was an ex-American destroyer, the old four-stacker type, and fortunately she had motorboats, not rowing boats, which was quite useful given the task at hand.

All day, we ferried material over to the *Bulldog* and the captain was quite anxious that nothing was damaged. The code books, for example, were soluble and all the writing goes when salt water touches them. By some miracle everything went over without getting at all wet. I also had a telegraphist with me. His job was to go straight to the wireless room and take a reading of all the settings so we could establish what frequencies they were using. Because everything is terribly close in a submarine, the wireless room was only 8 feet away from where I was standing in the control room and the telegraphist called me over – 'Look, sir' – and he pointed to what appeared to be an old typewriter. We both said it looked interesting and that we'd better send it over.

So there it was ... the famous Enigma machine, screwed down with four screws to the desk. My telegraphist, a very bright chap, had disconnected it in no time and had it passed back, up the ladders, through the conning towers, across the deck into this motorboat and on to *Bulldog*. Gradually, during the day we took various other bits of equipment, small wireless sets and anything we could remove and bits of machinery which looked interesting, unscrewed and sent up. Then I opened up the chart table and drawers and there were all these charts with heavy black lines coming out of all the French ports, which were obviously the German search channels. These were brand new, and it was the first time anyone had ever captured charts of all the German minefields and these were used, no doubt, for the next year at least. Next, I discovered what became famously known as the grid map, which the Allies had not seen before. It divided the Atlantic up into squares with U-boats assigned to patrol certain areas.

It took a long time to conduct a thorough search, and removing the material was at times quite a delicate operation. Many of these books were simply irreplaceable, some containing top-secret Nazi codes and ciphers, such as the Officers' Only Cipher Book which, again, we apparently had never previously seen. We were searching the U-boat for six hours, whereas usually boarding parties might dash in and out in twenty minutes. The captain very kindly sent some sandwiches over. And some tea. Everybody was thrilled and engrossed. There was a feeling of great excitement, yes, yes.

When it was all over, the captain decided to take things one step further. He decided we would try to take the U-boat in tow, and they began passing lines over. I stayed aboard with my crew. Eventually, we got her in tow but before long the wire parted so we then had to get a cable attached as well. We began moving along quite satisfactorily when suddenly an alert occurred. A U-boat periscope had been spotted, so *Bulldog* slipped the tow and went off to attack. She sailed off into the distance and eventually disappeared from sight. That was a very forlorn moment for us in this U-boat bouncing around in the middle of the Atlantic without power and leaking badly. We were very, very glad indeed to see her back again in due course. We managed to get the towlines hitched up again.

Soon afterwards, the captain ordered the boarding party back to *Bulldog*, and the U-boat remained under tow for the time being. It was slow progress in choppy seas but the following day, just before noon, Baker-Cresswell ordered the towline to be withdrawn and *U110*, now heavily flooded, sank almost immediately. The ship then progressed on to Iceland, where the surviving crew of *U110* was transferred to *Bulldog* for the journey back to base, at Scapa Flow, as prisoners of war. Balme continued:

It was ironic. Just through the bulkhead from where the prisoners were kept were all their ciphers, books and charts, just 6 yards away. They had no idea they were sleeping and eating within feet of all their secrets. We took 36 hours to get back to Scapa Flow, and as we went alongside we got rid of all the German prisoners. They were all blindfolded so they couldn't see what ships were in base. They all thought they were being blind-folded to be taken along to be shot. A Bletchley Park expert was there to greet us and to go through all the books and I helped him. It was only then that the significance of it began to dawn on us. It was a very exciting day. He said these things were absolutely untold heaven, particularly the ciphers, the machine and the settings, the list of settings, and so on. He photographed every single page of every book just in case they got lost in an aircraft or train going back to London and Bletchley.

Afterwards we were sworn to secrecy, never allowed to say anything to anybody. The captain was emphatic: 'You must never breathe a word to any of your family or anybody ever about what we had done.' I could see just a few months later in the *Intelligence Digest*, which we were all given to read, how the sinkings went down enormously. I knew it was largely because of this. It was the most closely guarded secret ever. There were some medals, of course, and they were also handled discreetly. I was awarded the DSC. King George VI made the presentation personally. He was frightfully well informed and really knew the significance of it. He was a remarkable man and when he decorated me he said: 'This is a most important event of the whole war at sea. I wish I was giving you a much higher decoration, but I can't because of security.'

The secrecy was maintained, and because of it authors and historians struggled for years to piece together the intricate web of code-breaking activity that emerged from Bletchley Park, known as Ultra, during the war years. Although at its peak 10,000 people worked there in cramped surroundings, it was cleared, dismantled and left virtually without trace in 1946. Even in the twenty-first century, the official website of the administrators of the historical building admits: 'The history of Bletchley Park is, to an extent, still shrouded in mystery.'

It was because of this lack of definite information that inaccuracies began to appear in post-war writings. An account of the capture of *U110* appeared in Germany and caused David Balme and his colleagues considerable anguish. He went on:

> It was claimed that the boarding officer – myself – shot dead the captain of the U-boat, Fritz Lemp. This theory was propagated by an author who was supposed to be an authority on the Battle of the Atlantic and thereafter every other writer seemed to take up the theme. A German Sunday newspaper began a long serialisation of the story. My name was mentioned as the officer who shot the captain, which was totally untrue. Through a friend of mine, another German writer came to England and interviewed me and soon afterwards published his story, stating that he could authentically state that David Balme did not shoot Lemp. He died in some other way.

In fact, 12 members of the *U110* crew were killed in the action, largely those who went to man the guns when the boat surfaced. Lemp was not among them. He dived overboard with the 32 survivors. The U-boat telegraphist, Hogel, was interviewed and remembered the captain swimming alongside him. Then he disappeared. He was a young man and a strong swimmer. So how did he die? That question brings us finally to the point of this diversion. Lemp, it seems, had expected *Bulldog* to proceed on its ramming course when he ordered 'Abandon ship!' However, *Bulldog* didn't ram the boat, and when he looked back and saw that *U110* was still afloat he realised she would give up all the German secrets. It can only be speculation as to his demise: either he committed suicide or he tried to swim back to the boat to scuttle it and drowned in the attempt.

The possibility of *U110* ever having completed its journey under tow into Iceland was also remote. Baker-Cresswell knew of the U-boat's value to British intelligence, which is why he had not rammed it. He also knew that if he took the boat into Iceland, the many Nazi spies there would know instantly that the British had captured an Enigma machine and all that went with it. By the following day, Berlin would have changed all codes and cipher systems. As it was, the capture of *U110* would remain the best-kept secret in the Royal Navy.

This, then, is how the machine and manuals from *U110* came into the hands of Bletchley Park. As history has now shown us, the Enigma cipher had been the backbone of German military and intelligence communications since 1918. They believed it to be unbreakable, and with good reason. Enigma's complexity was astonishing. Typing in a letter of plain German into the machine sent electrical impulses through a series of rotating wheels, electrical contacts and wires to produce the enciphered letter, which lit up on a panel above the keyboard. By typing the resulting code into his own machine, the recipient saw the deciphered message light up letter by letter. The rotors and wires of the machine could be configured in numerous different ways. The odds against anyone who did not know the settings being able to break Enigma were a staggering 150 million million million to one.

Polish mathematicians had broken Enigma in 1932 and

had even managed to reconstruct a machine. When war came, the code changed, effectively locking the Poles out. In July 1939 they had passed on their knowledge to the British. Armed with this knowledge, the code-breakers at Bletchley Park were already reading much of Germany's signals intelligence, aided eventually to even greater coverage and accuracy by the inventions of brilliant mathematician Alan Turing and the documents and equipment captured from *U110* and other German vessels boarded by the Royal Navy during the course of the war.

British sailors boarded German ships and seized Enigma material as early as 1940. They included Lieutenant Alec Dennis, for example, who led a boarding party that captured a German trawler with its Enigma code books in April 1940. Another important collection was captured 17 months after the *U110* incident. *U559* was depth-charged by the British destroyers *Pakenham*, *Petard* and *Hero* in the Mediterranean, north-east of Port Said, on 30 October 1942. Seven members of the crew were killed and thirty-two survived. Realising the value of the material on board, the sinking wreck was boarded by three members of the crew from *Petard*. They went into the boat and brought out numerous secret documents, a task they continued even as the boat was on the verge of going to the bottom. Unfortunately, the British sailors were still handing out files when she finally sank, and two of the three were drowned.

Stanley Reynolds, a 21-year-old able seaman at the time, recalled the incident: 'I could see the U-boat was sinking, although two of our men inside, including the first lieutenant, were still passing up equipment and confidential books. Then the U-boat's stern disappeared under the waves. Seconds later she plunged to the bottom of the sea. Although we searched around the place where the U-boat disappeared, we never saw the two men who had been inside the U-boat again.'

The next U-boat to be captured was *U505*, which fell into the hands of an American hunter-killer group consisting of USS *Guadalcanal* and four American destroyers off Cape Blanc in French West Africa on 4 June 1944 and was towed in triumph to Bermuda. Rear-Admiral Daniel V. Gallery, of the US navy, later wrote a vivid account in his book *We Captured a U-Boat*. By then, the contents of the U-boat were of far less significance. The British had collected masses of intelligence courtesy of Enigma and had finally given the Americans access to Bletchley Park's brilliant work some months before Gallery's men took their prize. The captured boat became a museum piece, and is maintained as such to this day.

Admiral Gallery's book raised considerable anger within the Royal Navy after its publication, and their official historian, Captain S.W. Roskill, was moved to write:

For one thing, no British officer who served in the Atlantic battle will accept the Admiral's implication that the idea of boarding and capturing a U-boat was an original inspiration on his part. He was wrong to claim that *U505* 'was the only German submarine boarded and captured at sea'. One can only presume that when he wrote his book, Admiral Gallery had never heard of the Royal Navy's achievement. Nor is that surprising, for the secret was so closely guarded that no one except the actual participants and a few highly placed officers in the Admiralty ever knew the whole story even though cooperation between the Royal Navy and the United States navy later became complete.

It is indeed a remarkable fact that although the crews

of three escort vessels and many survivors of recently sunk merchantmen who were on board them at the time – totalling at least 400 officers and men – all knew that *U110* had been captured, not one of them ever breathed a word about it. Rarely can discretion have been more severely tested or a secret better kept. But there is another very important fact regarding the capture of *U110*, and one which makes the accomplishment absolutely unique. Whereas the original crew of Admiral Gallery's *U505* was aware that their ship had been captured, so skilfully was the seizure of *U110* carried out that the German survivors never discovered that their ship fell into enemy hands. This greatly enhanced the value of the capture – more than three years before Gallery's men hoisted the Stars and Stripes above the Nazi cross.

Anger among British Second World War veterans about American claims was revived in April 2000 with the release of *U571*, starring Harvey Keitel, Matthew McConaughey and Jon Bon Jovi. It was a supposedly fictional account of how a US submarine was sent to recover the Enigma machine and its code books, but for British veterans the implication was clear: that the Americans won the war because they captured the crucial machine and code books. They rightly branded it as tasteless and misleading.

The vital fact was that the British were in possession of the material when it really mattered. Each new collection captured added to their knowledge; from the *Petard*, for example, came important documents that were greatly to aid the British submarine service, and at the same time put the German U-boats at greater risk of detection – a fact that was well borne out by the losses suffered by the two groups.

U-boat losses spiralled from the second half of 1941, and the more general effect of cutting the tonnage of ships sunk by the wolf pack marauders was equally dramatic. That is not to say that the attacks on Allied convoys were anything less than murderous.

In 1942 U-boats sank more than 6,266,000 tonnes of shipping targets. The sinkings peaked in March 1943 when, with 240 U-boats at sea, they torpedoed in that single month 627,377 tonnes of shipping. The total included the most excruciating battle, from the Allies' point of view, since the war began when 20 U-boats attacked a merged convoy of 77 ships and sank 21 of them, while losing only 1 of their own. At the end of that month, however, the tide began to turn. British anti-submarine warfare actions were stepped up considerably. British Coastal Command joined the over-all offensive, launching three major operations using radar-equipped aircraft that the Germans could not detect.

U-boats reported back to base that they were being attacked at night without warning. On 1 May Dönitz ordered that all U-boats fitted with guns 'should stay on the surface and fight back'. This merely added to the onslaught, and in that month of May 1943, generally considered to be the turning point in the Battle of the Atlantic, 41 U-boats were sunk, which represented more than a quarter of their operational strength at the time. Germany never recovered from this disaster. The following month, the U-boat tally fell below 100,000 tonnes of Allied shipping sunk. The crisis in the Atlantic was over.

CHAPTER EIGHT

In the Med . . . and 'the Finest Work Ever by British Submarines'

The Mediterranean had been necessarily neglected. The demands of the Norwegian campaign followed by the fear of invasion and then the appalling losses on the Atlantic convoys had simply prevented any build-up at British naval bases in Malta and Alexandria before the autumn of 1940. True, there had been a continuation of the phoney war in the Mediterranean of the kind that had initially affected Europe, and the needs were not as pressing as those closer to home. All that was about to change, but in the short term little could be done to meet the challenge. Warnings by GOC General Sir William Dobbie that the defences of Malta, for example, were woefully meagre, and included no aircraft, were soon proved to be entirely accurate.

Mussolini began the formalities when he threw his hand in with Hitler at the end of May 1940. Soon, he was ferrying his forces into North Africa to take on the British Army of the Nile, and General Sir Archibald Wavell, head of the British

1st Army, was amassing 300,000 Allied troops for the land battles. He was confident that he would rout the Italian advances in the land war. On the sea, however, British resources were stretched to the limit, especially for the submarine flotillas, such as they were. Overnight, traditional British supply routes to its eastern outposts in the Mediterranean and to the Middle East were closed down. The British war managers had to send their ships on the long journey, lasting two or three months, around the Cape of Good Hope for all supplies, other than those borne by special convoys with major fleet escort operations, which the Royal Navy could ill afford. At the time, neither Britain nor Germany had any great submarine presence in what was about to become the most vital arena in the war. With the lack of very serious competition, the Italian navy put up a very worthwhile case for supremacy in the Med – for the time being, at least – fielding a decent array of 5 capital ships, 25 cruisers, 90 destroyers and 90 submarines. They had a back-up of 2,000 frontline aircraft and were also experimenting with mini-subs, human torpedoes, underwater chariots and exploding motorboats to provide additional hazards for the British. When Mussolini entered the war, it soon became abundantly clear to the British that they had no real naval force between Gibraltar and the Italian fleet ports. The British base at Malta possessed a puny collection of just six submarines and no shoreline headquarters of any note. One. of the first operations of Mussolini's navy was to lay large new minefields all around the Italian coastline, and encircling Malta.

Consequently, three of the six British submarines based there, the minelayer *Grampus*, and *Odin* and *Orpheus*, were lost in the first week after Mussolini signed his pact with Hitler. It was believed that they were all sunk with no survivors by deeply laid Italian mines, in depths of up to 100 fathoms, although post-war investigations showed that all three had recently arrived from service in the Far East and had not yet adapted to the local conditions and dangers. This latter aspect proved to be a significant factor throughout the war, for both British and German submarines. The sinkings were followed by intense air raids on Malta, and the British naval base in particular.

These coincided with the beginning of large-scale Italian convoys making the trip across to Libya, and the British submarine operations were for the time being left to the base at Alexandria, Egypt. While these operations kept the enemy on its toes, it was clear that reinforcements were desperately needed at both bases. The new U-class submarines, now rolling out of British shipyards, were largely destined for Mediterranean patrols launched from Malta, but they were still completing trials in Scottish lochs when Italy joined the war and the bulk would not be available until well into 1941.

The 1st Flotilla, based at Alexandria, meanwhile, was bolstered in the autumn to include the submarine depot ship HMS *Medway*, along with five of the new T-class, three R-class, two P-class, one of the remaining O-class and the minelayer *Cachalot*. The Italians were soon being harassed as their ships carrying men, munitions and supplies made their way across to North Africa. The response, however spirited, was insufficient to stem the flow, and the British themselves found the Italian counter-measures equally difficult, particularly in the quantity of fresh and deep-laid mines and the new torpedo boats being brought out by the Italians.

At least Alexandria had a working base and an operations management. Malta was a vital location in the centre of the Mediterranean and a staging post for the British fleet passing through to the east, but it still had no organised structure for submarine operations. Commander Ronald Mills, whom we met in Chapter Six, was sent to the Mediterranean after the Norway campaign, bound for Malta with three other submarines:

> I was given overall command. There were four T-boats: my own, *Tetrarch*, Hugh Haggard in the *Truant*, Tiny Watkins in the *Triton*, and George Salt in command of *Triad*. The Admiral Commanding told me that I would have to give instructions to my team where I wanted them to operate. That was it, basically. There was no plan as such, no overall mapping out of what course of action we should take. Haggard was the only one of them, apart from myself, who had done a war patrol, so he and I discussed it and decided we would give the easier patrol positions to the *Triton* and the *Triad* while we ourselves went in close to the coast of Italy. We were all to meet up in Malta and use that as our base, although it was fairly risky because the Italian air force had been using it for target practice.

Haggard's *Truant*, formerly under the command of Lieutenant-Commander Hutchinson and badly damaged during the Norwegian campaign, had just returned from a refit, as Norman Jewell, then a 27-year-old first lieutenant, explained:

> We set off from Chatham and headed for the Mediterranean, sailing round the north of Scotland and down through the Irish Sea. Just as we got into the Bay of Biscay we saw two merchant ships coming towards us from Bordeaux. We surfaced to challenge them, and as we did so the sides of the ships were blown out. It

turned out that the ships were under the command of German prize crews, carrying men and secret equipment and documents from the *Graf Spee*,* as well as British and Norwegian prisoners. The ships' German captains were apparently under orders to scuttle if challenged and that is what they did. The crews and the prisoners took to the boats minutes before they scuttled. They included a woman, the wife of one of the captured captains. She had lost her handbag and had dived over the side to retrieve it. Thus she was soaking wet when we picked her up.† We took the prisoners aboard the submarine, about 30 in all, but we did not have room for the Germans. They complained bitterly but we signalled their position and they were eventually picked up by Sunderland flying boats. We landed those we had rescued in Gibraltar and continued on towards Malta.

Ronald Mills had already arrived at Malta in *Tetrarch* and was followed in later by Haggard in *Truant*. The other two boats, *Triad* and *Triton*, failed to make the rendezvous. *Triad* was torpedoed, and *Triton* was last reported on patrol off the coast of Italy. Nothing more was heard from her, although it is thought she may have been engaged by MV *Olympia*.

Ronald Mills had to set about establishing the Malta base, more or less off his own bat:

I felt it was essential to get a base up and running, and since I was the most senior of the COs there I made a signal to my admiral saying that I had decided to take

---

* *Graf Spee*, pride of the German fleet, was scuttled by her own crew and went down in flames after the famous Battle of the River Plate with three British warships in Uruguay on 17 December 1939.
† On record as the first woman ever to travel in a submarine.

over command there and to give command of my submarine *Tetrarch** to one of the spare crew officers. I remained in command of Malta for about three months until eventually Captain G.W.G. Simpson, who was designated for the job but was away on leave, came to take over. By the time he arrived it was very much a going concern. We had built an underground torpedo workshop, torpedo storage shops and we had definitely got the place going quite well under the guidance of my engineer officer, Sam MacGregor, who was a lieutenant-commander.

The Italians were bombing us daily, but we didn't really have very much fear of them even though we had just three aircraft, which we called Pip, Squeak and Wilfred. They were piloted by the governor's personal staff, and they contrived to keep the Italians from getting too close to us. When the Luftwaffe took over it was a very different matter altogether.

Indeed it was. Although the Italian bombing of Malta had been bad enough, the arrival close at hand of the Luftwaffe's crack dive-bombers at a base commandeered by the Germans on the island of Sicily, a short hop from Malta, brought unperceived terror to the island itself, and to the British fleet in general. Further German air bases were opened up on the Italian mainland to accommodate all varieties of the Luftwaffe strike force and, aware of the peculiarities of the Mediterranean, spotter planes and dive-bombers soon began to menace British surface ships and submarines. In late November 1940, for example, *Regulus*,

---

* *Tetrarch* was herself lost with all hands, mined in the Strait of Sicily in October 1941.

under Lieutenant-Commander F.B. Currie, was attacked from the air. She was one of four of the second batch of R-class boats originally built in 1930 for the Mediterranean but which had been in service in the Far East for the previous five years. Her crew was new to the arena. She was thought to have been sunk under attack from an Italian aircraft. This brought the number of British submarines lost with all hands in the Mediterranean in the six months since Mussolini entered the war to 9, along with 41 officers and 407 ratings.

These initial exchanges were a prelude to the German advance into North Africa, after Wavell's armies put the Italians to flight, captured Tobruk and took 100,000 prisoners. Three weeks later, on 14 February 1941, General Erwin Rommel's Afrika Korps landed at Tripoli with orders to rescue Mussolini's army. Now the real battles in the Western Desert began. German panzers and tens of thousands of troops sailed in every available craft across the Mediterranean to Libya and Tunisia.

Fresh to his command in Malta, Shrimp Simpson, RN, received a signal from his C-in-C which was brief and to the point: 'Stop all supplies from Italy to Tripoli.' The task fell almost exclusively to the slender Malta force, because the 1st Flotilla at Alexandria was 1,000 miles down the coast from Libya, and in any event had other pressing duties in the eastern Mediterranean and the Aegean, where Greece and the Greek islands were under attack first from the Italians and then with the invasion of the German land forces.

Malta, on the other hand, was within striking distance of all the shipping routes used by the Axis to cross the Mediterranean, and because of that the island became the object of intense bombing by the Luftwaffe as Rommel began his expedition into the Western Desert. The submarine base at Lazaretto Creek on the sheltered side of Valletta was a particular target, and by necessity bomb-proof shelters were carved out of thick sandstone walls behind the buildings and dived moorings also had to be established for submarines at the base during air raids. Not before time, Simpson was given delivery dates for his new U-class submarines, which would begin arriving from January 1941 onwards. Very soon, the Malta force began to show its mettle. Tonnage of ships sunk or severely damaged soon began to mount even though, initially, Simpson could put perhaps only four submarines on patrol at any one time in the central Mediterranean. In the first three months of operations under the new command, 11 supply ships, the Italian cruiser *Armando Diaz* and the Italian U-boat *Capponi* were sunk by the Malta-based *Regent*, *Upholder*, *Truant*, *Utmost*, *Rover*, *Upright* and *Ursula*.

The pressure to hit the Axis supply convoys became even more imperative when Rommel's Afrika Korps was in position to launch a full-scale land offensive at the beginning of April. The British Army of the Nile was put to flight, forced back towards Egypt, and 9,000 British troops and three British generals were captured. As Rommel's campaign gathered momentum, so did his need of supplies and fuel, which were still getting through without great hindrance. As more U-class submarines arrived to take up patrol, so the attacks became more frequent. John Stevens, whom we last met on the Atlantic patrols aboard *Thunderbolt*, now had his own command, *Unruffled*:

Our main priority was to intercept Rommel's convoys of two or three supply ships. *Unruffled* had a satisfactory number of hits, over time sinking well in excess of a dozen, amounting to 40,000 tonnes of shipping. We also knocked out four schooners with our gun. In the main, we didn't stop for survivors, because the convoys were usually escorted by three destroyers or other types of escorts and aircraft as well. Our primary targets were always the supply ships, not the escorts. We didn't have enough torpedoes to have a go at everything. The U-class boats were intended for short patrol operations, carrying just eight torpedoes, four in the tubes and four reloads. If you had maybe two torpedo attacks soon after you'd got out on patrol, you would have expended all your torpedoes and you would have to return to Malta. We did have a small 3-inch gun but there was no use staying out with that. So we had to be quite selective in our targets. We had a number of close shaves with counter-attacks, sometimes up to five hours with charges coming down. And quite often they might be able to see the boat or get reports from the air. That was one of the warnings commanders new to Mediterranean patrols were always given when they arrived at Malta – that they could be seen from the air to depths of perhaps 150 feet. They used to take us up in light aircraft to show us how easily you could be seen. The Axis forces had long ago cottoned on to this, and most of the convoys we were attacking now had two seaplanes prowling around, front and rear, looking for signs of submarines.

Because of the danger of being spotted from above and the heftily mined regions close to the Italian coastline, Shrimp Simpson worked out a plan to trap the supply boats. Rather than attack en route, his commanders perfected a way of lying in wait close to their destination, when the spotter planes may well have turned back or landed, and the surface craft felt more secure in sight of Tripoli harbour. It worked very effectively.

The Malta flotilla was soon notching up very substantial totals of enemy shipping sunk, and none better than *Upholder*, under the command of Lieutenant-Commander Malcolm Wanklyn. He became the most successful submarine commander in the Second World War in spite of what would prove to be a relatively short career. Launched at Vickers Armstrong, *Upholder* arrived for duty at Malta on 12 January 1941. On her first patrol, she sank a 5,000-tonne cargo vessel in one of the Axis convoys just off Tripoli, and in almost the same spot two days later sank an 8,000-tonne supply ship in an escorted convoy. This time, *Upholder* was counter-attacked and took the brunt of 32 depth charges before escaping under cover of darkness.

After a brief lay-off, *Upholder* returned to the fray and in April, again off Tripoli, severely damaged a cargo ship and the following day boarded the Italian supply ship *Arta*, which had been attacked by British destroyers. The boarding party accidentally set fire to the ship while attempting to blow open the safe but managed to recover a batch of confidential documents, along with a collection of souvenirs including German helmets and guns. Wanklyn, ever the joker, returned from patrol flying the German ensign, with a line of ratings on the casing wearing German helmets.

On 1 May 1941 *Upholder* was back in action and sank three separate targets in a single convoy: a destroyer, a 4,000-tonne supply ship and a 10,000-tonne supply ship. On 24 May Wanklyn sighted a troopship, the Italian liner *Conte Rosso* of 17,800 tonnes, carrying 4,000 troops, with an escort of three cruisers and several destroyers. He launched two torpedoes which both scored a direct hit amidships. The liner sank rapidly, killing 1,500 of the men on board. Wanklyn was awarded the DSO for this attack.

It might well have been the competitive spirit among the

Malta-based commanders that brought results, and certainly by mid-year the flotilla as a whole was scoring an increasing number of target hits, although around that time the flotilla lost four of its own boats in quick succession. *Usk* struck a mine at Cape Bon, *Undaunted* and *Union* were both depth-charged off Tripoli and the minelaying submarine *Cachalot* was rammed by an Italian torpedo boat while en route from Malta to Alexandria and was scuttled by her crew to avoid her being taken.

At Alexandria, naval successes were similarly the high point of an otherwise fairly dismal array of news for the Allies. The British had been forced to retreat ignominiously from Greece, leaving a mass of equipment and thousands of prisoners and casualties behind; they were being bombed out of Crete; Yugoslavia had fallen to the Nazi blitzkrieg; and, fortunately for the British, Hitler had just broken his pact with Russia and his troops were advancing towards Moscow. The only good news was that the Italians had surrendered in Abyssinia, and the Desert Rats of the 8th Army were now beginning to nibble away at Rommel's Afrika Korps.

Thus, with all the bad news around the Mediterranean and beyond, supply lines to Rommel's army remained a number-one priority if the British were to turn the tide in the Western Desert. Malcolm Wanklyn and his fellow commanders at Malta began to take greater risks and shorter breaks. In September 1941, as Wanklyn set out on his fourteenth patrol, he joined up with *Unbeaten*, *Upright* and *Ursula* for a prearranged assault to intercept and sink a troop-carrying convoy leaving the southern Italian port of Taranto bound for Tunisia. In an operation akin to the U-boat wolf packs, the four submarines took up position close to the enemy's route to the north of Misurta, on the north-west corner of Sirte. The three transports had an escort of three destroyers, and *Upholder* closed at full speed to penetrate the escort's screen. After reaching positions, Wanklyn's gyrocompass failed and he had to rely on the magnetic compass. He fired first, launching three torpedoes judged by the naked eye from 4,500 metres.

Two torpedoes hit the transport *Neptunia*, which sank in eight minutes, and the destroyers had to hurry to collect survivors. Wanklyn's third torpedo hit *Oceania* and ripped away her stern. The third transport, *Vulcania*, was hit by *Ursula* from long range, and *Utmost* finished her off as she tried to limp away. Meanwhile, *Utmost* now sighted three Italian cruisers and several destroyers and promptly sank one of the cruisers.

As a result of his latest exploits, Malcolm Wanklyn was awarded the Victoria Cross in December 1941. The citation read:

On the evening of 24 May 1941, whilst on patrol off the coast of Sicily, Lieutenant-Commander Wanklyn, in command of His Majesty's Submarine *Upholder*, sighted a south-bound enemy troop convoy, strongly escorted by destroyers. The failing light was such that observation by periscope could not be relied on but a surface attack would have been easily seen. *Upholder*'s listening gear was out of action. In spite of these severe handicaps Lieutenant-Commander Wanklyn decided to press home his attack at short range. He quickly steered his craft into a favourable position and closed in so as to make sure of his target. By this time the position of the escorting destroyers could not be made out. Lieutenant-Commander Wanklyn, while fully aware of the risks of being rammed by one of the escorts, continued to press on towards the enemy troopships. As he was about to fire, one of the enemy destroyers suddenly appeared out of the darkness at high speed, and he only just avoided being rammed. As soon as he was clear, he brought his periscope sights on and fired torpedoes, which sank a large troopship. The enemy destroyers at once made a strong counter-attack and during the next twenty minutes dropped thirty-seven depth charges near *Upholder*. The failure of his listening devices made it much harder for him to get away, but with the greatest courage, coolness and skill he brought *Upholder* clear of the enemy and safely back to harbour.

Before this outstanding attack, and since being appointed a Companion of the Distinguished Service Order, Lieutenant-Commander Wanklyn had torpedoed a tanker and a merchant vessel. He has continued to show the utmost bravery in the presence of the enemy. He has carried out his attacks on the enemy with skill and relentless determination; he has also sunk one destroyer, one U-boat, two troop-transports of 19,500 tonnes each, one tanker and three supply ships. He has besides probably destroyed by torpedoes one cruiser and one destroyer, and possibly hit another cruiser.

These attacks brought the reprisals everyone expected but hoped would never happen. Bombing raids over Malta and the submarine base were stepped up – and in merciless fashion. A relentless blitz of night attacks, dive-bombing and airdrop minelaying were deployed against the island and its military guests. The submarines not on patrol were moored in an arc so that a straight stick of bombs could not fall along it. The attacks continued almost daily, and on 13 February 1942 the Lazaretto submarine base was badly hit, with the sick-quarters and mess-decks flattened. Another wave of attacks on 17 February brought a deluge of armour-piercing bombs that sank several submarines.

The people of Malta were themselves now severely traumatised by the bombing raids and hungry through lack of supplies. For weeks, what became known locally as the Magic Carpet – the larger River-class or Narwhal-class boats – had been ferrying in supplies from Alexandria round the clock. The two most regular of these underwater freighters were the *Clyde* and the minelaying submarine *Porpoise*, whose mine-decks had been cleared to be stacked with stores, and occasionally passengers and VIPs. In fact, all submarines which had to pass Malta would invariably be detailed to drop off supplies for the island. The old destroyer HMS *Breconshire* made several trips, often under air fire. *Porpoise*, too, had a lucky escape on one of her supply runs when she was battered with 87 depth charges and a shower of aircraft bombs. In total, the cargo-carrying boats brought 383,135 litres of petrol, 378,860 litres of kerosene, 30 tonnes of general stores, 12 tonnes of mail, 6 tonnes of munitions and 126 essential personnel to Malta.

Meanwhile, one of Malta's greatest heroes, Malcolm Wanklyn, had come to the end of his term and was due to return *Upholder* to England for a refit. On 6 April 1942 *Upholder* sailed out of the base for her twenty-fifth and last patrol before heading off to Gibraltar and then home at the end of this final two-week stint. But she never made it back.

On 14 April *Upholder* was depth-charged and sunk by the Italian torpedo boat *Pegaso* north-east of Tripoli, where Wanklyn had himself sunk so many enemy ships. His was a remarkable record. During the 16 months with the 10th Submarine Flotilla, *Upholder* had sunk or damaged 22 enemy ships, including 3 U-boats, 2 destroyers and 1 cruiser as well as 119,000 tonnes of enemy supply ships. News of the loss was not formally announced by the Admiralty until 22 August 1942, when it released a statement that was quite unprecedented in naval history in that it included a tribute to the submarine and her captain:

> It is seldom proper for Their Lordships to draw distinction between different services rendered in the course of naval duty, but they take this opportunity of singling out those of HMS *Upholder*, under the command of Lieutenant-Commander Wanklyn, for special mention. She was long employed against enemy communications in the Central Mediterranean, and she became noted for the uniformly high quality of her services in that arduous and dangerous duty. Such was the standard of skill and daring that the ship and her officers and men became an inspiration not only to their own flotilla but to the fleet of which it was a part, and Malta, where for so long HMS *Upholder* was based. The ship and her company are gone, but the example and the inspiration remain.

Shrimp Simpson was said to be on the verge of quitting Malta but held on when he heard the news about *Upholder*. Pulling out was like giving in, and Simpson was not about to do that, although he knew that the extent of bombing raids being suffered by Malta now could not be endured much longer. The courage and resilience of the islanders were recognised on 16 April when King George VI announced the award of the George Cross, the civilian VC, to the island fortress which had withstood four months of almost daily bombing.

The latest disasters were the loss of several of the Spitfires which had finally arrived to help in the defence but which were reduced to a handful within 48 hours. Then the submarine base at Lazaretto was subjected to an all-out attack by the Luftwaffe, whose instructions, clearly, were to wipe it out – totally. Simpson's 10th Flotilla finally had to leave. Five of his remaining submarines were sent home to England for a refit. The remaining five (out of the original twenty that had joined the force) were assigned to Alexandria to join up with the T-class boats of the 1st Flotilla and later joined operations from Beirut, where another fine submarine base had been established. En route, another tragedy and another Malta hero lost: *Urge*, under the command of Lieutenant-Commander Tommo Tompkinson, was never seen again. She had completed 20 patrols.

Ten submarines had been lost in the first phase of the Malta operations, although the absence of the 10th Flotilla from the island lasted only ten weeks before Shrimp Simpson returned with *Unbroken*, *Unison*, *Unbending* and *United*, tooled up ready for work. The new Malta force was in place to support the famous mercy mission to relieve the besieged island with the convoy in August 1942, code-named Pedestal, which faced fierce bombardment from the Luftwaffe, sinking all but five supply ships out of fourteen that set out and dozens of the escort vessels that were amassed to drive the convoy into Valletta.

At the other end of the Mediterranean, the action was similarly frenetic for the Alexandria flotilla and more VCs were to be won. Among them was an incident involving *Thrasher*, a relatively new T-boat which had been in the Mediterranean only a couple of months and in February 1942 was operating off northern Crete. There, on 16 February, she penetrated an escort screen of five destroyers in broad daylight and torpedoed and sank a large Axis supply ship off Suda Bay. The destroyers gave chase, and as she crash-dived they remained overhead for an hour or more, sending down more than 30 depth charges. *Thrasher* stayed in the depths for two hours, and after dark surfaced to discover that the destroyers had left. She headed off towards the Gulf of Taranto, but very soon banging noises were heard on the casing. An investigation revealed that two unexploded bombs had become attached to the submarine.

Lieutenant Peter Roberts and Petty Officer Tommy Gould volunteered to go out and recover the bombs, one of which had lodged on the gun-deck and the second inside the casing. The first bomb was located and gently removed, wrapped in sacking and dropped over the stern. What happened next is described in the citation for the Victoria Cross subsequently awarded to each of them:

the bombs were of a type unknown to them. The danger in dealing with the second bomb was very great. To reach it they had to go through the casing, which was so low that they had to lie at full length to move in it. Through this narrow space, in complete darkness, they pushed and dragged the bomb for a distance of some 20 feet until it could be lowered over the side. Every time the bomb was moved there was a loud twanging noise as of a broken spring, which added nothing to their presence of mind. This deed was all the more gallant as HMS Submarine *Thrasher*'s presence was known to the enemy; she was close to the enemy coast and in waters where the patrols were known to be active day and night. There was a very great chance, and they knew it, that the submarine might have to crash-dive while they were under the casing. Had this happened they would have been drowned.

Throughout this period, as in the Malta arena, there were many acts of great gallantry and daring among the Alexandria flotilla, many of which resulted in their final demise. It is impossible to record all, but the names of several submarines became famous:

Triumph, under Lieutenant-Commander W.J.W. Woods, had figured prominently in the list of successes since her arrival in the Mediterranean. She had also carried out several special operations, landing commando units and teams from the Special Boat Service to perform sabotage missions all around the Italian coastline, always a highly dangerous occupation which demanded close inshore activity and delays while the commandos unloaded their folboats and paddled ashore. She carried out numerous attacks on Axis convoys. Her list of hits included the Italian submarine *Salpa*, sunk in June 1941, and she severely damaged the heavy cruiser *Bolzano* off Sicily in August, when she was on her way to deposit a sabotage unit off Palermo. The commandos had the unpleasant experience of being heavily depth-charged while *Triumph* made her escape, but the men landed successfully and blew up a railway bridge. The following day, however, *Triumph* surfaced at the prearranged rendezvous in the middle of a dense fog and was unable to make contact with the commando unit. The men were all captured and taken prisoner. Later in the year, on a similar mission, Woods was carrying a group of commandos for a clandestine landing near Athens, sailing from Alexandria on 26 December 1941. Four days later he signalled that the party had successfully reached its destination. *Triumph* was due to return to pick up the commandos on 9 January but failed to make the rendezvous. Nothing further was heard of the submarine. No Axis power claimed her destruction, and it is believed that she struck a mine.

Torbay had also conducted a number of special missions landing saboteurs and agents around the Mediterranean (see Chapter Nine) as well as continuing successful patrols, and soon after her arrival she sank the Italian submarine *Jantina* off Egypt in July 1941. But it was her attacks on shipping off Corfu in March 1942 that won particular attention and a Victoria Cross for her captain, Lieutenant-Commander Anthony Miers. The citation noted that while on patrol off the Greek coast on 4 March 1942, Lieutenant-Commander Miers sighted a north-bound convoy of four troopships entering the South Corfu Channel:

> They had been too far distant for him to attack initially, and he decided to follow in the hope of catching them in Corfu harbour. During the night, *Torbay* approached undetected up the channel and remained on the surface charging her battery. Unfortunately the convoy passed straight through the channel but on the morning of 5 March, in glassy sea conditions, Miers successfully attacked two store ships and then brought *Torbay* safely back to the open sea. The submarine endured 40 depth charges and had been in closely patrolled enemy waters for 17 hours.

Turbulent entered the Mediterranean theatre with some immediate and significant successes with a series of attacks on convoys bound for North Africa. The number of successes recorded against her name represented a remarkable achievement which eventually brought the award of a Victoria Cross for the 'great valour' of her captain, Commander John Wallace 'Tubby' Linton, at the end of what was ultimately a tragic journey. One member of his crew, with him almost to the last, was Lieutenant Tony Troup, who had volunteered for submarines when he was 19, which, he surmised, was youthful rebellion against his father, who didn't want him to:

And, of course, I was scared out of my pants the first time I went down in a submarine. I really was scared, and I thought, What the hell are you doing, you silly ass? I thought this wasn't really what I wanted to do, but there was no going back then and in fact this sort of thing was quite natural really, and I wouldn't have done anything else once I had got into it. After training in L-boats and a spell in *Trident*, I was assigned to *Turbulent*, which was building in Barrow-in-Furness, stood by her [i.e. posted to Barrow for final completion and trials] and we eventually went off to sea in December 1941.

We spent 1942 in the Mediterranean, all the time up to March 1943, so I spent the whole of that time at sea. I reckoned up the other day in the year of 1942 we did 254 days at sea, submerged for a lot of the time. There are many outstanding things that stick out in my mind. It was a time of high action and great drama. We sank a great deal of shipping, and our captain, Tubby Linton, was a very able man and marvellous captain. His intercepting Rommel's convoys for which he was famous was one thing. That went on throughout that year. We sank a lot of shipping, we were depth-charged, it seemed to me, a great deal of the time, we had lots of gun engagements with ships and then shot up railway trains on the west coast of Italy. We were bombed a good deal of the time, and when we were in the harbour in Malta, which was our advance base, we were bombed all the time, so one didn't stay in there very long. We eventually ended up with our main base in Beirut because our depot ship, *Medway*, which was trying to withdraw from Alexandria to get to Beirut, was sunk by a very brutal attack by a German submarine.

She was escorted by eight destroyers, but the U-boat got through the screen and sank her, so when we got back into harbour after spending rather a long time at sea, we had nothing, no clothes, no food, nothing. It was an incredible period of my life, and as a young man one's morale was kept going by thinking: It will never happen to me. Also, we had a particularly competent skipper, and our morale was pretty high all the time we were in the Mediterranean. Morale was affected very much by whether you got mail when you got back to harbour and how well you had done on that patrol, so it fluctuated a bit. If you didn't sink anything on your patrol, people were a bit down in the dumps, but on the whole we were full of confidence and good cheer, we were young and had a lot of fun.

In March 1943 Tony Troup left *Turbulent* to take the Perisher course (the name given to the course for officers to qualify as commanders, so called because of its intensity) prior to getting his own command. When he left, Tubby Linton had already been hailed as one of the greats in the submarine hall of fame, but his was not simply a story of 'big hits' in the Mediterranean. It went well beyond that, in terms of courage, daring and dedication to duty in the face of great adversity, as recorded in the citation for the VC he was awarded:

From the outbreak of war until HMS *Turbulent*'s last patrol, Commander Linton was constantly in command of submarines, and during that time inflicted great damage on the enemy. He sank one cruiser, one destroyer, one U-boat, twenty-eight supply ships, some 100,000 tonnes in all, and destroyed three trains by gunfire. In his last year he spent two hundred and fifty-four days at sea, submerged for more than half the time, and his ship was hunted thirteen times and had two hundred and fifty depth charges aimed at her. His many and brilliant successes were due to his constant activity and skill, and the daring which never failed him when there was an enemy to be attacked. On one occasion, for instance, in HMS *Turbulent*, he sighted a convoy of two merchantmen and two destroyers in mist and moonlight. He worked round ahead of the convoy and dived to attack it as it passed through the moon's rays. On bringing his sights to bear he found himself right ahead of a destroyer. Yet he held his course until the destroyer was almost on top of him, and when his sights came on the convoy, he fired. His great courage and determination were rewarded. He sank one merchantman and one destroyer outright, and set the other merchantman on fire so that she blew up.

The journey for Linton and his crew was drawing to a close in February 1943, when they sailed from Algiers for a patrol in the Tyrrhenian Sea. On 1 March she attacked and sank the Italian steamship *Vincenz*. On 11 March she torpedoed the mail and supply ship *Mafalda*. She was herself attacked the following morning by the anti-submarine trawler *Teti II* but escaped, only to hit a mine off Maddalena, Sardinia, on 23 March.

In conjunction with the surface patrols, the Fleet Air Arm

torpedo bombers and the RAF, the submarine flotillas had at the very least given the British 8th Army time to regroup by frustrating the deliveries of fresh men and machines to the armies of Mussolini and Rommel. It was a hard-fought battle but a crucial one for the Allies, and six months down the road the 8th Army sent the Afrika Korps packing, clearing the way for the Allies to plan the Operation Torch landings at Oran, and onwards to the invasion of Sicily and the Italian mainland.

The part played by the submarines of the 1st and 10th flotillas has perhaps not always been fully recognised by historians, although Commander F.W. Lipscomb was moved to record:* 'Although with the passage of time it is hard to realise what their patrols really meant in achievement, there is no doubt that the whole Mediterranean offensive can be regarded as the finest work ever accomplished by British submarines.' In the crucial two years between January 1941 and December 1942, the Italians lost 171 ships in the Mediterranean, totalling well over half a million tonnes, a large proportion of which were sunk by the submarine flotillas. On the debit side in that time, Britain lost 14 submarines in the Mediterranean, with 70 officers and 720 ratings.

As a postscript, the statistics are interesting when set against the losses of German U-boats in the Mediterranean. In the period from September 1941 to the end of 1944, the Germans sent 62 U-boats through the British-controlled Strait of Gibraltar. Nine were sunk in the attempt and another ten were severely damaged on the run. Although they did a fair bit of damage, not one of those 62 U-boats ever returned to the Atlantic. Most were sunk or severely

* *The British Submarine*, p. 113.

damaged in battle, and the remaining few were scuttled by their crews.

For the British submarine flotillas, it had been a brilliant performance in the Mediterranean – a performance that, of course, did not end with victory at El Alamein.

CHAPTER NINE

The Man Who Never Was and Other Special Ops

Cloak-and-dagger operations using submarines as the principal carrier of the missions were as a rule highly dangerous but vital to the war effort in every one of the theatres of the Second World War. They involved all kinds of activities that established the derring-do traditions on which special forces based their operations for the next half-century. Tug Wilson was a trailblazer in special operations with the cooperation of a number of submarine commanders who befriended him. As novelist John Lodwick, a later volunteer to the fledgling Special Boat Service, wrote of him: 'As leader of the first successful raids . . . he occupies a position in our hierarchy not unlike that of St Peter in Holy Mother Church.'

Wilson was handsome, slender and middle class. His partner, Marine Wally Hughes, was a small man but tough. They shared a common bond. They were canoe fanatics and were founder members of the SBS, which was at the time a modestly manned offshoot of the commandos formed in

1941 at the behest of Churchill himself. All the men of the SBS became frequent users of the submarine bus service, but Wilson and Hughes, both desperate for action, launched a particular brand of SBS work that involved a submarine nudging the shoreline, dropping the two men off the casing in a folboat and returning to pick them up after they'd blown up a local installation of some importance. That's the way it began, anyhow; it grew from there.

Shrimp Simpson was among those yet to be persuaded as to the value of such clandestine missions by free-ranging saboteurs, but he signed the docket which gave them permission to go to sea with *Urge* when she came into the Malta base to refuel in the third week of June 1941. The pair stowed their collapsible folboat, along with their cache of explosives, Tommy guns and knives, and set off on a hunting expedition towards the southern Italian coast. They had no particular target in mind. The plan was that they would scan the shore, looking for something important to blow up.

'Up periscope!' Lieutenant-Commander Tommo Tompkinson gave the order as *Urge* hovered under a calm sea 3 miles off the east coast of Sicily between Taormina and Catania. Upstairs, the Mediterranean was shimmering under the late-afternoon sun of that hot summer. Mount Etna was huge and very visible, a dramatic rising backdrop to this particular theatre of war as the periscope cut through the water. The date of his first mission and the first-ever successful sabotage strike of the war in the Mediterranean, which became the model for so many in the future,* was 22 June 1941. Tompkinson called Tug Wilson to the periscope. Almost at the foot of Mount Etna, he had spotted what

---

* Described fully in *SBS: The Inside Story of the Special Boat Service*, by John Parker, Headline, 1997.

looked like a tunnel serving the main railway line, which was surely a key transport link for Sicily's hefty population of Axis troops.

'Will that do you?' asked Tompkinson.

'Just the job,' Tug replied. 'Just the job.'

'OK. I'll drop you off a mile or so from the coast.'

Wilson and Hughes gathered their gear together, swallowed a couple of Benzedrine tablets and brought their flimsy-looking boat towards the forehatch, ready to launch when the submarine surfaced as darkness fell. Tompkinson took his vessel as close as he dared. Wilson and Hughes were ready, the adrenaline running high as the effects of the Bennies kicked in. With the water still surging over the casing, they moved their canoe through the forehatch, completed its assembly, replacing the timber cross-members that had been removed so that it could be squeezed through the hatch, and loaded 30 kilogrammes of explosives.

They positioned the canoe at the bow of the casing, clambered gingerly into their positions, faces blacked up, clothes greased, paddles in hand and Tommy guns slung over their shoulders. Wilson gave the signal and the submarine advanced slowly forward and then submerged, allowing the canoe to float off, leaving the duo paddling in unison towards the shore. Their training had been minimalist, and their equipment was of the make-do-and-mend variety. It did not include any form of communication other than a torch for signalling, covered by an old sock to dim the beam. Wilson recalled that nothing could prepare the human psyche for the nervous excitement that welled up inside as they pressed on cautiously towards the Sicilian beach.

Wilson glanced back. *Urge* had vanished from view. She would return at a given time to an agreed map reference and surface when the captain spotted the prearranged signal by torch that the two saboteurs were heading in. The disappearance of the mother vessel left a twinge of anguish: 'Will she be there when we get back? Will we find her in the dark?' One day, as Tug Wilson would discover to his cost, she would not be, and he would be left high and not very dry. This time, the first time, everything looked set fair. They were an hour and a half making their way to the tunnel and setting the charges. Then they made their way back to the beach and paddled out to the rendezvous, dodging a couple of fishing boats as they went. *Urge* surfaced to their starboard, and in a short time the two men were hauling themselves on to the gun platform and dragging their canoe on to the casing behind them. They stood for a moment looking back at the coastline with exhilarated satisfaction, tempered by concern that there had been no explosion. Had it failed to go off? Damp, perhaps, or wrongly connected? They quickly collapsed their canoe and loaded it back through the forehatch and headed below themselves as *Urge* glided towards deep water. As they went, the captain summoned Wilson and Hughes to the bridge on the conning tower. Through his binoculars, he had caught sight of dim lights on the shore. The train was just entering the tunnel when Tug saw it. He was counting the seconds . . . and then – boom! The distant sky was lit by a flash of red.

It marked the first successful raid for the Special Boat Service in the Mediterranean and set a pattern for the future that would be copied throughout the war in virtually every battle zone where there was a coastline and on into the post-war years and the development of the modern SBS.

For Wilson and Hughes, the Sicilian jaunt was not quite over. With the success of the raid confirmed, *Urge* resumed her patrol and moved on to the south of the Strait of Messina when a new target was spotted – a pair of 10,000-tonne Italian cruisers surrounded by six destroyers.

Tompkinson lost no time in selecting his target, the cruiser *Gorizia*. Within minutes, she was sinking with a couple of nasty gashes in her side, sustained from his salvo of torpedoes, and the Italian destroyers came looking for him. They dropped dozens of depth charges. The submarine shuddered and shook as if she was about to break into pieces and the noise was deafening and frightening.

Tug Wilson had never experienced anything like it and immediately recalled the words of his SBS commanding officer, Captain Roger Courtney: 'Those members of the SBS who have the privilege of being aboard one of HM submarines during a depth-charge attack should remain cool and calm, hide yourselves in some corner out of everyone's way, say nothing, do nothing and pretend to be reading a book.'

He didn't have a book, and the moment caused him to reflect: How in God's name was he, Robert Wilson, until recently quietly pursuing his rather staid career as a draughtsman in Bristol, harming no one and with a new young wife at home with whom he should have been raising a family, now holed up in the corner of the control room of a submarine being bombed by depth charges, having just blown up a railway line, and causing goodness knows what damage or loss of life and already thinking about his next mission? It was nothing like anything he had ever imagined when he had volunteered for service in the Territorial Army just before the war.

Over the next three months, Wilson and Hughes pulled off a series of raids, courtesy of 10th Flotilla's hitchhiker's guide to the Med, that caused mayhem to the Italian railway system. As well as Tompkinson, they travelled with Lieutenant-Commander Dick Cayley in *Utmost*, Hugh Haggard in *Truant*, Anthony Miers in *Torbay*, Malcolm Wanklyn in *Upholder*, Alistair Mars in *Unbroken* and Lieutenant D.E.

Watson in *Unbeaten*. The partnerships attacked targets in the main around the Italian coastline.

At the end of July 1941 Wilson and Hughes were assigned to *Utmost* under Lieutenant-Commander Cayley, a stocky man with whom Wilson struck up an immediate rapport. In the following three months, their raids brought total chaos to the railway system of southern Italy. None of them was without incident. The most spectacular was a huge railway bridge over the River Seracino in the Gulf of Taranto. It was such a vital bridge that the Italians, fearing it might be a target for saboteurs, had camouflaged the seaward side, which hampered reconnaissance. A clear view of it was possible only by daylight scanning from the submarine's periscope.

As darkness fell on the evening of 27 August, Dick Cayley brought *Utmost* as close as he dared to the beach as an extra-large load of explosives was required – eight charges of big-bang material, packed in bullet-proof and waterproof bags weighing around 14 kilogrammes apiece. The two men were floated off the casing, and Cayley kept the submarine on the surface to watch them go; it was lucky the sea was calm because the heavily laden canoe was low in the water. They were hyped up with nervous excitement as they began unloading their packages on the beach. Then Wilson looked seaward and saw that *Utmost* had not submerged. The black hull of the sub was clearly visible from the beach and too close for comfort as she might alert the Italians to their landing.

In spite of the precision-timing and with brilliant coolness, he climbed back into his canoe and paddled back to the sub to suggest politely that Cayley should bugger off! Back on the shore, he and Hughes, with Thompson sub-machine-guns armed and at the ready, began an initial sortie of the target, first climbing a steep incline of rocks and loose shale. Over the top, they saw the bridge looming up before them. It took four trips to carry the packages to the bridge site, and while Hughes unpacked and kept watch Wilson began his climb into the steel, carrying the lethal packs and swinging like a monkey between the girders and occasionally hanging one-handed from them while he set the charges and detonators into place. When it was done, Wilson made one last check of the connections, then rolled out a long length of slow-burn fuse to hang over the bridge and lit it.

'Run like hell!'

He was mentally ticking off the seconds as he and Hughes dashed away, crashing their way through the undergrowth back towards the sea. The whole lot went up in a cloud of shattered concrete, twisted metal and dust, some of it raining on *Utmost*, which had come to about half a mile offshore. As Wilson and Hughes came aboard, they were cheered by the crew, and the whole party received another heroes' welcome in Malta.

The action was hotting up, and for the next month *Utmost* continued her task of delivering the intrepid pair to their targets, while at the same time carrying out normal patrol duties. On 18 October Wilson and Hughes switched to *Truant*, with Lieutenant-Commander Haggard, who was on his way to Alexandria, and in doing so was to patrol the Strait of Otranto, between Italy and Albania. It turned out to be one of the most hazardous submarine journeys Wilson had ever had. *Truant* encountered a succession of high drama and activity, including mortar attack from surface vessels and aircraft, depth charges, torpedo action against enemy shipping, and, for a hair-raising four hours, the submarine was grounded on the ocean floor with only a bathtub of water over her periscope.

Even so, Haggard delivered Wilson to an important target, the main Milan to Brindisi railway line near Ancona. Wilson took prepared charges, which he attached to the rail in double-quick time just as a train was approaching. The explosion worked exactly as he had forecast, derailing the engine and 14 sleeping cars packed with Axis war executives and causing a good deal of disruption to the line.

Roger Courtney was in Alexandria to welcome Wilson back to the Special Boat Service depot ship, HMS *Medway*. By then 1SBS had extended its particular repertoire of special operations, working largely from submarines. The range of tasks covered beach recce for troop landings, sabotage operations on the lines of Wilson's own exploits, and rescuing Allied troops left behind after the fall of Crete in June 1941. In the month of August alone, one solitary SBS canoeist, Corporal G.C. Bremner, single-handedly rescued 125 British, Australian, New Zealand and Greek soldiers who had been hiding in the hills of Crete since it was overrun by the Germans. He brought them to safety via the submarine *Torbay* and on to Alexandria. He was eventually awarded a Distinguished Conduct Medal.

Another series of operations that became a speciality for submarine commanders in conjunction with the SBS during the latter half of 1941 was the insertion and evacuation of secret agents behind enemy lines across the whole of the Mediterranean theatre, and later in the Far East. These missions continued, often at great risk to all concerned, especially the submarines. One of the most risky of all of these was launched from Alexandria and involved *Torbay* and *Talisman*. They were earmarked to deliver a commando raiding party in what went down as a brave but ill-fated attack on Rommel's headquarters.

The task was placed in the hands of the remnants of

Colonel Robert Laycock's much-vaunted Layforce, which had originally consisted of 7, 8 and 11 Commando but had been decimated in covering the retreat of the Allied troops from Crete. Other operations had also taken a heavy toll, and by September 1941 Layforce was virtually wiped out; there remained only 53 men from the original group of 1,200 who had sailed full of hope and bravado from Scotland 10 months earlier.

Those remaining members of Layforce were now attached to the 8th Army as a special raiding force, led by Laycock himself and Lieutenant-Colonel Geoffrey Keyes, son of Admiral Sir Roger Keyes, the first director of Combined Operations, hero of the First World War raid on Zeebrugge, who had given such support to Layforce and had encouraged the partnership between submarines and the SBS.

The raid on Rommel's HQ, 200 miles inside enemy lines, would be made through a beach landing launched with the guiding arm of the SBS from *Torbay* and *Talisman* through canoes and rubber dinghies. On the night of 14 November, a storm was whipping up the surf, and two pairs of SBS men went ashore in their canoes to check the beaches prior to the main landing of the troops. When the all clear was given, the landing was ordered to proceed in spite of the rough sea. Landing canoes and dinghies from *Torbay* were repeatedly swamped on their way to the beach, and it took almost 7 hours to land the 36 men aboard *Torbay* instead of the 90 minutes which they had estimated the operation would take. By then, it was deemed impossible to land the remaining 18 men aboard *Talisman*. Laycock and Keyes were among those who made it ashore.

The depleted group none the less headed off in the direction of Rommel's communications centre and then on to the villa that was used as headquarters for his

Panzergruppe Afrika. Meanwhile, SBS Lieutenants Ingles and Allot, with their two aides, hid the rubber dinghies ready for the return of the raiding party. The disastrous start to the landing might have been an omen; the troubles kept on coming. The importance of the target buildings appeared to have been exaggerated and, as was eventually discovered, Rommel himself was not even there. He had gone to Rome.

There were, however, sufficient German troops there to put up a fierce fight in which the expedition leader, Geoffrey Keyes, was among those killed (he was later posthumously awarded the Victoria Cross). The raiding party retreated back to the beach to make their rendezvous with *Torbay*. By the time they reached the coast, there were only 22 survivors of the original 36, and to make matters worse the weather was appalling and the sea hugely choppy with a long swell running in from the north-west – i.e. straight at the beach. *Torbay* came back to the site at the appointed time to wait for the returning party, unaware of the shooting match that had ensued on shore. Soon after nightfall on 18 November, the first day of Operation Crusader, which was the 8th Army's offensive to relieve Tobruk, they arrived at the beach. The returning commandos, however, signalled that the rubber boats that had previously been hidden there had disappeared and thus they were stranded.

Torbay was in a risky position even in darkness, and with no apparent way of rescuing them the captain decided to put to sea and signalled he would return after dark the following day. Overnight, the 22 survivors of the raid were attacked by German troops; some were killed, others were captured and at least 4 others escaped into the hillside. Those who escaped included Colonel Laycock himself, who, with Sergeant Terry, made an incredible 36-day trek on foot through hostile countryside and desert. They reached British lines on Christmas Day.

For a while after this disaster, submarine operations with the saboteurs and raiders were vetoed from London, but in December *Torbay* once again had Tug Wilson and Wally Hughes as passengers when she set off for her next patrol in early December. It was an important and even more hazardous operation specifically to try out a new triple-limpet mine device Wilson had invented. *Torbay* took them to Navarino harbour and through the periscope located an enemy destroyer moored at the pier.

They set off in their canoe, paddling to within 135 metres of the ship. At this point, Wilson, wearing only greased-up long johns to protect him from the cold, slid into the water to swim the remaining distance, cautiously pushing six limpet mines ahead of him on a buoy. The limpets consisted of a kilogramme of plastic explosive in a metal case that would be clamped to the ship's hull by magnets. They would be detonated by the breaking of a glass ampoule of acid which in turn cut through a retaining plate which fired the detonator. Each mine could blast a 2-metre hole in the side of the destroyer. The hefty package needed careful manoeuvring, a slow task at the best of times but the December waters were ice-cold.

Hughes could see that his partner was in trouble within 70 metres or so. He signalled on the line attached to Wilson that he was pulling him in. Tug was hauled, protesting, back into the boat, with numb hands and chattering teeth. It was a disappointing end to their partnership. Hughes and Wilson would never work together again.

At the beginning of January, the 10th Flotilla welcomed Tug back to Malta to undertake a number of vital missions landing agents by submarine on the Tunisian coast complete with stores and radios. It was there, too, that he learned that he had been awarded the Distinguished Service Order for his exploits. He was to be sent home on leave to England to take his decoration from the King at Buckingham Palace.

'One last task . . .' said Shrimp Simpson, after revealing the award. Two agents had to be landed near Carthage.

'Of course,' said Wilson without hesitation.

He was to travel in *Upholder* with Lieutenant-Commander Malcolm Wanklyn. The landing was completed without a hitch, and Tug went back aboard *Upholder* to meet *Unbeaten* off the island of Lampedusa, where Wilson was to transfer between boats for the onward journey. *Unbeaten*, it turned out, was limping home, damaged in enemy action. By then, the sea looked too rough for Tug to attempt the transfer. Wanklyn suggested he remain aboard *Upholder*, return to Malta and there get a lift to Gibraltar. Tug, anxious to get on his way home, decided to take the risk. It was a fateful decision. As recorded in the previous chapter, *Upholder* was lost with all hands the following day. Tug Wilson was the last person to see them alive.

Tug, meanwhile, was summoned to the headquarters of Combined Operations, now under the command of Lord Mountbatten, who had a particular mission in mind. Tug was to test a new 'Q'-type gadget, which had been invented at one of Mountbatten's top-secret experimental stations by speed ace Sir Malcolm Campbell. It was a mini-torpedo that could be hand-launched from a canoe and was driven by a car windscreen-wiper motor. The idea was for SBS personnel to be equipped with a boatload of these items and go paddling around enemy harbours blowing up ships.

It was August when Tug returned, and Shrimp Simpson had already chosen a target after studying aerial photographs of ships in Crotone harbour. This time – and for the first time – he was without his usual partner, Wally Hughes, who was ill; in his place was another trusted commando, Bombardier Brittlebank. They were to be delivered to the harbour by Lieutenant A.C.G. Mars in *Unbroken*, which duly surfaced a mile and a half from the target area, and the pair disembarked with their canoe and supplies. They were to rendezvous again in five hours at the same spot.

Wilson and Brittlebank set off under a moonless sky around 11.30 p.m. and gained access to the harbour through a bomb-damaged boom. They had time to launch only one of the mini-torpedoes before they were spotted from a schooner. Wilson recalled:

> With the torpedo submerged, I took careful aim, and with a gentle push released it . . . During a few brief moments [before they were forced to retreat] I was able to follow it. The depth was about five feet, and it appeared to be running steadily. No definite explosion was heard during retreat, although there was now plenty of commotion and lights were beginning to appear in the Italian flotilla. My instructions were to ensure that on no account were we to be captured with the torpedoes still in our possession. So we paddled away towards my parent craft in waiting at the rendezvous 2,000 yards out.

Unbroken was still submerged, but the SBS pair hit trouble as they made their way towards the rendezvous. Two Italian destroyers appeared on the horizon heading towards them. As they approached, Wilson launched another of his mini-torpedoes, which sped away and appeared to hit one of them – but nothing happened. The destroyers bore down and passed on either side of the canoe without spotting it. They were almost certainly now looking for *Unbroken*, and Wilson realised that Mars would have picked up their approach from hydrophonic effects and taken evasive action.

By now the sea was rising, developing into a considerable swell with white horses running diagonally across the rendezvous area. For the next five hours, Wilson and Brittlebank patrolled up and down, until the back-up rendezvous time came round. They dropped a couple of four-second hand grenades over the side to attract the attention of the submarine if she was somewhere beneath them. *Unbroken* did not respond. They waited another hour and a half and, with the canoe now dangerously waterlogged, they decided they had to make land and dry her out and then attempt to get back to Malta under their own steam, paddling the whole 250 miles.

They began quite successfully until after one hasty retreat from the beach they damaged the canoe and had to make another stop. They were immediately surrounded by Italian soldiers and taken into captivity. Tug Wilson spent the rest of the war in – and escaping from – Italian and German prison camps, a classic POW story. In Germany he escaped twice, once from a moving train under heavy gunfire. He managed to get back into Italy in 1943 and became involved in the Rome escape route run by a Roman Catholic priest, before finally being betrayed and captured again. He spent the rest of the war in a German prisoner-of-war camp at Brunswick.

As a postscript to this last escapade of Tug Wilson and his friends at the Malta submarine flotilla, a second batch of hand-launched torpedoes was tried out by Major Harry Holden-White, of 2SBS, during the Allied Torch landings at Oran. He was also captured in the attempt, and gave this assessment:

In the midst of this massive operation involving 300 or

more ships, there was I and my number two, Corporal Ellis, paddling our way through the carnage of blazing ships and the screams of injured men to release these bloody mini-torpedoes on the approach to Oran harbour. I loosed off one, which hit an enemy ship. I didn't hear any explosion and the ship carried on, although it was sunk by one of our submarines just outside Oran harbour. I launched a second one, aimed at one of their submarines, which was just coming out of the harbour, but that went astray and hit the harbour wall. But at least it made a bang and the harbour master came out shouting and waving his arms. We let go with another, but the bloody thing died on us and, after we had been captured, I was horrified to see it floating in the harbour as we were marched away. It was supposed to be top secret.

The Mediterranean submarine flotillas were heavily involved in the Allied landings in North Africa in November 1942, which followed General Montgomery's famous victory at El Alamein. The newly appointed British commander hit the north flank of the Afrika Korps on 23 October with a methodically prepared offensive, and by 5 November forced Rommel into a retreat. Allied troops fighting under General Dwight D. Eisenhower began landing in Morocco and Algeria on 8 November, the American contingent at Casablanca and Oran. The submarine contribution to these landings was immense. With Malta back in business and at last having been given a mighty reinforcement of aircraft, up to 40 per cent of Axis shipping ferrying men and supplies to Rommel was being sunk, and submarines took a good proportion of that total.

The submarine service also supplied 18 boats to cover the

North African landings as markers and beacons for the surface task force of ships and landing craft, but equally significant was its contribution in the build-up to the landings themselves, particularly in that a fleet of more than 320 ships travelling from the British Isles had to deposit 140,000 men on the shores of Tunisia and Libya.

That very act required a good deal of advance reconnaissance of a kind never previously attempted, much of it completed in conjunction with the submarine flotilla. For the first time in history, submarines were to begin regular assignments with a new formation called COPPs, standing for Combined Operations Pilotage Parties. It came into being only six weeks earlier at Mountbatten's behest after his personal disaster of the Dieppe landings, small by comparison but in which there were more than 3,000 casualties. The Coppists (as the members of COPPs were known) were the creation of Lieutenant-Commander Nigel Clogstoun Willmott, a veteran of Narvik and the early days of the Mediterranean campaign. He proposed the idea to Mountbatten and was given top priority to see it to fruition, with an impossible deadline – in time for the Torch landings. COPPs were elite, top-secret units, recruited mostly from the ranks of Royal Navy officers, whose real duties were not revealed until some 15 years after the war (because basically they were still at it, and in some rather sensitive places, like Iraq, and by then combined with the Special Boat Service).

The COPPs' men were swimmer-canoeists who were trained in the art of navigation and hydrography. They would be delivered by submarine to carry out a complete reconnaissance of assault beaches, which of course were in enemy territory, often with sentries, shore batteries and various other defences in place. Their task was to draw maps and charts to guide the Allied armies to a safe and smooth passage over the assault beaches. The whole landing area had to be examined in detail, checking gradients of underwater approaches, obstacles, sandbars, rocks, beach consistency to warn of vehicles bogging down, land surfaces, mined areas, beach defences and, most important, beach exits for the assault troops. The task at any one beach would take many hours and a good deal of patience and caution by the submarine commanders who brought them.

Although submarines had been used for limited explorations of assault beaches, usually with SBS personnel, the first submarine commander to become involved with the Coppists was Norman 'Bill' Jewell, whom we met in the previous chapter when he was second-in-command of *Truant* to Hugh Haggard. Since then, he had returned to the UK, taken his commander's course and in the summer of 1942 had taken delivery of a brand-new S-class, *Seraph*, from Vickers at Barrow-in-Furness. Like most new captains he was standing by her during commissioning waiting to get going in what would become one of the most famous wartime boats of all:

They were very good at Barrow and listened to anything we wanted to have done to the submarine. We went to our work-up in the Clyde area, and from there we went on our first war patrol in the North Sea. Our first action with the new submarine came as we approached our patrol area. We were on the surface and spotted what we thought was a periscope. We opened fire – and blew up a whale. Eventually, we were sent on to the Mediterranean to join up with the squadron in Gibraltar, and except for being bombed by our own aircraft in the Bay of Biscay we had a relatively uneventful voyage out. An RAF anti-submarine patrol dropped a stick of bombs on us,* and we dived and stayed down for about half an hour before we moved on.

On arrival in Gibraltar we were sent on patrol off the North African coast from Algiers to Oran in preparation – although we didn't know it – for the Allied invasion of North Africa. We came back to Gibraltar to take on board the COPPs party who were to map the beaches of the North African coast. We spent our time off the coast while the COPPs parties went ashore at night in folboats. In the daytime we took photographs of the beaches and the coastline through the periscope so that they had a complete picture of the landing areas.

It was the first such operation and was so successful that it would be adopted for every Allied landing for the remainder of the war. The war planners were truly amazed at the amount of detail they received back. The very nature of it demonstrated the hazards of assault beaches which might otherwise have gone unnoticed. They ruled that in future no large-scale beach landings would be attempted by Allied assault troops without the Coppists going in first, and that usually meant a submarine delivery.

As the invasion plans neared fruition, Jewell's knowledge of the area made him a natural choice for a special mission, and on his return to Gibraltar he received a mysterious signal which read: SERAPH IS ALLOCATED TO SPECIAL POLITICAL OPERATIONS FROM THIS DATE. UTMOST DISCRETION OF

---

* This was not unusual. From mid-1942 the RAF were on round-the-clock anti-submarine patrols, logging thousands of flying hours every month and knocking out dozens of U-boats. Pilots and observers suffering eyestrain from peering into the sea were responsible for a good many incidents of friendly fire.

OFFICERS NECESSARY AND ALL FURTHER ORDERS TO BE
DESTROYED AFTER COMMITTAL TO MEMORY.

Jewell could not imagine what that entailed, but before the
day was out he discovered his task. It was to be part of an
operation that Winston Churchill would later describe as
having 'saved countless lives'.

> I was asked to come ashore to meet a party of Americans
> who wanted to be landed. I had no idea who they might
> be, but I was soon to be enlightened. There were six of
> them altogether, including General Mark Wayne Clark
> [Eisenhower's deputy and deputy commander of Opera-
> tion Torch] and Brigadier-General Lyman Lemnitzer
> [principal US planner on Eisenhower's staff]. We were
> apparently going to have to land them on one of the
> wadis off North Africa, close to Algiers in Vichy French
> territory – i.e. controlled by the Germans. They would
> have a small SBS escort and that's all.

Having been reminded that what took place at the meeting
was at the absolute top level of secrecy, they discussed the
operation and how Jewell, then 28 years old, saw it unwind-
ing. They ran through the plan for the approach and landing
but no more, and Jewell was eventually informed that the
landing would take place on 20 October. On that night, the
six Americans came on board *Seraph* accompanied by just
three SBS men, Captain 'Gruff' Courtney, brother of the
founder of the SBS, with Lieutenants R.P. Livingstone and
J.P. Foot, all of whom had the usual accoutrements of SBS
weaponry about their person.

It now transpired that the Americans were to be put ashore
and make for a small white-walled farmhouse at the top of a
hill close to the beach. There they would meet General Mast,

commander of the Vichy French forces, and Robert Murphy, President Roosevelt's diplomatic representative in North Africa. The object of the mission was to persuade the Vichy general to cooperate and offer little or no resistance to the Allied landings. And so, after dark on 20 October, *Seraph* closed to within half a mile of the shore and the SBS men prepared to unload the canoes in which they would ferry the Americans to the beach. Jewell continued:

We were told that if it were safe for them to come ashore there would be a light shining in the window. Well, we found the farmhouse but spent all evening and then into the night hanging around off the coast. Eventually, just before dawn, we saw the light come on. It was, however, by then too late to complete the landing operation safely, so we left and came back again the following night. Sure enough, the light came on after dark and we managed to get the six Americans in folboats floated off the submarine casing.

We kept in touch with them by radio, and then on the following night, about midnight, we got a signal that they wanted to be taken off. The weather had deteriorated by then, with a heavy swell running, and we went in as close as we could, probably within 400 metres. As they made their way back, the folboats were tossed around unmercifully and all three overturned. The generals and their associates were thrashing around, fully clothed in deep water, and had to swim to the shore, with difficulty, while the SBS men manhandled their upturned folboats and dragged them to the beach. They went into hiding while the SBS dried out the folboats. For the moment, we had to back off. The situation was getting critical, but just before dawn the weather calmed down and we went back in and this time, one by one, they came back, soaking wet. We dived, reported their safe return and then waited until a message came through that a seaplane would rendezvous with us and take them off.

We arrived at the spot and the plane duly arrived. They were transferred once again by folboat and set off home. Actually, the generals had been jolly good company while on board. They joined in games to pass the time while we were in transit and waiting to land them. Before they left, Mark Clark said we might have another similar job to do, and a week later I was contacted by US navy Captain Jerauld Wright [Eisenhower's naval liaison officer] in company with an American air-force officer.

The outcome of the clandestine meeting with General Mast now fell into place. The Vichy General Mast had agreed to cooperate and guarantee the loyalty of the Algerian garrison he commanded. The French forces at Oran and Casablanca were strongly pro-Vichy, but there was one man in France whom they might follow if he made the call. That man was a popular hero, General Henri Honoré Giraud, who had recently escaped from a German prisoner-of-war camp where he had been incarcerated because of doubts of his loyalty to Vichy France and who was living in hiding near Lyon. However, his whereabouts was known to Marshal Pétain, who was on the verge of having him arrested and handed back to the Germans in exchange for further concessions from Hitler. A secret courier was sent to locate Giraud to ascertain his willingness to be smuggled out of France. He agreed, on condition that he could take his family, was given a command in keeping with his rank and was taken aboard an American boat because he hated the British for sinking the French fleet.

On 25 October Lieutenant Jewell and the SBS were once more summoned to stand by for Operation Kingpin – to rescue Giraud and take him on board *Seraph*, which for the duration was to be named USS *Seraph*, with an American captain joining in. The operation was considered so vital that a duplicate back-up ran parallel using *Seraph*'s sister submarine, *Sybil*, under Lieutenant E.J.D. Turner. Time was already running short. On 27 October *Seraph* was ordered to a point off the south coast of France. The hours, then days ticked by, waiting for news from Gibraltar confirming the time and place for Giraud and his party to be picked up. For seven days, the submarine remained dived by day and came up for air and battery-charging at night. No news had been received by 4 November – four days before the invasion of North Africa. Then, at 8 p.m. that night, all hell broke loose. General Giraud was on his way from Lyon, moving overnight. He would be ready to board a shoreboat 1,000 yards east of La Lavandou the following night. Jewell set off to get in position, with *Sybil* not far behind:

> We got around the corner and were told to watch for a signal from the shore. This was spotted, and it told us to wait one hour. We backed off, dived and sat on the bottom for an hour. At the end of the hour we surfaced, and after a while a little white boat was spotted heading towards us in the darkness. It came alongside, and General Giraud and five others, including his son, clambered on to the deck casing. Unfortunately, he slipped and fell on to the ballast tanks, but no harm was done apart from a soaking. We turned, and went back the way we'd come to rendezvous with a

seaplane which would take him on to England.

General Giraud in the meantime asked for a map of North Africa. He was a bit full of himself and thought he was going to be the commanding general for the landings in North Africa, and I understand he was a bit surprised when he met up with Eisenhower to find that he wasn't going to be.

The landings were, of course, highly successful. After initial opposition around Oran, some Vichy French troops pulled back, although that cooperation was not universal, especially among some elements of the French Foreign Legion. Among those who famously switched sides after the Allied landings was Admiral Jean François Darlan, High Commissioner for French North Africa, who was subsequently shot dead by an assassin. He was immediately succeeded by General Henri Honoré Giraud, and Lieutenant Jewell and his crew on *Seraph* had the satisfaction of hearing in a speech by Winston Churchill that many thousands of lives were saved through the operation in which the submarine service provided the key component: fast and efficient transport.

Soon afterwards, Jewell's *Seraph* was damaged in a collision with an enemy submarine off the coast of north-west Africa. She went back to the United Kingdom for repairs, and while in the UK a new mission appeared for her captain:

I was told to report to naval intelligence and there met up with a team concocting an incredible scheme. In brief, we were to try to fool the Germans into accepting false invasion plans. A body was to be washed up on the coast of Spain which would carry in an attaché case secret papers, a letter for Eisenhower, the Commander-in-Chief in North Africa, saying that rather than going for Sicily the invasion would be on the south coast of Greece. I was not, at that time, fully briefed on the plan, merely on the preparation of a background for the body – that of a recently deceased civilian whose real name was never revealed – and the creation of the Man Who Never Was.

My knowledge was limited exactly to that which I needed to know in order to carry out my part of the plan. However, we spent a good deal of time building up a background for this body, who was to be called Major Martin, providing him with a life, a girlfriend, and in his pockets theatre tickets, restaurant receipts, a letter and so on. They knew it would be checked out by German spies in London. I had the enjoyment of acting the role of Major Martin in the days prior, going to the theatre, restaurants and nightclubs and so on, collecting the items that would form part of the story of his life. Then when the repairs were completed to *Seraph*, the body of Major Martin was placed in a canister about the size of a torpedo.

The body was packed in ice so that it would be the right age when washed up. We were given clear passage down to the coast of Spain, which meant that the RAF was aware of our presence. We were also told that we would not be required to attack anything en route because our mission was too important. However, we were taken out of our safe passage line to attack some shipping going to Bordeaux. We never saw them, but thanks to that instruction we were then bombed three times by the RAF.

We eventually arrived off the coast of Spain at the point where Spain joins Portugal. We went up towards the coast at night and were just about to surface when a fishing fleet went over the top of us, going out to collect sardines. We surfaced behind them, and closed inshore at a suitable point where I thought the currents would carry the body inshore. This was perhaps the most difficult time from my own point of view. Until that point, no one on board – apart from myself – knew that the canister contained a body.

The cover story was that it was carrying meteorological equipment to fill in the reporting gap for the Meteorological Office in London. But now, the body was to be retrieved from the canister to be put over the side. I had to tell the officers because I could not do the whole thing on my own. I did not give details of the plan, but in any event I had to swear them to secrecy.

They were surprised; some were shocked. Very few of them had seen a dead body at that time, let alone dispatched the body of an unknown man into the sea in this manner. I posted officers on the bridge as lookouts. Myself and the engineer officer went down on the casing because we had to take the canister to bits to get the body out. It was a tubular canister, about the width of a man.

We took off the end of the canister and brought the body out. It was the first time I had seen it. We made a final check to make sure that his papers and attaché case containing the secret 'invasion' plans were intact and attached to his wrist, and then slid him over the side. We went full astern on the motor so that he would be pushed on his way. We said a few words as a funeral service over him and then secured the canister on the casing and dived. At daybreak we surfaced to try to get rid of the canister and we had a hell of a time.

It had been so designed to keep the ice from melting

that it had air pockets all the way around it, and even though we had put about 200 bullet holes through it from a machine-gun nothing happened at all. We then had to go alongside it again and put some plastic explosives inside and outside and then withdrew while it blew up. It then disappeared finally. We then went on to Gibraltar, arriving the next evening. As we arrived, someone came over the gangway carrying a telegram for me, which said the parcel had been received: so the body had arrived safely. As would be discovered later, the Germans went to great lengths to discover the background of Major Martin through their spies in London and could not discredit the information that we had placed about him. In due course, the Germans withdrew an armoured division and sent it through Italy and down the other side towards Greece. They were at least a division less in Sicily when the landings eventually took place. I was very glad indeed to see that it had all gone according to plan.

We then had a short period in Gibraltar before being told to take all our torpedoes out and to fill up the torpedo tubes and the magazine and torpedo racks with wines and spirits for the depot ship in Algiers. From there, we moved on to Oran, where we were going to be briefed on the Sicily landings by the American General Patton. He came down to see us, replete with pearl-handled revolver, and made it quite obvious that he didn't think very much of his allies going into Sicily; he was very short with us, rudely outspoken and quite conceited. Admiral King was also there and thanked us for taking part. Anyway, we had a description of what General Patton wanted of us. We went back to Algiers and prepared to go to our marking position off the west coast of Sicily. We were given a marker to put on the bottom to give out signals for beach landings. While we were putting it down in fairly thick fog, an E-boat came practically alongside. Fortunately, he did not see us and we dived and kept out of the way for about half an hour before surfacing again. Later that night, we were to surface to become the marker for the first landing ships as the invasion began.

That task completed, we were given the all clear to set off back to Malta. As we did so, we heard someone shouting in the water. It turned out to be an American soldier who had apparently jumped over the side, and then a little further on we found another and then another. They were just swimming around, and were in fairly good condition. It was very fortunate for them that we heard them. They had lifebelts on and had apparently dropped over the side so as not to be involved in the initial landings.

From Malta we were sent to patrol across the gulf between Sicily and North Africa when the Germans were putting in fairly heavy reinforcements. Two lines of submarines were put right across the way so that any troop transport ships would have to break through. On the very first night, our inshore squadron came right over the top of us, so we had to dive to get out of the way of them. We lost about two hours, and while they were doing their stuff on top we came up and saw what looked like three large liners on fire on the surface. Then nothing else came through that night, and when we surfaced at dawn the whole area was covered with bodies floating in the water. Shortly afterwards, a destroyer flotilla appeared and started picking them up. We had no instructions as to what to do, but decided not to attack these ships because it didn't seem quite the right thing to do in the circumstances; it would have been immoral.

During the invasion of Sicily, *Seraph* acted as a guide and a beacon for the invading US forces. For this, and in recognition of previous services, Lieutenant Jewell was awarded the Legion of Merit at the instigation of Eisenhower. Apart from their massive contribution to the general attacks on Axis shipping, 18 submarines supported the Torch landings in North Africa in November 1942, and a total of 47 Allied submarines were pulled in for a variety of vital tasks for the invasion of Sicily and, later, the Italian mainland.

It was perhaps fitting that *Unrivalled*, under Lieutenant H.B. Turner, steamed tentatively into Bari harbour on hearing the news of the surrender of Italy on 7 September 1943. There he found a mass of Italian ships, and there was an air of controlled panic: the word was that the Germans had turned on the Italians and were taking every opportunity to sink their ships. Turner quickly grasped the opportunity and sent word around the harbour that he was organising a convoy to deliver them to safety. Now with the help of *Unruly*, he commanded the Italian captains to 'follow me', which they did.

Within a few days, virtually all the remaining ships of the Italian fleet were gathered in the Grand Harbour of Malta. It was an ironic final touch to a devastating statistic: in three years of war, the Italians lost 1 battleship, 2 aircraft carriers, 14 cruisers, a monitor, 2 anti-aircraft ships, 2 fast minelayers, 44 destroyers, 41 submarines, 7 corvettes, 8 fleet minesweepers, 94 other ships and craft of all kinds, along with the thousands of men in the ships' companies who perished. It was to the George Cross island they had consistently bombarded that the remnants were delivered like a trophy, and on 11 September 1943 the Commander-in-Chief, Sir Andrew Cunningham, signalled the Admiralty in London: 'Be pleased to inform their Lordships that the Italian battle fleet now lies at anchor under the guns of the fortress of Malta.'

CHAPTER TEN

Human Torpedoes and Mini-Subs Attack the Nazi 'Beast'

The exploits of the Mediterranean submarine force drew attention to the wider sphere of the covert underwater assault on the enemy using both submarines and submarine technology as platforms. The possibilities drew the interest of a number of leading naval and scientific brains and inventors from the 'specialist equipment unit' attached to Lord Mount-batten's Combined Operations group. His lordship actively encouraged the submission of all manner of weird and wonderful schemes that might be used against the enemy. He wanted assaults and sabotage aplenty around the enemy-held coastlines, and in that he was parroting the speeches of Winston Churchill, notably in his famous call to arms 'to set Europe ablaze'. Mountbatten did, however, have his own passions, especially in the area of small-party raiders. He loved the idea of the SBS linking up with the submarine service. He saw it as a brilliant concept, amalgamating the skills and the bravado of the boat commanders with the sheer guile of the commandos.

What the inventors and the thinkers came up with as various avenues were explored in turn attracted the interest of volunteers for special groups to be engaged in tasks that were broadly advertised on the military noticeboards as being 'special and hazardous service'. In other words, the chances of coming back alive were probably a lot less than 50–50. In spite of that, there was no shortage of takers.

Mountbatten, it must be said, went against the thoughts of conventional military and naval minds in giving his support to smaller-group raiders and such projects as the building of various underwater craft for specific purposes. There was broad dissension across all three services as these various groups began to get a toehold, and some still thought that the SBS raiders were more trouble than they were worth, pointing out that, with or without them, the submarine commanders themselves had done a very good job of shooting up Italian trains and coastal installations whenever the opportunity arose. Hanging around while the canoeists went there and back was a danger not only to the crews but to a very expensive piece of hardware.

New schemes were coming forward to Combined OPs every day, and one that had been rejected several times by the top brass finally came to fruition after much persistence from Mountbatten himself in December 1942. It became another famous wartime story: the Cockleshell Heroes.* Twelve men in six canoes were to be delivered to the mouth of the River Gironde by the submarine *Tuna*. The man who dreamed it up was Major H.G. 'Blondie' Hasler, a tall and hefty 28-year-old with a well-known passion for small boats. It was his idea that he would lead the team of 12 in canoes, packed with

---

* Described in detail in *SBS: The Inside Story of the Special Boat Service*.

limpet mines and explosives, in a daring and highly dangerous paddle 90 miles up the Gironde and blow up enemy
shipping moored in what was considered to be a safe haven.
In fact, only ten men in five boats set off from *Tuna*, the sixth
boat having been damaged getting it out of the submarine.
Of the ten who left that day, only Hasler and his partner,
Marine Ned Sparks, survived. Of the remainder, two were
drowned when their boat capsized and the others were
captured and shot by the Germans.

Mountbatten, however, sent a memo to the Chiefs of Staff,
pointing out that 'this brilliant little operation was carried
through with great determination and courage and is a good
example of the successful use of limpeteers'.

His thoughts were perhaps akin to the Italian way of sea
wolf activity, filled with ideas involving gadgetry and
motorisation and experimentation. From the beginning of
the war, the Italians had shown themselves to be well ahead
of everyone in their perfection of seaborne guerrilla warfare.
They also possessed an impressive array of deadly bathtime
toys, such as effective breathing apparatus for underwater
swimmers, double limpets, human torpedoes, piloted torpedoes, miniature torpedoes and exploding motorboats. These
weapons were largely in the hands of teams of dedicated
and highly trained men – inspired by the famous Commander Belloni and the infamous Prince Julio Valerio
Borghese – from the 10th Light Flotilla of the Italian navy.
This particular skill of the Italians really began to worry the
Allies in 1941, at a time when the British fleet was reduced
to two battleships in the Mediterranean, HMS *Valiant* and
HMS *Queen Elizabeth*, which lay sheltered behind torpedo
nets at Alexandria. At 3.30 a.m. on 19 December, two
Italians were discovered clinging to the anchor buoy of
Valiant. They surrendered immediately and were taken

ashore for interrogation and then, to their dismay, back to *Valiant*, where they confessed that the battleship was about to blow up. The crew was mustered on deck and the watertight doors were closed, but shortly after 6 a.m. the ship rocked and shuddered as the charge set by the two Italians blasted a large hole in her stern. Soon afterwards, *Queen Elizabeth* reared up from two explosions from charges attached below the water line, and both ships were temporarily out of the war. It soon emerged that they had been attacked by three human torpedoes known as Maiali ('sea pigs') driven by a team of six men from the 10th Light Flotilla, trained to remain under water for miles wearing flexible rubber suits, breathing gear and fins. They had been launched from Prince Borghese's submarine *Scire* off Alexandria, two astride each of the human torpedoes. They travelled to the target ship where the time-fused warheads from each one were disconnected and attached to the ships' hulls. They then made their exit on the remaining part of the torpedo and returned whence they came. The operation even drew praise from Churchill as an example of 'extraordinary courage and ingenuity'.

Mountbatten drew together a number of eminent military and scientific experts to look at new weapons and methods for his men to 'study, coordinate and develop all forms of stealthy seaborne attack by small parties and pay particular attention to attacking ships in harbour'. Among the projects launched immediately was the Chariot, a hefty torpedo-shaped submersible which was a copy of the two-man Maiali used by the Italians (one had been captured off Crete). Its crew, equipped with breathing sets that would allow six hours of diving, sat in the open astride the Chariot, which could travel at about 16 knots and carried one 272-kilogramme charge. They were hazardous and slow. The first torpedo force came into operation in September 1942, operating under the auspices of the submarine service, in an operation to attack *Tirpitz*, the largest and strongest warship ever built in Germany at 53,000 tonnes.

She was even more powerful than her elder sister *Bismarck* and was based in occupied Norway from January 1942. From there, she and her supporting ships would sally forth to attack Allied shipping – at least, that was the theory. In fact, the Germans seldom used her for such operations. She was hardly ever seen; if the British had but known it, the Germans were fearful of losing her. Even so, her very presence, skulking in the fjords of Norway, was sufficient to worry ships travelling the most dangerous convoy route to north-west Russia. The dilemma for the British ships was potentially fatal: if attacked by submarines or aircraft, ships and escorts stayed together to maximise their combined defensive capacity, but if they were hit by surface ships they were ordered to scatter. U-boat chief Dönitz thus used a dual attack, horrifically demonstrated against the PQ17 convoy in July 1942. The convoy was ordered personally by the First Sea Lord, Admiral Sir Dudley Pound, to scatter because he believed *Tirpitz* was about to attack. She did not even come close as the convoy dispersed, and the unprotected ships fell prey to the waiting U-boats and German aircraft. Two-thirds of the convoy and almost 100,000 tonnes of munitions for Russia went to the bottom. *Tirpitz* did not fire a single shot.

Unaware of the Germans' fear of losing her, the British began to consider every scheme to destroy the German 'beast', and in October 1942 an audacious plan was launched to sink her using the Chariots. Two of the Chariots were hidden in a double bulkhead of a Norwegian fishing trawler which would then proceed to Trondheim; there, they would be released with crews to attack *Tirpitz* in her berth behind anti-submarine nets in a fjord north of Trondheim. Although the trawler managed to get through three German check-points, the expedition was hit by a sudden change in the weather as the Chariots were being launched. They had to be abandoned, and the crews swam ashore and escaped into Sweden. No further attempts could be launched because of the low temperatures that year.

More than 50 Chariots were built, and their crews experienced mixed fortunes. Their best results were in the Mediterranean, although they were never really considered a success. Operation Principal, for example, was an attack on Palermo harbour on 3 January 1943. Five Chariots were used. Each, with a crew of two, was embarked on the deck in watertight containers in the submarines *Trooper* and *Thunderbolt* (ex-*Thetis*). *Unruffled* took part as the recovery boat after the operation was complete. One Chariot sank the Italian cruiser *Ulpio Traiano* and another damaged the liner *Viminale*, which sank later in the year. Of the remaining three, one broke down en route and was picked up by *Unruffled* six hours later, a second sank through unknown causes, and on the third the driver ripped his diving suit negotiating harbour defences and drowned. His number two turned and took the Chariot out to sea and blew it up.

The next attack on *Tirpitz* would be handed over to another new unit in the submarine service – the as yet unused and untried X-craft flotilla. This consisted of fully equipped miniature submarines. They were originally devised in 1942 by two naval commanders, Varley and Bell, for penetrating enemy harbours, but it was soon realised that their engine capacity and fuel tanks meant they were equally suitable for longer-range work, even if the ride would be mightily uncomfortable.

The final version had a range of 1,200 miles on the surface

and perhaps a total of 150 miles dived before the batteries needed recharging. The method of attack was for them to go under enemy ships in the harbour, and for a diver to go out and attach limpet mines to the hull of the enemy ship. Later there was an addition of large side charges, attached one on each side, each containing 2.25 tonnes of Torpex. They had buoyancy tanks in them, which on release would be flooded and left under the target. They could be time-fused up to six hours with a minimum delay of fifteen minutes to let the boats get away. They were set to counter mines, and, if one went up, every one in the vicinity would go up, so that in the case of multiple attacks all the charges would explode together.

The crew of the boat was initially three people, but then one diver was lost in an accident so they brought more expert divers from the Charioteers' unit who were continuously diving and much more experienced. At that point the crew was increased to four.

Successful trials were carried out, and in the late summer of 1943 the opportunity arose for their use on a major expedition. The target was the elusive giant battleship *Tirpitz*, which continued to give the Allies nightmares. At the beginning of 1943 Admiral Dönitz became head of the German navy and made it clear he was placing its entire resources to the submarine war. Heavy ships and U-boat reinforcements were moved to Norwegian ports to avoid the long run back to Germany, and from there they could proceed at will against Allied shipping. *Tirpitz* was moved north from Trondheim, to put her out of range of British reconnaissance flights, and so supply convoys to Russia were halted for the second time. Later in the year, Spitzbergen in the far north, which had been occupied partly by the Allies and serviced by British submarines, came under attack.

Tirpitz, together with *Scharnhorst* and seven destroyers, launched a fairly ineffective bombardment and then sailed away.

It was decided then that the time had come to try the X-craft in an attack on *Tirpitz*, by now holed up in Altenfjord. In June 1943 RAF reconnaissance pilot John Dixon, flying alone as usual in his unarmed, long-range Spitfire with cameras in its nose, located *Tirpitz*. His discovery enabled the Admiralty to go ahead with a raid by the midget submarines.

The plan of attack was for six X-craft to be towed by conventional submarines for the main part of the 1,000-mile journey. They would then proceed, submerged, under their own steam towards their target, which was 80 miles from the open sea. Lieutenant Basil Charles Place takes up the story, beginning with the formation of the X-craft unit:

I was just coming back from ordinary submarine service in the Mediterranean and was sent for by the captain of submarines of what was then the 5th Submarine Flotilla in Fort Blockhouse in Gosport who just said: 'How would you like to sink the *Tirpitz*?' I said yes immediately. From there I went up to northern base* for instruction about the boat and then went back to take on the second prototype which was being built at Portsmouth dockyard. After trials in the dockyards, we went back up to Scotland and ran that one as a training boat while Vickers Armstrong were building in Barrow six operational boats. Four or five regulars came in at that time; one was an Australian who was not a submariner who

* HMS *Varbel*, which was the shore base at Rothesay for the 12th Submarine Flotilla. It was the flotilla that dealt in all special projects, like midget submarines, human torpedoes and different types of underwater craft.

happened to be officer of the watch on the battleship *Queen Elizabeth* when she was attacked by the Italian Charioteers in Alexandria harbour and the captain said to the Australian: 'You'd better go and do the same thing.'

Another one happened to be around in another boat in home waters, and they appeared to be recruiting men of our seniority and experience and were regular officers in that they had been midshipmen and were tolerably adept at coastal navigation and that sort of thing. The two original stalwarts were William Eke, who had been first lieutenant of *Sturgeon*, and Donald Cameron, who had been third hand on *Sturgeon* and who did all the original trials and proof trials to get the show on the road. We were in Scotland for a certain amount of training and then coming down to Portsmouth for trials, which had to be done at night because of security, then going along for breakfast, back into the conference room at nine and sitting down in a slide room and looking at results of the trials.

The next stage, from November 1942, we were trialling everything including living conditions and what sort of food we could take and so on. A five-day trial never seemed to do very well because the boat did suffer enormously from defects, mostly electrical. I think what had not been appreciated was how very damp the inside of those small boats could get.* There was also an inherent defect in the stability of the boat, and unfortunately my first lieutenant was washed over the side because of this and was killed during a

---

* So damp that the labels fell off food tins and no one knew what they were about to eat.

five-day endurance trial. Another first lieutenant of mine was killed a little later in the net-cutting part of the operation.

The latter was a fascinating and in some ways entertaining thing to do. We sometimes wondered at the sheer practicality of it in daylight in an enemy harbour. The process of getting out of the boat was by filling up a tank in which the diver sat. When the pressure equalised, the diver went out through the hatch, swam to the submarine net and cut it to let the boat through. It took us a little time to discover a technique for doing this. The prospect of getting through an anti-torpedo net was, we found, absolutely nil. But an anti-submarine net is a crisscross of quite wide spaces all designed to stop a submarine of sizeable dimensions. A four-foot mesh was of fairly conventional size so that something like five or six cuts would let the X-craft through.

If everything went right, it was quite exciting to make the last cuts and the boat comes through and you're sitting in front of it, then climb back inside and the boat goes on its way. But it was one of those things where if one thing goes wrong everything goes wrong. It is an occasion when you cannot exercise any brute force at all, and before we had telephones the diver had to tap on the side to indicate up a bit or down a bit so that the boat would come through.

The disadvantage of it was that the line of buoys that supported the net could be seen with a great kink where the boat was in it, and watchers from shore would immediately know there was something amiss. With your diver out, he is a sacrificial lamb to some extent and has got to decide that he does not jeopardise the boat by making sure that if he was killed, the wire-cutter did not fall in such a manner that it held the boat in the net. Various things like that did make one feel that it was of doubtful practicability to cut nets, certainly in daylight.

Around Christmastime 1942 we went to Barrow to see the new boats coming out – *X5* to *X10* – by which time most of the problems with the prototype had been ironed out. The new design was very good and did not give a great deal of trouble. From about 5 September, Spitfires operating from the Shetlands and landing in north Russia for refuelling did a daily reconnaissance, and there was a specific simple code for us to be told about ships, if *Tirpitz* had moved or whatever. It was a simple code broadcast over the BBC, which was all we had – no communications – and a distinctive phrase was repeated on two news programmes. They would not have made anyone the least bit suspicious.

The work-up was for the operation planned for March, but the three new boats didn't come off the stocks until mid-February and by the end of March there would be too much daylight to allow for charging, and so it was decided to put it off until September. We spent the summer working up, and by late August we had *Malaya*, an old battleship anchored in one of the Scottish lochs, and all boats, six of them by then, attacked without difficulty at all in fairly accurately simulated conditions. So there was a good deal of confidence among the individual crews by then. The boats were brought on board for full checking and loading with the side charges.

At that time there was William Eke, the grand old man of the party – he was about 28. He was pushed back in the summer to ordinary submarines. His first lieutenant, Crabbe, took over his boat. Don Cameron had the second boat, *X6*; he had been with William Eke from the beginning, which was about two years by then. I had the third, *X7*, Terence Martin had the fourth, *X8*, the Australian Macfarlane had *X9* and Ken Hudspeth, also an Australian, had *X10*. There were spare crews and passage crews. Six towing submarines came up in early September for final preparation, two T-boats and four S-boats. Morale was very good indeed. One of the hitches was that we didn't tow for long enough. We used special ropes with a telephone cable running down the centre of it for communications between the two vessels.

The two big ones, the T-boats, towing *X5* and *X6*, survived the journey intact, but all the other tows parted company once or more. September was the earliest month we could attempt the operation because of the daylight. It was perfectly possible in the dark to lie up among the rocks to charge the batteries, but you couldn't reasonably expect to get in and out of the 80 miles or so without a charge in the middle.

And so for the operation itself: the six craft set off on 10 September over a period of 48 hours, going on their respective routes, towed by the submarines *Thrasher*, *Truculent*, *Stubborn*, *Syrtis*, *Sceptre* and *Sea Nymph*. They put to sea from Loch Cairnbawm on the north-west coast of Scotland in the first phase of Operation Source. Each X-craft was armed with two 2-tonne explosive charges. Basil Place remembers two particular disasters:

In towing, the X-craft stays dived for six hours at a time and then in liaison with the towing boat comes to the surface. The X-craft then ventilates the boat by running the engine with an outboard induction and also puts a certain amount of charge in the battery, usually about twenty minutes every six hours. Telephone communications, however, were not good, and when they failed we had a system of explosive charges for signalling.

The first disaster was when *X8*, being towed by *Sceptre*, was signalled to come up. There was no response from below, and when the towing rope was hauled in there was nothing at the end of it. *X8* was never seen again. The other one was *Stubborn* towing *X7*, my boat. They spotted an X-craft on the surface at night – remarkably, because they are very small. It was *X9* and it had lost its towing submarine. *Stubborn* waited by it while sending a signal to its towing boat to return to the spot. They did make contact but by then the buoyancy chambers in the X-craft had got so loosened bumping against the side of the hull in the heavy seas that one of the seams cracked and flooded so that the boat had a list of 30 degrees.

When its towing boat reappeared, *X9* began to be manoeuvred towards it. They released a side charge to be connected up to the submarine and for no known reason it exploded. Fortunately, they were moving ahead at the time, so the damage was not extensive. But it was sufficient for the X-craft to be rendered a hopeless state and it was decided to abandon it. The crew was taken off into the submarine. So that left only four boats in a position of attacking. The weather had been fairly poor for the first four or five days. We decided to slip tow on 20 September. We exchanged crews, the passage crews going into the towing submarine and me with the operational crew being transferred to the X-craft. In the course of doing this for my boat, we picked up a mine, which got entangled with the tow gear. Fortunately, I managed to disentangle it. Then, during the changeover, the towline parted yet again, this time irreparably, and we had to complete the journey being towed by one of the submarine's berthing wires and thus lost our ability for quick release.

Even so, we managed to reach our slipping position with masses of time and finally slipped at 8 p.m. on 20 September. *X5*, *X6*, *X7* and *X10* all slipped in a relatively short time of each other, making their independent way into Standshund over a declared German anti-submarine minefield. We deemed it wisest to go on the surface, since it would have been designed for German heavy ships to go over the top of it. By then the weather was much improved. The boats were not expected to see each other or coordinate their attacks except that every four hours for one hour was explosion time and it was unwise to go too close to the target.

We eventually dived at around 2.30 a.m. and made our way up to Altenfjord proper, coming up to periscope depth every so often. We dived deep and the weather by then was quite pleasant. Altenfjord is about the same size as Scapa Flow and was obviously used for minor fleet exercises, anti-aircraft exercises and so on. We surfaced just after dark among some small islands just outside the main fleet anchorage and the auxiliary fleet anchorage where they held all the oilers and store ships. The coasts were very steep, and we were beside some rocks where we could not be seen. We needed to get a full charge at that point, which we did, although we also discovered a bit of a problem.

The exhaust was leaking, which we had to mend, and then dived the following morning at around 1.30 a.m. to make our way eventually through the anti-submarine boom up towards *Tirpitz*, seemingly with all the time in the world. We had about five and a half hours to do the 4 or 5 miles finally required. We hung about for a bit until daylight before moving forward towards the anti-submarine boom, which was strung across the neck of the fjord. Then we dived deep to avoid a minesweeper coming out and ran straight into an empty anti-torpedo boom with no ship inside but forming a square. Unfortunately, a piece of metal from the broken towing gear got us lodged on the torpedo net around the empty berth, and it took quite a while to get out. We didn't break surface, but I was rather worried we had revealed our presence.

There was, however, no reaction and we moved ahead and gained first sight of our target, *Tirpitz*, at about 5.45, quite plainly, very clear. We approach-fixed ourselves and went deep to go under the anti-torpedo nets that were surrounding the ship. Now, all of our knowledge of German anti-torpedo nets had been based on air reconnaissance or our own nets. Our own nets didn't go below more than 40 or 50 feet at the most. They were made of heavy steel rings, interlocking. It was said that there were two lines of buoys on the surface and by measuring the buoys it had been assumed that the nets could not possibly go below 40 feet but if they had one on hangers it might go deeper, to 70 feet. The water was 110 feet deep there and so in theory we should have been able to go easily underneath. But as it turned out their nets weren't like that at all. They were very fine 4-inch mesh, just like crisscross stitching, with very fine, thin wire which went a very great deal deeper.

My impression was that they had one net from the surface down to, say, 40 feet deep. The next one went from 30 feet deep to 70 feet deep. There was then a net that came up from the bottom, hanging permanently from submerged buoys, which overlapped the second net. So it did take us a considerable amount of time to get in. In fact, at one stage I contemplated doing an about-turn and going in through the boat passage which had been apparent from aerial photography. I didn't personally think we could make an adequate turn without a severe risk of running aground. In the end, having tried to get through at all depths, I decided there was no option but to come up to the surface and have a look properly through the night periscope, a binocular periscope.

Miraculously, when we came up to the surface there was no intervening net and *Tirpitz* was just a matter of 50 or 60 feet away. We went down as soon as we could and collided with the ship's bow at about 25 feet and slid on gently underneath in the full shadow of the hull. It was then that we heard the first charges levied, as we thought against us, but by then we were in an ideal position for attacking.

We dropped our two charges and, being in some doubt as to how we had got in, I decided to go back to the point where we had penetrated the nets. That was easier said than done, and we spent the next three-quarters of an hour trying to find a way out. Our charges were set for an hour; thus, we had only 15 minutes before they would blow. Drastic measures were required, and we did a sort of flop operation of hitting the net, holding ourselves down and blowing the bow tank to absolute full buoyancy as fast as we could so that we came up at a terrific angle and at the same time going full ahead on the motor. We just scraped the top of the net and got out. I'm afraid that led to the toppling of our gyrocompass. We hoped we were steering towards the open sea, but unfortunately we seemed to have come back into the net again at about 50 feet; the explosions went with quite a considerable amount of noise and we were too close for comfort.

The after-hatch lifted and quite a volume of water came in. There were one or two spurting leaks around and about, and so we backed out of that particular piece of net at periscope depth, which we could maintain, and had to surface. At the same time, I had a look around and it was very galling to discover that *Tirpitz* did not seem to have settled in the water or anything at all. I really had some doubt then whether that explosion had been our own charges going up or whether it was a depth charge from a surface ship.

However, we went back to the bottom for a while and decided that we would have to get further away. In the next half-hour, however, we discovered we were unable to maintain any sort of depth. There was so much water in the boat that as soon as you got a bow-up angle it all swished down to the back end and you came up to the surface. And as soon as you got a bow-down angle it swished down to the other end and you went rocketing down to the bottom. We were fired at almost immediately we surfaced and, having lost the night periscope, we knew we were in grave danger of running up the beach. We'd always said that the security aspect of the operation that really counted was that it could be done, and once it had been done the security had been lost.

The boats were very much stronger than the enemy were likely to suspect. They may have thought that we were human torpedoes. What we didn't want to do was run the boat up the beach blind and present them immediately with knowledge. We had a conference and decided we had really better bale out. We considered going up by Davis's gate [the DSEA equipment] but decided that we should wave a white flag on the surface and when picked up would give the others the opportunity of making an escape. There was quite a lot of firing going on and it seemed logical that I should go outside and wave a sweater. Unfortunately, the boat started taking in water. I shut the hatch and the small amount of water that she took in was enough to put her back down to the bottom again where the other three, as we'd worked out, were to wait about an hour until the worst of things had finished up top and then make a Davis escape, which they were reasonably well trained in. A Davis escape is always very risky, although 110 feet of water was not a huge amount. But unfortunately something occurred and two of them got stuck in the boat, perhaps overcome by oxygen poisoning, before they had a chance to get fully flooded and only one of them escaped, who was picked up like myself about an hour and a half later.

As for the other boats, it was against Cameron in *X6* that the charges we had heard inside the net were directed. He had suffered some really disquieting defects, one of which was the flooding of one of the side charges. So he was coming in at an angle of about 15 degrees. As the attack periscope was at an angle we could see the sky on one side and the water on the other and not a lot in between. He decided to do his last bit of attack through the boat passage and take a chance of running aground. In fact, he did run aground in about 15 or 20 feet of water, broke surface, rushed in – we must have been very close together at the time – and made his attack, hit *Tirpitz* on the port side, let go the charges, and all the crew baled out as the boat was flooding up and were picked up.

X5 we know got into the vicinity of the target because Cameron saw her from the deck of *Tirpitz* after he was picked up. Some years later, a thorough search was made of the area and his boat was not found, although Cameron was of the opinion that the boat he saw was sunk at that time. Ken Hudspeth in *X10*, the fourth boat that went in, had so many defects that he had to lie up in a deserted part of the fjord for four or five days, trying to repair leaks and the gyrocompass. He didn't get into the target area until ten days after slipping, and by then the place was so teeming with boats that he couldn't get in at all. He returned to the rendezvous zone and was picked up by *Stubborn*, which by then had only one wire left to use for towing; the rest had been broken on the outward journey. Then a gale blew up and it was decided that *X10* would have to be sunk.

Meanwhile, those of us who were picked up were taken on board *Tirpitz* and then transferred to another vessel to be transported to a prisoner-of-war camp in Germany.

The four explosions from the X-craft charges had in fact inflicted crippling damage, and one of them, from Place's *X7*, went off exactly below the battleship's engine rooms, severely damaging both her main turbine and fire-control system. *Tirpitz* was put out of action and Place and Donald Cameron were both awarded the Victoria Cross for

a most daring and successful attack on the German

battleship *Tirpitz*, moored in the protected anchorage of Kaa fjord. To reach the anchorage necessitated the penetration of an enemy minefield and a passage of 50 miles up the fjord, known to be vigilantly patrolled by the enemy and to be guarded by nets, gun defences and listening posts, this after a passage of at least a thousand miles from base. Having successfully eluded all these hazards and entered the fleet anchorage, Lieutenants Place and Cameron, with complete disregard for danger, worked their small craft past the close anti-submarine and torpedo nets surrounding *Tirpitz*, and from a position inside these nets, carried out a cool and determined attack. Whilst they were still inside the nets a fierce enemy counter-attack by guns and depth charges developed which made their withdrawal impossible. Lieutenants Place and Cameron therefore scuttled their craft to prevent them falling into the hands of the enemy. Before doing so they took every measure to ensure the safety of their crews, the majority of whom, together with themselves, were taken prisoner. In the course of the operation these small craft pressed home their attack to the full, in doing so accepting all the dangers inherent in such vessels and facing every possible hazard which ingenuity could have devised for the protection in harbour of vitally important capital ships. The courage and utter contempt for danger in the immediate face of the enemy shown by Lieutenants Place and Cameron during their determined and successful attack were supreme.

With *Tirpitz* in dock, there was further bad news for the German navy. *Scharnhorst* was sunk by *Duke of York* and her escort on 26 December 1943, which meant that *Tirpitz* was the only major battleship left. And so the British redoubled their efforts to ensure she never came back to trouble them. On 3 April 1944 Fleet Air Arm bombers and fighters from *Victorious*, *Formidable* and three other aircraft carriers attacked the ship in her Norwegian anchorage. Two waves of aircraft, consisting in total of 42 Fairey Barracuda torpedo bombers and 80 American-built Grumman Wildcat and Hellcat fighters, had to dodge 68 anti-aircraft guns now surrounding *Tirpitz* but managed to score a number of direct hits which put her out of action again. Four more attacks were launched by the Fleet Air Arm in July and August and then, finally, 28 Lancaster bombers dropped another load on their way to England from Russia. Dönitz finally conceded that the pride of the German fleet was done for and had her towed to Tromsøfjord to act as a coastal defence battery. Even that plan was thwarted when the RAF made one more run and bombed her. This time she went up with her own ammunition store, and fewer than 90 of her trapped crew of 1,000 were rescued from the warship.

Meanwhile, the X-craft were used for other attacks. *X24*, under the command of Lieutenant Ian Fraser, went to Bergen harbour on 13 April to attack a large floating dock and sank a 7,800-tonne ship, leaving the port's loading facility badly damaged. Two others, *X20* and *X23*, were used in conjunction with the Coppists for preliminary surveys and to mark invasion beaches for the D-Day landings. With their usefulness in Europe now virtually at an end, the midget submarines were moved to the Far East to begin operations against Japanese shipping.

CHAPTER ELEVEN

Bad Days (and Good) in the
Strait of Malacca

In comparison with the mêlée of activity on the home station, the Battle of the Atlantic and the incredible adventures of submarines in the Mediterranean, the Far East had been seriously neglected, although quite evidently not by choice. As we have already discovered from earlier recollections, the China station in Hong Kong had been the busiest of overseas billets for the submarine service for almost 20 years prior to the outbreak of war. It was a posting that the crews enjoyed, and at its peak 15 submarines were based on the station, trained and equipped for a defensive role around Britain's vast eastern interests. When war came, Britain needed every submarine she could lay her hands on in the home region, and the Far Eastern boats were progressively withdrawn. Within a year of their reporting for duty attached to the British and Mediterranean flotillas, seven of the fifteen had been sunk.

When the Japanese attack on Pearl Harbor at last brought

the Americans into the conflict the Royal Navy had just one submarine, *Rover*, dry-docked in Singapore undergoing repairs. Seven Dutch submarines, previously looking after their own nation's interests in the region, also came under British control, but by Christmas 1941 four of them had been sunk. After the Pearl Harbor attack, Admiral Sir Geoffrey Layton, commander of the Eastern Fleet, literally pleaded for reinforcements. He received just two submarines, the new T-boat *Trusty*, which sailed from the Mediterranean on 26 December 1941, followed by *Truant* under Commander Haggard on 3 January, the latter having just completed five months' continuous service in the Mediterranean.

Commander William King was a veteran of the China station. It will be recalled from his earlier reminiscences that he first went there in 1932. Lately he had also seen a great deal of action in both the Norwegian campaign and the Mediterranean in command of *Snapper*, which was withdrawn from service in the autumn of 1941 for a refit. He recalled:

> I turned in *Snapper** and went to Barrow-in-Furness to draw my second submarine, *Trusty*, bigger but not much better in terms of on-board conditions. There was no air-conditioning or anything like that. We went out to the Mediterranean for patrols and then were sent on to the Far East, to bolster defences in Singapore. We arrived at a dockyard on the north side of the island and realised that there was no one in charge. I was then informed that the Japanese were expected on the other side of the causeway at any moment. I went over to the

---

* Under a new commander, *Snapper* left the UK for the Bay of Biscay patrol and was not heard from again. She was assumed mined or depth-charged off Brest between 10 and 12 February 1942 with the loss of all 42 crew.

other side of the island, and did what we had to do and attempted to find some food to take on board. All that we could get was Horlicks malted milk and Australian cough drops, which had to do us for the next patrol. We moved out of the harbour and immediately confronted a 20,000-tonne Japanese transport ship. The whole of the deck was covered with vehicles, and we opened up with gunfire. It went up in a sheet of flames and sank. I was given a reprimand. I was told I should have torpedoed it but I had deliberately not done that because we might easily have run into the Japanese main fleet and the nearest reload for torpedoes was a thousand miles away.

I then heard on the radio that Singapore had fallen. We had taken some damage and were leaking oil. We made for Sourabaya, which was already being attacked. We desperately needed to take on food, fuel and water. The harbour was already under fire and I made the decision to stay on the surface. A Dutch submarine that dived was lost with all hands after being depth-charged in shallow water. We then made for Ceylon, limping, and were based on Colombo, where we spent some time in dry dock for repairs. In fact, we got out just in time for the Easter Day raid on Ceylon by the Japanese. We were alongside the depot ship taking on torpedoes when the Japanese aircraft came over.

The rest of the Allied ships had gone out into the Indian Ocean, and we were the only modern boat left in the harbour so the whole bloody lot attacked us in a stream, line ahead at about masthead level. I could actually see the pilots in their cockpits. Fortunately, we had replaced our Lewis gun with a Bren, which worked beautifully. I also had a very good yeoman of signals who plastered these chaps as they came over and as they went away. He was firing away, hitting them as they came in and again as they went out. Consequently, their bombs missed. You could see them making holes in the harbour just beside us, anxious to get away from the Bren spitting out its load. A lot of them didn't make it back to their carriers. They were simply too brave and came too low.

We then went on patrol on the Malacca Strait under conditions that frankly would not support human life. We had many men who were sick; I fell sick and I don't think I was performing very well. It was all down to the lack of air-conditioning. It is at those times that the submarine is at its worst. You were living in the most filthy stench, a mixture of human smells, excrement, cooking, battery gas, fuel, washing, everything – an unbelievable cocktail. Fortunately, nature is merciful; if you are locked into a bad smell your olfactory nerves become fatigued and you don't smell it any more. When you come to the surface and get fresh air past you and then get a smell of the situation below, you realise exactly what you've been living in. Smokers told me you had to have three cigarettes before you could enjoy a smoke because your whole system was saturated with this nastiness. Smells were an unbelievable discomfort, not least because when we went to the toilet, we used to store it up in buckets, in big sort of cans, and at the end of the day or when we were able to surface we'd throw it over the side using these buckets.

You can imagine the scene, climbing up through the conning tower in an 80-mile-an-hour wind [because of the engine down-draught] carrying these buckets covered only by a sack and throwing them to leeward. I used to steam away from our position, throw all the excrement and gash away from where we were. Never blow anything up to the surface, either, because aircraft above us were waiting for exactly such signs. That's the way it was in those days.

The other thing is that when you're dived, you want to use up as little oxygen as you can so you encourage everyone to rest and keep quiet. There was always a good comradeship among the crew in submarines, which seems to hold them together in difficult circumstances. Obviously, tempers do flare on occasions, but not for long because everyone knows they would soon be panting again. The fact is that our submarines were slums compared with American boats. If you have to do something, like loading torpedoes or some other emergency, you find that the oxygen goes away very quickly indeed. It was necessary then to reload torpedoes when dived, well under water level and well under control. So you tried to keep everyone as quiet and as still as possible, and all the chatter would come alive when you surfaced at night. In the Far East, in those conditions, it was never comfortable, and the only consolation was that the poor buggers on land were having it much worse than ourselves.

Six more submarines eventually arrived at the Colombo base between March and August 1943 to link up with the depot ship *Lucia*. It was still a paltry number for the long patrols that were necessary in the Far East now that Singapore had fallen, but repeated requests for more boats were being denied. Like Field Marshal William Slim's 14th Army, the submariners in the Far East became isolated on the forgotten frontier – and no wonder, with the supreme effort being displayed in the Mediterranean and the Atlantic. Nothing more than rather tentative patrols could be launched in the Far East before the Italian surrender in September 1943, by which time the situation had become critical. At the beginning of that month, the Eastern Fleet had just one submarine, the Dutch *O24*, in operation, the rest having been sunk or withdrawn.

The Italian surrender allowed a modest replenishment to occur in the early months of 1944. The 4th Flotilla was formed with seven T-boats and five S-class. By April the 8th Flotilla was brought into being with six S-class, and between the two almost ninety patrols were launched between January and September 1944. In August, as more boats were freed from the demands of the Mediterranean, the 3rd Flotilla, formed on the Clyde, arrived at Trincomalee, on Ceylon's east coast, in September, bringing the total complement of the Eastern Fleet to 26 submarines.

Further reinforcements were promised, and all new S- and T-class submarines commissioned in the British shipyards in the latter part of 1944 and early 1945 were destined for the Far East. Very soon, there was an outright shooting match going on, with torpedoes zooming around the eastern seas and dozens of enemy craft and supply vessels, albeit many of them small fry, sent to the bottom.

Tony Troup, whom we met earlier as first lieutenant on Tubby Linton's *Turbulent*, had, it will be recalled, left that submarine shortly before she was lost with all hands to begin training for his own command. Still only 24, he came through his Perisher (CO's) course with flying colours and began the next phase of his submarine life as captain of a brand-new S-class, *Strongbow*, with a scratch crew made up mostly of 'hostilities-only' (HO) recruits who had been in the navy for only about six months.

So one was holding one's breath a bit but, true enough, they knuckled down – it was great. I think there was a difference between an HO and a regular, but it was quite hard after a bit to discern it. The regulars were very steady and they knew their stuff and didn't have to be told and that sort of thing, but the HOs were very enthusiastic. Some of them weren't very good, but on the whole I think they were an eager bunch. They had been taken from all sorts of walks of life and thrown into a submarine. We went off to the Far East just before D-Day in 1944 in a convoy of merchant ships.

By that time the Battle of the Atlantic had been really won, and we convoyed right down to Gibraltar and we were way out in the Atlantic when the D-Day landings happened. I was sad not to be there. However, we then went on through to the Med and we were detained at Malta for about a week or ten days because it was undecided whether I was going to be used in the Aegean, because at that time the Germans still occupied the Greek islands.

Sadly, we didn't and went off to the Far East, arriving in Trincomalee in late August. After ten days alongside, we went on patrol and then patrolled continuously virtually without a break well into the next year. I was on patrol in the Indian Ocean in May when V-E Day was declared, so that was about the span of my time there – about a year. During that time I did patrols from Trincomalee right across the assignment area from Burma along the west coast of Sumatra to the Malacca Strait down to Singapore. We had excellent Admiralty charts of the area, which we relied on implicitly because in those days we had very primitive radar, and navigation of the strait was very difficult indeed. There were minefields down either side of Sumatra and the Malaysian coast, so we used to navigate using celestial rather than anything else, and using soundings because the coast is quite flat and it was difficult to find out where you were. The targets we found were generally known in the Royal Navy as supply ships. We always sank supply ships, but the enemy always sank merchant ships – they were exactly the same. There was nothing much over 5,000 tonnes, mostly coastal stuff, many small craft and junks. This was what they were resorting to using – junks and coasters, which quickly sank.

We occasionally passed off targets either because we thought they were too small or because the water was too shallow and you couldn't get at them. We hit that problem on several occasions. I did start an attack at the top of the Malacca Strait, which was full of sandbanks. The echo-sounding got down to 12 feet under the keel and that meant that I couldn't fire because when the torpedo went out it would hit the bottom right away. That was what you were up against. I, for one, had a sort of unwritten rule that I wouldn't go inside 60 feet because you couldn't dive and you couldn't defend yourself, remembering always that the only defence from attacking aircraft was to submerge.

This was particularly difficult when we began to intersperse our patrols with a good deal of secret service work in Japanese-controlled waters, such as landing agents and saboteurs, very similar to what we had carried out in the Mediterranean. One landing was into Thailand, but unfortunately they were all captured. We did one run where we were to pick up a group sitting off an island on the west coast of Sumatra. There was an

American, a black man and a native. We were to take them off, replenish them with stores and put them back. They had been there for ages recording all the shipping movements; amazing people. From our point of view it was also a difficult operation. We were told to rendez-vous at the island where we would see these people in an outrigger canoe. We saw them paddling around, and they saw the periscope in the daylight, but we couldn't come up because of Japanese air activity, and we had to wait until dark. But they began paddling after the periscope, trying to catch us up.

They had clearly exhausted themselves and there was nothing we could do. Eventually, I decided to send them a message in a bottle. We compiled a careful message, saying simply 'anchor and wait until dusk' and I put it in a sherry bottle. We then had to decide how to get it to them. We had an underwater gun for firing out smoke candles. So we put this inside the gun and it worked. I went underneath them and the bottle came up right alongside them, but unfortunately, as it came up, they saw the periscope and began paddling furiously after me again and completely missed the bottle. I then withdrew, knowing where they were, and waited until it was nearly dark. We then returned, got them on board and gave them every blinking thing we could lay our hands on. By the time they were to depart back to the island, a storm was blowing up and I said I would tow them back to the island because we had drifted miles off. We tied them on astern and then, of course, it was so rough we towed them under. By now it was beginning to get light and we had to rig a torpedo derrick to hoist their canoe out of the water and do it all over again. By the time we had finished, it was broad daylight and I was getting hellishly worried. The wind eased, they paddled off and I shot off on the surface to get away as far as possible so as not to compromise them. Subsequently, I found out they survived and were plucked off when the war ended. It was very similar to some of those incredible skylarks in the Mediterranean [in *Turbulent*], but it was extremely risky, going very close inshore where there was no protection and it was impossible to dive. We were very vulnerable, and the agents were unspeakably brave. They were never any trouble – they were all super people.

We had one or two narrow escapes. Once, while running on the surface down towards the Malacca Strait, we saw some smoke on the beam in the distance. It appeared to be a merchant ship. We started to charge along parallel with it to get ahead of it, but when I got up into the periscope standings and had a look, I could see that it was a destroyer. He turned towards me the same moment, so we dived and he came absolutely straight at me, zigzagging like mad. He depth-charged me, although it wasn't too bad; just a few leaks. The Japanese depth-charge attacks compared with the Germans' differed in competence in that the Japanese had good sonar and they were really quite good at it, contrary to general view. We thought they would be fairly primitive and only using hydrophones, but they used both, and they used sonar quite effectively, especially from my point of view because eventually I got badly caught right at the top of the narrowest end of the Malacca Strait.

It was at a place known as the One Fathom Back Channel, and I got caught by five anti-submarine vessels, a couple of frigates and three ace trawlers. They gave us a really bad time, very bad, and the damage was such that we had to try to get back to harbour, which was a thousand miles away. So it took a little time. The damage was irreparable, which was infuriating. We had the pressure hull pushed in, and in those days the submarines were (at least mine was) riveted, and the force of the explosion had pushed in what's called the double butt strap so that the water came in between the joint. Our main engines also moved on their beds and that caused a great deal of vibration.

We had the torpedoes jammed in the tubes, the air compressors were smashed and generally we were in a bad way. But we did finally get home, but it was really the end of our time. The damage assessment was that the submarine shouldn't go below 150 feet, and that wasn't any good to anybody. So we came home. In one respect it was infuriating, but on the other hand it had not been the best of billets. There was a difference of attitude between the Japanese enemy and the German enemy. I, and I think everybody, disliked the Japanese intensely. They were bestial towards their prisoners, and we knew they did some shocking things to people. My cousin, Pat Pelly, was in command of the submarine *Stratagem* in the same flotilla, and he was sunk in the Malacca Strait, just about a couple of months beforehand. There was only one surviving officer. They had a hell of a time and were brutally treated. We all knew this. One didn't like the Germans but one respected their navy in particular. They were good, clean fighting people, better than the Italians really, but not so the Japanese.

The latter aspects were also noted by another commander, Lieutenant-Commander (later Rear-Admiral Sir) Hugh

Mackenzie, who arrived in the brand-new submarine *Tantalus* in April. He had previously been involved in the Mediterranean campaign as CO of *Thrasher* and found the two assignments as different as chalk and cheese. His operational patrols were also heavily interspersed with the landing of agents and saboteurs right across the Far East, sometimes directly for Mountbatten's South-East Asia Command intelligence unit, others for the Special Operations Executive, which had spread itself to all key areas in spite of a general shortage of supplies, difficulties with other Allied government departments or military controllers and trouble getting their agents shifted into position. It fell largely to the British submarine flotilla to achieve the last, often with unhappy results, as Mackenzie recalled:

> From April until September we engaged in patrols down the Malacca Strait. It was very shallow, hot, dirty water, difficult navigation, with sandbanks everywhere and very few targets. On virtually every patrol we were engaged in landing agents. They were usually dropped off the west coast of Malaya. One went close inshore and landed them by folboat. We nearly always managed to land them successfully but seldom picked them up and nearly always got surprised by Japanese forces when we tried to reach them. The Japanese clearly knew too much. The story was that they captured too many of the agents ashore and they had some horrible methods of extracting information from them, through torture, and that's how they knew when a pick-up was likely to take place. They were very brave men because they knew the risks they were running and not many of them came back. They were mostly British, who had been out in Malaya before the war.

Mackenzie was also involved in one of the most controversial incidents of the war in the Far East: an attempt to blow up Japanese shipping at Singapore. It was one of 81 missions into Japanese-held territory launched by the Australian section of the Special Operations Executive or, to give it its title at that time, the Services Reconnaissance Department, also known as Z Special Unit. This particular mission went under the name of Operation Rimau, the Malay word for 'tiger'. It turned out to be an ill-fated, tragic mission which, apart from the ambitious nature of the operation itself, became bogged down in interplay between rival administrative officials in the British and American military establishments. General Douglas MacArthur, for one, had been giving the Australians the impression that he was dissatisfied with their contribution to the war in the Pacific. His 'I know better than any of you' tactics were evidently not uncommon in any situation. According to Gruff Courtney (who, it will be recalled, accompanied General Mark Clark on his special mission to Oran), Z Special Unit (SRD) was suspected of being a British Trojan horse planted in a US theatre of war to regain lost British colonies (in this case Singapore) as the war came to a close, and to restore her pre-war influence in the Far East. In consequence, GHQ would tolerate SRD out of political politeness to an ally but render it impotent until it could be safely ignored, and diverted into a sideshow in company with the rest of the Australian army. So every project of SRD had to receive approval of GHQ, and even if it were at long last grudgingly approved, then the necessary air and sea transport had to be obtained from the appropriate air and naval commander, who had the right of refusal. GHQ also had indirect but vital control over SRD's finances, and any proposed operation of which it did not approve would die stillborn of financial anaemia.

Operation Rimau was dreamed up in the wake of an earlier attack on Japanese shipping launched from Australia. This was Operation Jaywick, in which Lieutenant-Colonel Ivan Lyon, on detachment from the Gordon Highlanders to intelligence and special operations, led a very successful raid on Singapore harbour, using folboats launched from a captured Japanese fishing vessel, the now-famous *Krait*, damaging seven ships totalling 40,000 tonnes. In the autumn of 1944 he was planning another, bigger raid, this time using new and supposedly secret 'canvas' submarines, known as Sleeping Beauties. Their official title was Motorised Submersible Canoes (MSCs), and they were the invention of Blondie Hasler, leader of the Cockleshell Heroes, who was by then on the staff of Mountbatten's South-East Asia Command. The idea was to take 15 of these craft by submarine to an island off Singapore and from there to launch their attack, in what were basically canoes that travelled under water, and attach limpet mines to Japanese ships. It would be the first time the Sleeping Beauties had been used in any major operation.

In the scheme of things, the operation did not get great priority from GHQ, given that by then the Far East arena was a busy one although Australia figured more prominently in submarine operations. Between 1942 and 1945, 122 American, 31 British and 11 Dutch submarines used Australian ports, with Fremantle having the largest role. More than 60 submarines used the port as an operational base.

In August Operation Rimau was given the green light, and it was once again to be led by Lieutenant-Colonel Lyon, leading a mixed team recruited from the British and Australian armies, the Royal Marines, the Royal Australian Navy and the Royal Naval Volunteer Reserve. A previously classified document prepared by Australian investigating authorities states:

The original plans were prepared in London and provided for the following:

1. Submarine transport to the operational area.

2. A reconnaissance from the submarine for a base, located about 70 miles from Singapore harbour, the island of Merapas being tentatively selected.

3. The provisioning of this base from the submarine.

4. The seizure of a local junk and the transshipment to it from the submarine of the party and operational stores and equipment.

5. The sailing of the junk, as a depot ship, to a forward rendezvous from which a coordinated attack by 15 MSCs could be launched against the target areas.

6. A withdrawal to the rendezvous and thence a further withdrawal in folboats to the provisional base.

7. Evacuation by submarine from the base.

Ominously, the instructions from London also stated: 'Should the pick-up not take place on the scheduled date, the party was to wait a further 30 days, after which they were at liberty to make their own arrangements for escape.' Exactly how they were to make their way home was not explained.

The party left Fremantle on 11 September 1944 in the

large minelaying submarine *Porpoise* (Lieutenant-Commander Marsham), which made her name running the blockade of Malta with food and fuel stacked on her mine-deck. Now she had stores weighing 14 tonnes stacked aboard for the Rimau expedition. Also on board were 11 folboats and 15 motorised submersible canoes. The uneventful journey took them first to Merapas, a small, thickly wooded island 70 miles east of Singapore. It was reached on 23 September, and an after-dark reconnaissance revealed that Merapas was a suitable base with excellent cover and a good water supply. On the night of 24 September, stores were unloaded from *Porpoise* and taken ashore. One officer stayed behind to guard the stores; the rest re-embarked *Porpoise* and set off in search of a native junk.

Four days passed before a suitable vessel was spotted, a junk called *Mustika*, sighted off the coast of Borneo. She was stopped and captured by seven of the Rimau party. *Porpoise* submerged and *Mustika* was sailed towards Pejantan island, reaching the north coast early in the afternoon. That night the operational stores and equipment, including the submersibles, were transferred from *Porpoise* to *Mustika* and the submarine set off back for Australia, arriving at Fremantle on 11 October 1944 with the Malay captain and eight crew members of the junk who were interrogated and 'some useful intelligence was obtained'.

On the journey back, *Porpoise* had developed engine trouble, and so when Hugh Mackenzie, in *Tantalus*, left Fremantle on an offensive patrol on 16 October, he found himself with an additional task: to pick up the Rimau party from the rendezvous point at Merapas island. It was suggested that Mackenzie might leave that patrol to make the pick-up around 7 November. When that day arrived he still had on board 15 torpedoes and sufficient fuel and stores for another fortnight's patrolling. The summary of events prepared in Australia goes on:

As his main object was offensive action against the Japanese, Mackenzie was loath to abandon his patrol at that stage in order to pick up Rimau. In addition, the orders for the party were that they might expect to be picked up any time within a month after the initial date, 8 November. Consequently, Mackenzie [having consulted submarine HQ] had to delay leaving his patrol until such time as fuel and stores and expenditure of torpedoes demanded. Major Chapman [Rimau liaison officer] was consulted and he concurred with these arrangements. Finally, it was decided to make the rendezvous on the 21/22 November. At 0706 hours on 21 November, having made a landfall on the surface, *Tantalus* dived and approached the northern end of Merapas island.

A periscope reconnaissance showed nothing suspicious, although there was no sign of the party. Well clear of the island, the submarine surfaced at 1916 hours. Conditions were suitable for landings, and it was decided to drop the folboat close to the north-east corner of the island soon after moonset at 2345. From there the rescue party could land on the northern shore. At 0100 hours on 22 November, *Tantalus* stopped about 600 yards off the north-east corner of the island, and Major Chapman and Corporal Croton disembarked in the folboat. *Tantalus* then put to sea with the intention of returning the following night.

At 2150 hours on 22 November, *Tantalus* arrived a few hundred yards off the north-west corner of Merapas. Shortly afterwards a folboat containing only Major

Chapman and Corporal Croton coming off, Chapman reported that there was no sign of the Rimau party on the island. It was agreed that nothing was to be gained by remaining any longer in the vicinity and trying again at later date, so *Tantalus* proceeded clear and sailed for Fremantle. On the island Major Chapman had discovered signs which showed that the whole party had been there, and had apparently left in a hurry. The evidence indicated that they had left at least 14 days previously. No message had been left and there was no sign of any fight or struggle.

The following account of the loss of the Rimau party was compiled after the war from the interrogation of Japanese prisoners and natives. In respect of the party's movements, it is somewhat hypothetical:

On 1 October, the Rimau party in the junk *Mustika* sailed for Pulau Laban via Tamiang and Sugi straits. Pulau Laban, located 11 miles south-west of Keppel harbour, was the intended forward point from which the attack was to be delivered. On 6 October in the vicinity of Pulau Laban (and probably while preparing to discharge MSCs), the Rimau party in *Mustika* was approached by a native police boat. Mistaking the craft for a Japanese patrol craft, Rimau opened fire, killing all the natives in the boat. Lieutenant-Colonel Lyon then decided that as the security of the operation was lost, the operation must be cancelled owing to the necessity of protecting the secret of the MSC equipment. The latter was therefore destroyed, and the party split into four groups. Each group had rubber boats and was ordered to make its own way back to Merapas island. Three days later the Japanese learned of the action with the native police and all island garrisons were warned to be on the lookout. By coincidence all four parties met on Sole island where they clashed with the Japanese.

During the gun battle, the party leader, Lieutenant-Colonel Lyon, and one other officer were killed. The remainder of the party escaped and pushed on to Merapas. Another senior officer, Lieutenant-Colonel Davidson, was killed en route. They remained on the island until 4 November, when they were found once again by the Japanese and attacked. A number of Japanese were killed in this action but the party suffered no further casualties. The party then split into small groups and moved south. From here their movements are obscure. Three were known to have [boarded a Chinese junk] heading for an island east of Timor. One of the three was taken by a shark, another was killed by a Chinese member of the crew and the third, Lieutenant Sargent, was taken prisoner and was not seen again.

Over the next few days, 11 other members of the party were captured at various points and were all taken to Singapore in December 1944, where one of them later died from illness. The fate of the remaining personnel was never discovered, but they were assumed to have been killed in firefights with Japanese search parties.

The ten surviving prisoners in captivity were eventually arraigned before a Japanese court martial and sentenced to death. The sentence was carried out on 7 July 1945, one month before the Japanese surrendered. They were 'given the honour' of being ceremonially beheaded. So ended an ill-fated and tragic operation that the Australians have never forgotten, and when the issue is mentioned there is still criticism of the manner in which the Rimau party was more or less abandoned for a month in territory infested with Japanese while the submarine destined to pick them up carried on her patrol. Thus, once again, the split between war patrols and secret missions that the submarine service had, according to some, been 'lumbered with' throughout the war became the topic of heated debate. Another unfortunate element of this whole affair was that Operation Rimau was scrapped because security had been compromised, as London demanded, so as not to jeopardise the 'secret MSCs'. The lives of 22 men were seemingly less important than saving 15 useless toys from falling into the hands of the Japanese.

Attempts to blow up shipping in Singapore harbour were not abandoned. The X-craft were on their way! After the Bergen attack, there were few targets left in Europe and it was decided that X-craft should be sent to the Far East. Six boats were hoisted on board a depot ship, HMS *Bonaventure*, a converted Clan liner that used to sail the Scottish Highlands and arrived in the first week of April 1945. Captain W.R. Fell placed his command at the disposal of the United States 7th Fleet, but the X-craft seemed destined to be scrapped until, in July, they were tasked for special operations, cutting undersea communications cables between Singapore and Hong Kong while simultaneously attacking cruisers in the Johore Strait, Singapore. On 27 July the submarines *Spark*, *Stygian* and *Spearhead* left Brunei, Borneo, and *Selene* left Subic, Philippines, each with a midget submarine in tow.

D-day was 31 July. Lieutenant M.H. Shean, RANVR, and his team in *XE4* succeeded in cutting the Hong Kong to Saigon cable, and the Saigon to Singapore cable. The operation was perfectly performed under extremely difficult conditions, and, as usual on such operations, a foot of each cable was brought back as proof. Lieutenant Westmacott and his crew in *XE5* had a rough passage to their target in the heavily defended waters of Hong Kong. There, they spent three and a half days struggling with their task, often having to dash out to the open sea as patrol vessels came in sight. But the attempt failed and they had to return to base.

Lieutenant Ian Fraser, meanwhile, was delegated to go into Singapore harbour in *XE3* and place explosives on the Japanese battle cruiser *Takao*, while Lieutenant Smart in *XE1* was to perform a similar task against the *Myoko*, Fraser recalled:

From Labuan in Borneo to the Singapore Strait was a tow of about 600 miles. So we set sail in the last week of July 1945, towed by *Stygian*. At the entrance to Singapore Strait, we did the crew change. The passage crew got off and I and my operational crew took over. We slipped the tow and began our journey up the Strait of Singapore until we came to the island of Singapore itself. The cruiser we'd been detailed to attack was lying at the old Admiralty dockyard on the north side of Singapore island, which meant a journey of 12 miles up a narrow channel round the north end of Singapore island called the Johore Strait.

We went through the boom, the gate of which was open at the entrance to the harbour, at about nine o'clock in the morning on 31 July. We navigated our way along the channel until we saw *Takao* looming up in front of us. She was heavily camouflaged, lying very close inshore. It was thought that she was going to be used as a bombardment centre against British troops coming down through Burma. I let all my crew have a look through the periscope. One of them was a New Zealander, Kiwi Smith. I never knew his Christian name. I had an engine artificer called Charlie Reid. And my diver was Leading Seaman Magennis. I let them all have a look at *Takao* through the periscope before we started the attack because it was all very exciting, especially as we dived and could see the hull of the boat through the porthole.

We ran in and went underneath the ship and settled on the bottom. The diver, Magennis, got out and found to his horror that the bottom was heavily encrusted with barnacles. He had to scrape the bottom of the ship with his diving knife to attach the magnets. It was quite a considerable job and it took him about forty minutes to fix the six limpet mines. They were all primed ready to blow. He returned to the submarine and I flooded down – and nothing happened. We couldn't move. The tide had gone down and we were stuck in a very narrow hole under the ship on which we had just hung a daisy-chain of limpet mines. It appeared that the water levels had dropped a foot or so, and *Takao* had sunk down also.

The submarine would not budge. The only thing we could do was to try to power our way out in some manner. I started going full ahead, full astern, blowing tanks, filling tanks. This went on for a good 20 minutes, and by then I was getting a bit frantic. Eventually, by continuing with that procedure I managed to nudge a hole through the seabed, and we finally forced our way through. We came out on to the seabed proper where we discovered another problem. We released the side cargo tanks after placing the limpet mines but found that one of them had been damaged and was stuck firm, so we had a situation of having one on and one off, which of course caused the submarine to be lopsided. We were over to the starboard all the time. Magennis had to go out again in his diving suit and lever this thing off. This he did, about 50 yards away from this cruiser in about 30 feet of very clear water. Anybody looking down would have seen a black shape instantly. To make matters worse, his diving suit was leaking and he was sending a stream of bubbles to the surface.

Eventually, he released the side cargo tank, got in again and we made our way out of the Johore Strait and out to sea. The time-fuse was set for six hours. In other words, it was due to go off about nine o'clock that night. We were quite tired by this time because we had been in the submarine something like 56 hours and we'd been taking Benzedrine tablets to keep ourselves awake. At nine o'clock I stopped the submarine. I got them all on deck, just to see if we could see anything when the charges were due to go off. And at the precise time there was a violent explosion. It really was a magnificent blast. We brought out a little cheer, then got under way again and eventually made contact with *Stygian*. We changed the crews again and it was towed back to Labuan.

But all was not well. A couple of days later, I went with Captain Fell to have a look at aerial photographs taken over the spot. The old *Takao* was still there, sitting on the bottom presumably. You couldn't really tell because she was in very shallow water. But she had definitely not been blown to smithereens, as we'd imagined given the size of the explosion.

Captain Fell said: 'Well, there's only one thing for it. You'll have to go back again and have another go at it.'

Well, that really did upset me, having done what I thought was a very successful attack, now to have to go back again . . . well! But nevertheless we said OK and we fixed to go back eight days later. On 9 August I was sitting on deck of *Bonaventure* watching a film. The X-craft was all ready to go that day, victualled up with new stores and explosives. Suddenly, the film was stopped and the captain came out to announce that an atom bomb had been dropped on Nagasaki. Our minuscule operation was to be put on hold. In the end, of course, the Japanese capitulated so we didn't have to go back to Singapore. I was very grateful for that.

Instead, I was made senior officer of submarines, Sydney, and eventually I learned that myself and Magennis had been awarded the Victoria Cross. We were both to receive our awards from the King at Buckingham Palace. It was suggested that I should go to Singapore on the way back to find out just what had happened to *Takao*, which I did. I was taken on board by the Japanese officers. One of them had been educated at Oxford and spoke with a very refined Oxford accent. He showed me over the ship, right down to the bottom. The explanation was that *Takao* was lying in such shallow water inshore, and the only place that we in the X-craft could possibly have got underneath was in the middle where there was a depth of about 18 feet. For'ard and aft, there was only about 4 to 6 feet underneath. All the charges had gone off but did not explode in the anticipated manner. The charges were supposed to set off the ammunition aboard the ship but there was none. She had been de-ammunitioned. The theory that she was going to be used as a battery to fire against British forces was wrong. There was only a maintenance crew aboard. Hence the reason why she sank only 6 feet lower than she was in the first place. I was still intrigued because we all saw the spectacular explosion at the time the charges went off. It was then that I discovered that the fiery explosion that we had seen resulted from a plane that crashed on landing at the airport. So that was the end of that story. The Japanese didn't see the irony of the situation. They were quite indifferent towards us.

The citation for Fraser's VC filled in a few of the gaps that he had missed out in his own account:

During the long approach up the Singapore Strait, *XE3* deliberately left the believed safe channel and entered the mined waters to avoid suspected hydrophone posts. The courage and determination of Lieutenant Fraser are beyond all praise. The approach and withdrawal entailed a passage of 80 miles through water which had been mined by both the enemy and ourselves, past hydrophone positions, over loops and controlled mine-fields, and through an anti-submarine boom.

And for Leading Seaman James Magennis:

A lesser man would have been content to place a few limpets and then return to the craft. Magennis, however, persisted until he had placed his full outfit before return-ing to the craft in an exhausted condition. Shortly after withdrawing [and] despite his exhaustion, his oxygen leak and the fact that there was every probability of his being sighted, Magennis at once again volunteered to leave the craft and free the damaged limpet carrier. He displayed very great courage and devotion to duty and complete disregard for his own safety.

And so the Far Eastern encounter had also come to a close.

In the final year, between September 1944 and August 1945, British and Dutch submarines carried out 94 patrols in the SEAC area, based on Ceylon, and 79 in the south-west Pacific area, based on Fremantle or Subic Bay. Hugh Mackenzie in *Tantalus* took the record for enduring the longest patrol of any British submarine in the final months, spending 39 days in his patrol area and travelling 11,692 miles. Commander Arthur Hezlet in *Trenchant* was acclaimed hero of the final weeks of the conventional submarine. He sank the Japanese heavy cruiser *Ashigara* in June 1945 as she was transporting thousands of troops to reinforce Singapore. In addition to his DSO, Hezlet was awarded the United States Legion of Merit for what was regarded as a brilliant attack in which a full salvo of 8 torpedoes was fired from 3,650 metres and 5 hit.

The old warhorse *Porpoise*, which had stayed the course in every campaign in every theatre since the beginning, failed to return from her fourth patrol, laying mines in the Malacca Strait. She was believed to have been sunk by a mine between 16 and 19 January and was lost with all 59 men on board. She was the seventh-fourth – and last – British submarine to be lost in the Second World War.

CHAPTER TWELVE

Thousands of Men, Hundreds of Ships: The Final Reckoning

Britain's home-based submarines ended the war where they had begun, patrolling Norwegian waters and beyond as German opposition became increasingly faint. U-boats still roamed, but in vastly fewer numbers, and the Allied convoys of food and supplies to Russia, then in a desperate plight, succeeded in progressing to the northern ports without great hindrance. Although there had been desperate losses to Allied shipping during the peak of U-boat activity, the arrival of radar equipment in aircraft and the concerted anti-submarine efforts finally put the U-boats to flight.

The marked difference in the strategy of the two nations is dramatically demonstrated when the statistics of the British submarine service are examined and compared with the U-boat records. The submarine service never represented more than 3 per cent of the entire personnel of the Royal Navy. The British relied to a far greater extent on the surface fleet in every theatre to protect the passage of essential supplies of food and raw materials for Britain and to deny the trading routes to the Axis powers. The Germans, on the other hand, used their U-boat force as the principal weapon of seaborne attack. It was their blunt instrument as well as playing the leading role in protecting the nation's coasts and defending its sea communications.

It will be recalled that Germany and Britain began the war possessing similar numbers of submarines. The Royal Navy's peak in submarine strength was reached early in 1942 when just 88 submarines were classed as operational, along with a further 9 Allied boats under British control. At no point during the war years was Britain able to field the magical number of 100 operational submarines. Dönitz's strategy, which he made clear from the outset, was rapidly to build the largest submarine force the world had ever seen. Soon there were 100 U-boats, then 200.

During the war years, Germany built 1,162 U-boats and around 300 more were in the pipeline at the time of capitulation in May 1945. They were used in pursuit of the Germans' avowed policy of unrestricted U-boat warfare which had virtually brought Britain to her knees in the First World War and was repeated during 1939–45, with the same result. But again the Allies eventually retrieved their position, and Germany faced a relentless toll among U-boats: 727 manned by crews totalling 26,918 were lost, the majority sunk by Allied surface ships and shore-based aircraft. The submarine service sank 35.

The progression of those U-boat losses paints a mini-portrait of the way the fortune of war proceeded:

1939: 9 lost with 204 crew.
1940: 24 lost; 643 crew.
1941: 34 lost; 887 crew.

1942: 85 lost; 3,277 crew.
1943: 235 lost; 10,081 crew.
1944: 219 lost; 8,020 crew.
1945: 121 lost; 3,806 crew.

The British, with far fewer submarines, lost 74 boats during the war years, manned by crews totalling 341 officers and 2,801 ratings. In addition, 50 officers and 309 ratings became prisoners of war.

There had been a resurgence of successful U-boat activity towards the autumn of 1944, when freshly launched German submarines were fitted with an important new invention: the snorkel ventilating tube. This took the form of a retractable device containing air-intake and exhaust pipes for the engines and general ventilation. The telescopic tube fed air into the diesel engine and carried off exhaust gases. A U-boat equipped with the snorkel could run submerged on her diesel engine while also charging her batteries. While the boat could do so only at a slow speed and at shallow depth, the chances of being picked up by radar were greatly reduced and, when they heard of it, Allied naval commanders breathed a sigh of relief that its development had not arrived earlier in the war. It was one of a number of significant developments in German U-boat technology which were about to come on stream as the war reached the final stages.

Among them were two new classes of U-boat, the XXI and XXIII, known as Elektro boats, which were more streamlined, faster under water and could stay submerged for longer than anything that existed at that time, anywhere. There were orders in the German shipyards for the production of more than 350 of the new boats, and around 35 were already on the point of being launched. Delays in delivery through Allied bombing raids on shipyards and the decreasing facilities for the six-month training required for the crews meant that only limited operations were carried out before the war ended.

Another important development was a revolutionary submarine engine invented by the brilliant engineer Dr Helmuth Walther. British naval intelligence had already gleaned information about these engines, which, along with all aspects of German submarine development, would be specifically targeted by the teams of British, US and Russian specialists who swept across Germany behind the assault troops. These men were charged with the task of plundering the vaults of a thousand and one areas of German technology, covering everything from rocket science to sausage-making. Allied scientists rubbed their hands in anticipation as tonnes of documents and hundreds of samples were loaded into trucks, on to aircraft or into ships to be returned to Britain, America and Soviet Russia even before the war had ended.

Dönitz anticipating this move, devised a plan for the scuttling of German submarines and capital ships to avoid a repeat of the humiliation that their captains had suffered at the end of the First World War. He ordered that on transmission of the codeword Regenbogen* the entire fleet should be scuttled, leaving only ships required for fishing, transport and mine clearance after the war. Dönitz was forced to rescind the order after surrendering to the Allies, but U-boat commanders in the western Baltic ignored the cancellation and scuttled every one of their 231 boats. It was one of the new XXIII boats that fired the last shots of the war for Germany – two days after capitulation. On 7 May she claimed to have sunk two ships totalling 4,669 tonnes and

---

* From *U-boat Fates and Histories*, articles and lists on the highly detailed website www.uboat.net

according to the U-boat histories missed the surrender signal because of a faulty radio.

The Allies took possession of 154 U-boats of all classes under the surrender-of-ships order. Around 120 were eventually sunk in deep water off the west coast of Ireland in 1945 and 1946 under Operation Deadlight. Another three dozen or so found their way into the hands of various naval intelligence and general departments for dissection and evaluation; some were even converted for use in the Royal Navy. Even so, as in 1918, the Royal Navy was confronted with the need for a major shake-out of submarine stock as the war ended, but, as will be seen in the next chapter, U-boat technology was to provide a stepping stone to significant advances in the development of submarine power for the remainder of the century.

In the meantime, thousands of men returned to civilian clothes, although the British submarine service was engaged in many activities ranging through people-moving, gathering up the spoils of war and keeping watch in volatile parts of the globe where Britain had interests and could not grant immediate release to many of those who wanted out. As Commander W.D.A. King, who had spent his life in submarines and had seen heavy action in all theatres, recalled: 'At the end of the war I was thirty-five and I looked fifty-five. I was a wreck, physically, morally, socially, financially and in every other way. I wanted to get out of the navy, but of course they wouldn't let us go. It took me two years to struggle out by writing letters.'

That situation would be resolved within a couple of years, and by then it was clear that much of the British submarine stock was already tired out and to some extent antique. A half-dozen old First World War H-class boats were still in service along with a small number of L-class. The H-boats had been good servants, and particularly useful lately as so-called 'clockwork mice' (dummy targets) on ASDIC exercises. After the war, they were all scrapped. The three classes that had been the mainstay of the submarine force from 1939 – S, T and U – also underwent a severe pruning.

Eighteen S-class boats had been lost during the war years. A small number were scrapped in the late 1940s and thereafter progressively until the 1960s, by which time around 16 remained in service. The T-class lost 17 boats in the war; 13 were scrapped or sold in the late 1940s, including some famous names such as *Torbay*, *Truant* and *Thrasher*, and most of the remaining 23 stayed in service well into the late 1960s. It was, however, the end of the road for the U-class. Nineteen were lost in the war and the remainder scrapped or sold by the end of the 1940s.

The new A-class, designed to overcome the deficiencies of the ageing T-class, had a speed of 18.5 knots on the surface, were 85.6 metres long and had four 21-inch bow tubes and two 21-inch internal stern tubes. New innovations included radar operated from periscope depth and a night periscope. Mass production started before the end of the war, but none saw active service, and to some, especially left-wing Labour politicians, it all now seemed a bit academic.

By then, it was already clear that submarine technology was on the threshold of dramatic developments. The Allies made a dash for the German U-boats and their accompanying manuals, which were to provide some inspiration for a new breed of submarines built on both sides of the Iron Curtain after it had slammed down at the start of the Cold War. The Walther engine, used in the four U-boats built before the war ended, was put under the microscope. It was a steam-generating power plant of a kind that had eluded British and American submarine engineers for years. It worked on the principle that hydrogen peroxide, when passed over a catalyst, produced oxygen and water. The oxygen and water were fed into a combustion chamber, sprayed with fuel, and the resulting mixture generated steam that powered a turbine. Walther had been working on the engine for four years, but because of its revolutionary principles there was little chance of proving it at the time of increasing pressure on the U-boat command.

One of the Walther boats commissioned in March 1945 was scuttled at the German port of Cuxhaven on 5 May 1945. The British had already learned of its existence and raised the boat by the end of the month. It was recovered, towed back to England, rebuilt and commissioned as *Meteorite* for evaluation. Professor Walther and his staff were brought from Germany to Barrow-in-Furness to advise during the rebuilding. Vickers carried out trials, which led to the building of two hydrogen peroxide-fuelled submarines, *Explorer* and *Excalibur*. They were unarmed and built for speed. Development was slow, with Britain hit by financial constraints across the board, as well as political infighting with a split in the Labour government over defence spending at a time when the country was on its knees. Consequently, they did not make an appearance until the mid-1950s. Even so, the results were remarkable, with speeds of up to 25 knots submerged, but by then developments elsewhere and the volatile nature of the chemical structure meant they were already obsolete.

America also carried out experiments with captured German submarines, and also honed in on underwater speed trials. A boat similar to British experimental submarines, *Albacore*, was unarmed and was built with a short, fat, streamlined hull that gave the best underwater speeds from a single screw. *Albacore* achieved a top speed of 35 knots. For the time being, however, the major powers continued to bolster their stock of boats with new submarines of conventional design, which by and large owed some of their innovative features to German XXI technology.

The US navy converted 52 war-built submarines to the Guppy configuration, standing for 'greater underwater propulsive power' (with the 'y' added for phonetics). These submarines had their deck guns removed and streamlined conning towers fitted. They were quite clearly aimed towards intelligence missions rather than operations that relied on their firepower. Other advances came in the field of weapons and sensors. Torpedoes capable of 50 knots, homed in to their targets acoustically, were a breakthrough. They could also be guided by electronic commands passed to them through a threadlike wire paid out behind the speeding projectile. Submarine sonar, for detecting both surface ships and other submarines, was also dramatically improved.

The Soviet Union, meanwhile, also poured massive development effort into conventional submarine production which, disturbingly for the British, not only mirrored the latest U-boat technology but also the Second World War production levels of Germany. As the first signs of the Cold War set in, Stalin set in motion a fast-track production programme designed to provide the Soviets with an instant and highly capable submarine force of 500 boats. He died before the target was achieved, but even so almost 270 boats, labelled Whiskey and Zulu class by NATO observers, were completed between 1950 and 1958. Taking the comparison further, the Soviets built more submarines than all the world's other navies combined between 1945 and 1970, with a production total of 560 new vessels extending through their complete range of conventional and nuclear boats.

Another important development followed quickly.

Towards the end of the war, the US Pacific Fleet had suffered heavy surface casualties in radar picket destroyers, and therefore decided to convert some submarines to carry out this role under water, particularly for those escorting aircraft carriers. US designers now focused on developing a missile-carrying submarine. The *Regulus* cruise missile was carried in a hangar and was similar in many respects to the German V1 rocket. At a stroke, the Americans had introduced an entirely new role into submarine warfare, which would be taken further by a small group of scientists working on theories of nuclear-fuelled, missile-firing submarines. The Soviets swiftly followed suit, introducing SS-N-3 Shaddock cruise and SS-N-4 Sark short-range missiles to a number of selected vessels. These missiles, however, had to be launched from the surface, and the submarines themselves could not remain submerged indefinitely.

Thus, barely had the dust settled than the submarine branch of the Royal Navy discovered it would have to provide a major presence at the forefront of intelligence-gathering as the Cold War began to gather momentum. Far from downgrading the number of submarines supplied to the defence of the United Kingdom and her contribution to the newly formed North Atlantic Treaty Organisation, new boats ordered towards the end of the war were coming out of the shipyards and were deployed immediately.

The Admiralty found it necessary to add to its strength of conventional boats to supplement the ageing technology of the A-, S- and T-classes that now represented the bulk of the submarine force. In 1948 anti-submarine warfare was declared to be the primary mission of the submarine service, and in any event budgetary restrictions limited new orders to eight new Porpoise-class and thirteen Oberon-class boats. Like most of the other contemporary Western designs, they were heavily influenced by the German XXI, with the emphasis on speed and, in the case of Oberon, a maximum diving depth of 198 metres. The designs were approved in 1948, but even these did not begin to appear until 1955 and beyond. All were designated as patrol submarines and were a godsend to the struggling British shipyards.

With the added advantage of the snorkel system, they could remain submerged for a far greater length of time. They were also very quiet under water, a good deal of attention having been paid to internal noise and the simple movement of crew. Sonar techniques were also upgraded into the most modern form for underwater listening. These boats were equipped with air-conditioning to travel the globe, in hot or cold climates, and indeed there was plenty of renewed military activity around the world to keep them occupied as communism spread throughout the Far East, and Britain began her painful withdrawal from her protectorates and colonies, a process that would last well into the 1960s.

Although the colonial wars were troublesome enough, the more vital aspect of submarine work was soon to come in the form of a head-to-head with former friend the Soviet Union, a task that generally was about listening and one that would become a prime task of the submarine force for the remainder of the twentieth century. Bryan Tilley joined the navy in 1947 at the age of 17 and began his training. He volunteered for submarines but was sent initially into the battle-class destroyer *St James*, where he was trained in submarine weapons. He eventually moved into submarines to specialise in ASDIC and sonar operations on board the A-, T- and Porpoise-class boats before later joining the first of Britain's nuclear-powered submarines:

The qualities of a first-rate sonar man were good hearing, good concentration and eventually intuition. Piano-tuners used to be the experts because they had this ear for being able to get the pitch, the tone of the note on the sonar, signifying a ship's position. Later, it became a situation of having to differentiate the engines and background noise and eventually, with a bit of experience, you could pick out the difference between, say, American and Russian submarines. The British submarines had already gone into noise-abatement techniques, on such things as engine mounting and insulation. We also had what were called steam boots, with leather bottoms. We all wore comfortable shoes at sea, monkey rig it was called. The Russian submarines tended to be noisiest, especially their engines, which were cruder than the Americans' or ours. I was on *Acheron*, one of the earlier A-boats, which were much better than the T-class. The A-boat seemed a better boat to me, although they were a very bad boat on the surface. They rolled around a lot, but she was much more comfortable when dived. You went down 100 feet to get out of any rough weather on the surface. Even so, the longest patrol you could do was four to six weeks and that would be up in the naughty area, listening in on northern Russia gathering information of sonar nature and wireless transmissions. The object of those patrols, apart from spying, was to gain knowledge relating to the movement of submarines around the ocean that in the event of war would have to be put out of action.

I was then present for the building and commissioning of *Grampus*, the second of the new Porpoise class built at Birkenhead. The comparison in accommodation between the *Grampus* and the A-boats was atrocious from the senior ratings' point of view. It was a little box because it was loaded with additional gear. They were good boats tactically but terrible for accommodation. The sonar equipment was a big improvement. I had the prototype for new equipment. A lot of experiments were carried out in *Grampus*. It was the pacemaker leading on to the next stage of development. A dome on the bow housed a tank with the equipment in it [which was later a feature of the nuclear-powered boats]. The office was down below within the submarine, and there we tape-recorded everything that was picked up and it was sent away for analysis, and there were increasing amounts of that.

The advances in the technical qualities of conventional submarines were indeed very welcome, especially as the British force had such a wide-ranging arena of operations. Apart from the shadowing of Soviet submarine activity, which burgeoned almost from the end of the war, submarine cover for British naval operations was required in the Middle East during the withdrawal from Suez, and other colonial hot spots, as well as the Far East during the international tension during and after the Korean War, with its implications for the British in Hong Kong. Australia once again became a regular berth for submarine commanders, and a new flotilla was built up with accommodation for families of submariners on longer tours of duty.

To that point in time there seemed little prospect of any immediate change of seaborne tactics. The Russians were hellbent on copying Germany's wartime submarine production, going for numbers in a big way. Many naval chieftains, in various countries, saw no reason to alter course from the policies that had brought them through two world wars in the space of half a century. The use of conventional submarines seemed likely to proceed and progress in much the same way as it had since the beginning of the century. But a massive upheaval was already imminent.

There was also some unfinished business to attend to in the aftermath of war in regard to safety and escape systems for British submarines. A special committee formed in 1939 after the *Thetis* disaster under the chairmanship of First World War hero Admiral Sir Martin Dunbar-Nasmith had more or less been put on hold. The war interrupted a full deliberation of the reasons why a submarine surrounded by a ring of ships and with a man standing on her stern went down with 99 people still trapped inside. A new inquiry was set up a year after the war ended, this time under the chairmanship of Rear-Admiral P. Ruck-Keene, and there was a vast wealth of experience to be drawn on. He was given a large team of experts to assist, and they began by taking detailed statements from survivors of 32 submarine incidents involving British, American, Norwegian and German vessels. All past methods of escape were examined, and new ideas were brought forward, extended training programmes drawn up and a better system for rescue response recommended and acted on. It would be quite some time before these new elements came into effect, and too late to save two more major peacetime disasters.

At the time, the main escape systems still involved the use of the Davis Submerged Escape Apparatus (DSEA). This consisted of a mouthpiece connected by a flexible tube to a rubber bag, which had an attached canister of oxygen, enabling the wearer to breathe under water during escape. There was a clip to go over the nose and goggles to protect the eyes. On the way, it was necessary to operate control valves and remove the mouthpiece on the surface, which was not always possible in times of difficulty, and lung damage or even suffocation could be caused by incorrect use. The escape was supposed to be made in separate sections of the boat, sealed off by watertight doors and valves. In each section, what was known as the twill trunk was lowered from the escape hatch to form a funnel through which the escape could be made, although this could not be attempted until the flooding up of the boat equalised the pressure inside and outside the boat. When this was reached, the escape would begin through the trunk and hatch.

The second method to get out of a stricken boat was through an escape chamber at either end of the submarine. This entailed a lengthy process of flooding up the whole escape compartment before the hatch could be opened, and it could take no more than two men at a time, i.e. two escapes every twenty minutes or so. From the stories of survivors interviewed by the Ruck-Keene Committee, however, it became evident that fewer than 15 per cent of all those who were alive immediately after their submarine sank made escapes, and of those who did get out a similar proportion had no escape apparatus. One of the key findings for the low survival rates was that too much time was spent in trying to save the ship before the men themselves finally began to evacuate, which was perhaps natural when they might have been in the middle of an ocean, where there was no assistance on the surface, or in another form of extremely hostile environment.

The figure was astonishing. Eighty-four per cent of those who were alive at the time of the disaster died attempting to save the ship. The delay in evacuating meant that the level of carbon dioxide in the air was such that within ten hours or so many were seriously affected by the gas. By the time the effort to save the vessel was given up, most of the crew might be too badly affected by carbon dioxide at atmospheric pressure even to attempt to get out. They may even have lapsed into unconsciousness when flooding up took place. Examples were evident from *Thetis* and the experience of Commander Lonsdale in *Seal*, who, when he called his men to the control room for prayers after nineteen hours on the bottom, discovered that only six were able to respond, and it was for that reason that he finally surrendered his submarine to the Germans.

The safety investigations went on for some years, although quite early on a number of firm recommendations were made. They included warnings about the use of the DSEA, which the experts felt should not be used at depths of more than 46 metres and that greater awareness of the problems of using it should be included in training. For instance, it was felt that men reaching the final stage of ascent might be in no condition to remove the mouthpiece before the oxygen ran out and, having completed the escape successfully, might die of suffocation. Further, it was felt that escape chambers should be made smaller to cut down the time for flooding up, and generally work should be done on internal systems to improve air purifying to curb the effects of carbon dioxide poisoning. The immediate outcome of the early testimony was to improve escape training for crews. For this a 30-metre water-filled tower, 5.5 metres in diameter, was built at the submarine school at Fort Blockhouse, although it was not completed until 1952. The rescue alerts for submarines in distress, with particular attention to reaction times, were also overhauled as part of the two systems called SUBSMASH and SUBSUNK.

Some of the modifications to submarine safety and rescue procedures were to be tested sooner than anyone could possibly imagine. Less than five years after the end of the war, Britain suffered two major submarine disasters. It was

all the more poignant because it occurred at the mouth of
what was then one of Britain's busiest seaways, that controlled by the Port of London Authority.

On 12 January 1950 the submarine *Truculent* spent the day
at sea off the Thames Estuary carrying out trials, following a
long refit in Chatham dockyard. On board was her crew of
59, plus 18 civilian dockyard technicians who were to check
the final performance before officially handing her back to
the Royal Navy. Among the crew was Leslie Stickland, who
was 20 when he went into the submarine service during the
war and stayed on, eventually joining *Truculent*:

In March 1949 she was paid off for a major refit, and as
I was the engineer in charge of outside machinery –
diving, tanks, pumps and so on – I was detailed to stand
by her on the refit. By early January 1950 we were ready
to go again. The ship was crewed up again with its full
complement, and this had some bearing. The crew had
only just come together, and there wasn't the same
knowledge and communication that would be normal;
we were mostly new to each other. But we got on pretty
well, checked everything over and agreed a date for
post-refit trials for 12 and 13 January. The normal
routine would be to do the engine trials first and the
diving trials last. The 13th was a Friday, so we did the
diving trials first.

We went out on a perfect day. No wind, visibility
was perfect, but it was bitterly cold. We carried out the
diving trials with complete success by about four in the
afternoon and started to make our way back to
Sheerness. During the run-out and back we had occasional troubles with the engines which necessitated
stopping the engines, but that had no bearing on the

accident. We were in the middle of our meal at about 6.45 p.m. when the engines stopped again, but almost immediately there was an impact. We had no idea what had happened, and even conjectured that we had hit a mine.

Only later did the handful of survivors discover the truth. As *Truculent* made her way back to Sheerness, the officer of the watch saw another craft approaching from the starboard side. She was displaying a red light he could not identify. The craft was a Swedish tanker, *Divina*, on passage from Purfleet bound for Sweden with a cargo of paraffin. The red light was being shown in accordance with Port of London Authority regulations to denote a dangerous cargo. *Truculent*'s officer of the watch called his captain to the conning tower. He in turn called for the manual and eventually concluded that the light denoted a stationary ship, and he ordered the submarine to steer to port. Unknown to him, *Divina* was in the process of changing course to head north as she came out of the channel, and now the two vessels were on a collision course. The captain ordered, 'Hard to port . . . Full astern'. Watertight doors were secured as the ice-breaking bows of *Divina* crunched over the top of the submarine, which began to sink, bow down, within minutes.

The captain and his party on the bridge were washed into the sea and were swept away by the tide. Forty minutes later, the Dutch vessel *Almdijk* heard shouts for help coming from the water and found the group of men. Five survivors, including the captain and the officer of the watch, were picked up and taken below. The Dutch ship had a ship-to-shore radio facility, and the captain raised the alarm. His submarine, meanwhile, was sliding towards the bottom, as Leslie Stickland recalls:

The boat took a steep bow-down angle. I checked that the main vents were shut and blew the forward tanks in an attempt to correct her, without success. Although at that time I had seen no water, it was apparent that the forward compartments were flooding. My primary concern was to keep the boat up and to get the crew back into the engine room before we hit the bottom. When it became apparent that we could not hold the boat, the first lieutenant ordered the control room to be cleared and for us to go to the engine room. We shut off the engine-room compartment doors and isolated it. By this time we were settling on the bottom.

We realised that escape would be necessary, although there was no reason why this should not be successfully achieved. We decided that escape should be attempted as soon as possible because we wouldn't last too long with the air supply now available to the men with half the boat shut off. We could also constantly hear propeller noises over the top of us and we assumed, wrongly as it turned out, that they were rescue vessels.

We then allocated the escape apparatus. The apparatuses are evened out through the submarine with a required number in each compartment, but with everyone now in the after-part of the boat there was never going to be enough. I gave mine to a good friend who worked in the dockyard and I went up without one. They were allocated on the basis of who could swim and who was the strongest. Even so, there was no feeling of impending disaster. We could see no good reason why we should not all get out. There were no difficulties arising, and I don't think anyone felt we would not escape. The atmosphere during the escape was wonderful. Some took it as a bit of a joke and that we would all be OK. Everyone was confident that in a few moments after going out they would be picked up. The escape procedures went very well and we all got out. There was not a member of the crew left in the submarine.

Well, when we got to the surface, there was nothing. Not another boat in sight, and we were all floundering around in a strong tide. The other thing was that in the submarine, although we had flooded up to escape, the engine had been running for several hours, the oil was hot and the temperature was OK. When we hit the surface, the water was exceedingly cold. No one would be able to survive in that for long, and quite quickly there were shouts from people going down or being swept away. Very soon there were only a few of us left. I have no real idea how long I was in the water, but it was certainly long enough, when we sighted a rowing boat crewed by the vessel that had hit us. They had come back to look around after a crew member reported that he thought they had hit something, perhaps a motor-boat. So they picked us up and did what they could. But there were few of us left by then.

In the end, just eight naval people and three dockyard technicians were picked up. An hour or so later we were transferred by lifeboat to HMS *Cowdray*, the duty destroyer which had answered the SUBSMASH call. About the same time the navy were alerted, we were popping up on to the surface. So there were no naval vessels anywhere near as we surfaced. The tragedy of it all was so many were lost when it had been an almost flawless escape routine. Everybody got out, but there was a strong tide running and it was very, very cold.

Afterwards, I was asked to go down to Sheerness when they were discussing whether the *Truculent* should be raised. In the end it was decided to raise the boat. The salvage was conducted quite well using two German vessels. The boat was raised to the surface, and it was horrifying to see the mess it was in. There must have been 2,000 or 3,000 tonnes of silt and sand inside. No one could get into the vessel until the mud had been shovelled out. The boat was brought back to Sheerness but was completely beyond repair. The port side of the forward end of the boat was hanging off like a door on hinges. The collision damage extended a third of the way through the pressure hull. She finished her days in a breaker's yard.

Sixty-seven men made a near-perfect escape from the sunken submarine and, apart from one or two problems with untrained technicians, the Davis gate saw everyone get to the surface alive. But in the end, only 11 men were picked up alive; the remainder drowned, died of the cold or were swept away by the tide.

At the subsequent inquiry, blame was apportioned jointly between the two collided vessels. It was observed that had the men remained inside the submarine for 20 or 30 minutes longer, the rescue ships sent under the SUBSUNK alert would have arrived over *Truculent* to save them. By the same token, it was also pointed out that because of the flooding and the closure of all but the after-compartments of the submarine, the 67 men on board were already beginning to feel the effects of carbon dioxide poisoning when the first officer made the decision to get them to the surface. He had little choice. If he had delayed, they might have been in no state to make the attempt, as had been the case in so many previous incidents examined in recent times.

It was their bad luck that when they came to the surface

there was a sudden lull in the traffic, which had been very busy, and the propeller noises they had heard earlier had given way to the paddling of the oars of the single rowing boat from *Divina* – the only rescue craft that came to their assistance before most of them simply disappeared beneath the waves.

The *Truculent* disaster was comparatively fresh in the memories of submariners when a second post-war tragedy struck, with further implications.

At 4.30 on the afternoon of Monday, 16 April 1951, the six-year-old A-class submarine *Affray* left Portsmouth for a war patrol exercise with an unusually large number of men on board. Under the command of Lieutenant John Blackburn, she carried his team of four officers and fifty-five ratings. There were also twenty-three young sub-lieutenants in training, who came along to observe a simulated war patrol, and a party of four marines. Blackburn's orders were to proceed down the Channel to the Western Approaches, carry out dummy attacks for three days to give experience to the junior officers and then land the marines at a bay on the Cornish coast.

At 8.56 p.m., Blackburn signalled from the Isle of Wight that he intended to dive and proceed westwards down the Channel. He would surface at eight the next morning. No surfacing signal was received, and at 9 a.m. on the 17th a SUBSUNK operation was launched. By midday, forty ships, eight submarines, various aircraft from the RAF and Fleet Air Arm and a flotilla of US destroyers visiting Plymouth were all engaged in the search for *Affray*. The nation, then the world looked on with a kind of edge-of-seat fascination, counting the hours that the submarine had been missing and knowing, from the highly detailed press, radio and newsreel accounts, that the men could not possibly survive beyond a given time. Hopes were raised when a number of ships in the search reported faint ASDIC signals and *Affray*'s sister submarine, *Ambush*, decoded a message stating, 'We are trapped on the bottom'. But *Affray* still could not be found, and the boat was edging to the point when the air finally expired, becoming a coffin for all aboard.

The point was reached when, after 46 hours, the massive search operation was stood down. The navy announced its regret that all on board *Affray* – wherever she was – would by now have perished. The task of locating her would be handed over to a smaller team, consisting of four frigates and three minesweepers equipped with all the special electronics available for underwater location. The flotilla carried out a sonar search and the diving ship HMS *Reclaim* followed up any likely contacts. The Admiralty Research Laboratory also installed an underwater television camera on *Reclaim*, the first time such a device had been used. The search naturally attracted great interest in the media, especially when, at the end of the second week after *Affray*'s disappearance, there was still no sign of her. By the third week, speculation was beginning to run rife, and not least that she may have been a target of sabotage or, worse, that she may have been sunk by the Russians as the Cold War moved into deep freeze. Indeed, a secret Admiralty report to James Callaghan, then junior Admiralty minister and a former seaman, stated how 'a submarine containing 20 officers of the submarine course would be a worthwhile target'.

The Royal Navy's embarrassment continued as MPs began to raise the issue on an almost daily basis, first in sensitive tones requesting information on behalf of grieving relatives, but later turning to acid comments such as 'What hope has our navy got of finding Russian submarines when it can't even find one of its own?' Politically, this was a particularly bad time for Prime Minister Clement Attlee, whose Labour government was facing both a revolt over defence spending and a general election later in the year. The growing furore heightened when the *Sunday Pictorial* published a series of earlier letters home written by a member of *Affray*'s crew. Engine-room artificer David Bennington, who had died in the disaster, wrote to his family after war patrol exercise: 'It really is a terrible boat. When I get home I'll try to describe the scares and pandemonium that reign at times . . . I think the boat is about finished.'

This was hardly a recommendation for the A-class craft, which, for the time being, were in the front line of Britain's submarine force, especially as *Affray* was only six years old and had many years of anticipated service left in her. The public and the media were getting increasingly vocal. The submarine had been missing for 56 days. The search ships had covered 23,000 miles between them and had made 150 contacts of wrecks on the seabed, of which 9 were investigated by divers. It was only when the flotilla decided to retrace the steps of the initial SUBSUNK operation that they finally struck lucky. One of the team, Captain Roy Foster-Brown, calculated the likely speed and distance travelled, pored over the charts alone in his cabin and eventually came out with an X marking a spot south-west of the Channel Islands. He told his navigation officer, James Diggle: 'Tomorrow we shall search the Hurd Deep and we will find *Affray*.'

The Hurd Deep is a series of underwater chasms in the English Channel, 37 miles from *Affray*'s known diving position. Foster-Brown was convinced that the original ASDIC soundings had missed *Affray* because of the nature of the ravines. Next day, the search began a fresh trawl of the area using Type 162, a sophisticated form of sonar, and within an hour a shape emerged. Underwater television cameras were lowered along with a diver,* and very soon the shape was confirmed as the missing submarine. She had both radar mast and after-periscope raised. This suggested she had been at periscope depth when she sank. Further examination revealed the probable cause of the disaster, in which 75 men lost their lives. The snort mast had snapped a metre above the deck, allowing water into the boat through a 25-centimetre hole at the rate of a tonne a second.

The Board of Inquiry heard testimony from survivors of wartime submarine disasters about how the crew probably met their death. Even so, there remained an element of mystery to the whole affair in that the possibility of an explosion of battery gases may have occurred, causing a split in the ventilation shaft, and thus allowing water to flood the battery. Whatever the cause, it could never be known for certain. *Affray* was never salvaged.

The disaster, however, did have one historical note that brought at least some form of comfort to submariners and those engaged in ensuring the safety of boats. The *Affray* sinking was the last incident involving a British submarine in which 'all hands were lost' in the twentieth century. There were only two more serious incidents involving conventional submarines from then until the time of writing (2001). The first was on 16 June 1955, when one of the wartime S-boats, *Sidon*, was badly damaged by an explosion while moored alongside her parent ship, HMS *Maidstone*, in Portland harbour. She was waiting her allotted time to cast away for torpedo-firing trials. At 8.25 a.m. a loud explosion shook the submarine as one of the highly volatile hydrogen peroxide motors of the torpedoes exploded in its tube. A cloud of

* Commander Lionel 'Buster' Crabbe, whose headless body was found after he was engaged on a spying mission under the ship that brought Soviet leaders Khrushchev and Bulganin to Britain in April 1956.

smoke rose from the conning tower hatch, and as the order to abandon ship was given as *Sidon* began to sink, 12 crew members, including the captain, Lieutenant-Commander Hugh Verry, were trapped inside. Surgeon-Lieutenant Charles Rhodes, a 27-year-old national service officer who went down into the explosion area to help injured men, brought one out on his shoulders and then went in again. He never came back. The boat went down within minutes, despite valiant efforts by the crew of the mooring vessel *Moordale* to secure her with a cable. Several divers at once entered the water and began tapping messages on *Sidon*'s hull to those trapped inside the submarine. By early afternoon it was apparent that all 12 inside were dead or incapable of replying. The submarine was raised ten days later and the bodies extracted and buried on 28 June in a small naval cemetery in Portland. On 14 June 1957 *Sidon* was towed from Portland and sunk.

The last incident as these pages are being written involved *Artemis*, of the new A-class and built in 1946. On 1 July 1971 *Artemis* sank alongside HMS *Dolphin* when water entered through the upper torpedo hatch, which could not be shut because it had been snared by electrical shore supply cables. Twelve men escaped but three others were trapped in the fore ends under water for several hours. The boat was raised after five days and sold for scrap.

At the time of the *Artemis* incident, however, a whole new breed of submarines was already in operation: safer, faster, floating palaces almost, compared with those that submariners thus far had been used to. They were, of course, those powered by nuclear energy.

CHAPTER THIRTEEN

The True Submarine, Just as Jules Verne Foresaw

The arrival of a US nuclear-powered submarine programme, from which the Royal Navy would ultimately benefit, was brought to fruition under the control of a short-tempered but brilliant naval engineer who was also an experienced submariner: Captain Hyman Rickover. He began his project in 1946 without the benefit of any great enthusiasm from more senior naval figures. He was joined in 1948 by Dr Ross Gunn of the US Naval Research Laboratory and Dr Philip Abelson of the Carnegie Institute, both of whom had been working on similar themes that would bring about a revolution in submarine propulsion on similar lines to the Walther boat. Gunn had been advocating the idea of steam propulsion for submarines since 1939. Unlike Walther, who had used highly concentrated hydrogen peroxide, Gunn was now proposing the use of nuclear fission. In the simplest terms, a reactor would generate steam, which would drive the turbine. There was little interest shown in his work as America pushed on towards the creation of the atomic bomb until he teamed up with Abelson. Together they produced a document outlining their proposals. It came into the hands of Rickover, who invited the two scientists to join his own team.

For the next two years they struggled with the theory of a nuclear-powered submarine while at the same time fighting a relentless rearguard action against formidable opponents. Early in 1950 they were finally able to show positive results. Rickover's team produced designs for a land-based nuclear reactor as a prototype for one that could power a very substantial submarine. They demonstrated in precise language how a single power plant could provide the propulsion for unlimited surface and submerged travel. A small quantity of enriched uranium would produce enough power to run for years, and the nuclear submarine would be able to operate at high speed, completely and indefinitely submerged and restricted only by human endurance.

Against this, Rickover drew the comparable portrait of even the most modern conventional diesel/electric submarines, in which the submerged approach to a target had to be made at very low speed of no more than 2 or 3 knots to avoid wasting battery power and whose ability to stay submerged was limited to the state of on-board batteries. As every submarine commander well knew, this was critical in any attack situation because sufficient power always had to be husbanded in case of counter-attack and the possibility of having to sit on the bottom until the danger had passed. The need to conserve battery power had always meant that submarines had to be cautious about engaging fast surface warships, such as aircraft carriers and battleships. Nuclear submarines, said Rickover, would end all those problems overnight. They would be fast, they could travel at top speed without ever having to surface and they could remain submerged for great distances. The size of the nuclear reactor and its shielding meant that the submarine had to be 97 metres long and displace 3,539 tonnes on the surface, which was more or less the size of a modern cruiser.

Many were unconvinced by these claims; some were even scared by them. Even so, the US Congress approved a $30 million budget to build the world's first nuclear-powered submarine, and her keel was laid down by President Harry Truman at the Electric Boat Company shipyard – the same company that had produced the first *Holland*s at the turn of the century – in Groton, Connecticut, on 14 June 1952. She was to be named *Nautilus*, the eighth American ship to be so called and, it will be recalled, the name of the vessel in the Jules Verne story of a submarine that could travel the globe without ever surfacing. That fictional prediction was on the brink of becoming reality.

Nautilus was launched by Mamie Eisenhower, wife of the then president, Dwight D. Eisenhower, and eight months later, on 30 September 1954, became the first commissioned nuclear-powered ship in the United States navy. On the morning of 17 January 1955, the first commanding officer, Commander Eugene P. Wilkinson, ordered all lines cast off and signalled the historic message: 'Under way on nuclear power'.

Very soon, *Nautilus* began to shatter all speed and distance records, and in August 1958, then under Commander Bill Anderson and with 116 men on board, became the first ship to cross the North Pole. With a pronouncement that would be echoed by the moon landing team a few years later, he said: 'For the world, our country and the navy – the North Pole.'

These developments came at a time of mounting East–West tension and, we now know, were to have a profound effect on the race for nuclear domination by the superpowers. The Soviet Union was only a fraction behind America in its development of nuclear-powered boats, and by 1955 had also successfully launched the first ballistic missile from a submarine. Thereafter, the Russians added to their nuclear fleet with remarkable speed and efficiency, and by the mid-1960s they possessed a formidable force. The prospect of a nuclear holocaust became ever more feasible, and the Ban-the-Bomb logo became a worldwide symbol of protest. Britain had been rather left behind in these developments. Under the post-war austerity measures and the vast regeneration programme for bombed-out cities, the Labour government had no facility for such exploration. The first question asked when any new proposal came forward was: 'How much?'

The Admiralty had enough trouble begging the cash for the new Porpoise and Oberon boats, let alone the millions required for even one nuclear-powered submarine. Only a small naval unit at the atomic research centre at Harwell had been studying nuclear-powered submarines but had made little progress by 1955. Lord Mountbatten, First Sea Lord, was a strong campaigner for a British nuclear submarine force, and he finally won approval to get a development project moving. At that point it was discovered that, because of a shortage of funding, the United Kingdom Atomic Energy Authority had concentrated on reactors that were too large to fit in a submarine. Mountbatten immediately flew to the USA, hoping to sweet-talk the Americans into helping out. He asked for a ride in *Nautilus*, but the all-powerful Admiral Rickover refused to meet him and refused to give him permission to go aboard the submarine. He merely sent a message stating that the Anglo-American Agreement on Military Atomic Cooperation did not extend to *Nautilus*. Further, he made no secret of his 'supreme contempt' for the

British nuclear programme and flatly refused to give any assistance.

There it rested until 1956, when Rickover visited Britain and Mountbatten made a determined effort to woo him for the sole purpose of getting a nuclear power pack. It so happened that the two men struck up a rapport immediately, Mountbatten having been supplied with a long briefing on the character of the foul-tempered, outspoken American. 'At the end of Rickover's sojourn,' wrote Denys Wyatt, one of Mountbatten's staff officers, 'Rickover didn't give a damn whether we as a country got the submarine, but he did care whether Mountbatten got one or not.' Eventually, terms were agreed to provide a power plant and reactor – by then in manufacture for the fleet of *Nautilus*-class submarines approved for immediate building by the US Congress.

This agreement between the UK and the USA was temporarily put on hold when Prime Minister Anthony Eden joined forces with the French to invade Egypt after President Nasser nationalised the Suez Canal. Eisenhower was apoplectic with rage, not so much because of the act of invasion but because it occurred on the day of the US election in which he sought a second term. Even more important, Eden had not bothered to consult him. Eisenhower's sulk lasted a couple of years, until February 1958, when the British were still no nearer constructing their own submarine. A new hull had then to be designed to accommodate the American machinery, and construction by Vickers Armstrong finally got under way, laid down by the Duke of Edinburgh on 12 June 1959. It was, after all, his uncle, Lord Mountbatten, who had smoothed the path for Britain to possess this powerful addition to her fleet and who was convinced that without it the country would be at the mercy of Soviet Russia. It was also Mountbatten who, during a visit to the

USA in October 1958, persuaded Rickover to approve the supply of the very latest plant used for USS *Skipjack* instead of being 'fobbed off' with an earlier version. Mountbatten was given the grand tour by Rickover and was allowed to crawl all over his nuclear submarines. 'It was', said the First Sea Lord, 'a fantastic peep into the future.' This time, Rickover showed him over the Atomic Top Secret Room, if only to berate his lordship about Britain's 'lousy set-up'.

'What you want to run a show like this', said Rickover, 'is a real son of a bitch.'

Mountbatten countered: 'That is where you Americans have the edge on us – you have the only real son of a bitch in the business.'

The Americans were already well on their way towards the launch of Polaris, the submarine-launched ballistic-missile system, and, according to his biographer, Philip Ziegler, Mountbatten dreamed of the day when Britain's nuclear deterrent would depend not on land-based missiles or the RAF's bombers but on the efforts of the Royal Navy. He had the statistics: that 70 per cent of the surface of the globe was sea, 50 per cent of the world's population lived within 50 miles of the sea, 40 of the 55 cities with more than a million inhabitants were seaports – it was obvious that the future deterrent must come from under water. He argued that 'if the British can put their share of the deterrent into submarines, there would be no call for the Russians to attack our missile sites and bomber fields as an act of self-preservation if they feared a possible attack'.

Polaris was a long way off for the British. It was not even at the point of consideration when the building of Britain's first nuclear submarine finally got under way. She was to be christened *Dreadnought*, the ninth ship in naval history to carry that most famous name. In a subliminal way this perhaps demonstrated that the Admiralty had finally acknowledged that the submarine had graduated to capital ship. She was launched by the Queen at Barrow-in-Furness on Trafalgar Day, 21 October 1960, by which time, incidentally, America had already built 15 nuclear boats, had another 14 under construction and had stopped building conventional submarines altogether.

Dreadnought had a surface displacement of 3,500 tonnes and 4,000 tonnes submerged. She was 78 metres long, had a beam of 10 metres, could travel effortlessly at 28 knots submerged and had a crew of 88. She was classed as a hunter-killer fleet submarine, armed with six conventional bow torpedoes. She was to be the prototype for an immediate expansion of Britain's nuclear submarine force, which from now on would be built entirely by British scientists, engineers and shipbuilders, with more planned for the immediate future, to form the Valiant class. The price the First Sea Lord had to pay for that agreement was a halt on the building of further diesel/electric submarines, which in turn left Britain very short of boats a decade later.

Meanwhile, *Dreadnought* herself finally delivered the long-awaited revolution to the British submarine force. She was new in every regard, handled by telemotor controls using a joystick and a dazzling array of dials that made up the elaborate instrument panel. For the crew going aboard for the first time, it was a jaw-dropping experience, with accommodation the like of which they had never seen before, even in surface vessels. Apart from an efficient air-conditioning and purification system, there were numerous luxuries, such as showers, washing facilities, a laundry, a large galley equipped for serving very decent meals, separate messes for junior and senior ratings, well-furnished recreational spaces and a range of leisure facilities, such as a cinema, a library and other features to relieve the monotony of long periods submerged.

By then, the British government had approved the building of Valiant-class boats for which *Dreadnought* was the prototype. Five were to be laid down for construction between 1962 and 1970, and with that approval came a major operation in recruitment and retraining to prepare the crews and shore bases to take control of boats the like of which they had never experienced before. Nor was it simply a question of training.

As had been discovered in the USA, the unique qualities of life aboard a nuclear submarine required commanders of outstanding leadership skills and crews capable of withstanding the particular pressures that came with long periods of life beneath the waves. There was no precedent to the experience. The whole point of nuclear boats was that they would submerge as soon as they left their base and, if necessary, remain submerged for the duration of their patrol. From the very beginning, crews might go for weeks without seeing daylight or having any contact whatsoever with the outside world. Most on board would not have the slightest inclination of their whereabouts, the time zone they were in or even whether it was night or day.

Later, as more boats came on stream and two- or three-month patrols submerged became common, the aspects of crew welfare necessarily became a priority in both selection and training. The fact of life that had faced all submariners since the beginning, i.e. the confined and restricted nature of travelling in a boat tight for space and packed with quite dangerous gear, was no less pronounced in the comparatively palatial surroundings of the nuclear boats. If anything, they were heightened by the longer periods of time spent submerged in what was still a confining, if not confined, space.

Greater studies would follow, but from the early American experience, repeated in Britain, it was immediately evident that prospective crews needed careful screening for temperament, intelligence and fitness. They had to be sufficiently adept mentally to overcome any feelings of boredom through what might seem to the outsider to be intensely monotonous procedure of alternating their period of watch with an equal time of leisure and sleep. A sonar operator who might not have his mind fully on the task, for example, might miss the first trace or sound that is vital to subsequent developments. Boredom and irritability might lead to low morale, and put pressure on the officers. Selection and training of commanders, officers and senior ratings in turn became perhaps the most crucial elements of all. In their hands rested the responsibility for all elements, human and mechanical, in these highly sophisticated war machines. Testing the abilities of these men went well beyond the technical skills previously recognised as measures of leadership qualities.

The American way, introduced by Admiral Rickover for the early nuclear commanders, became legendary. He would consider only officers whom *he believed* possessed superior qualifications. He challenged them with confrontational interviews that often degenerated into verbal abuse liberally sprayed with the f-word, insults and harassment. This, he said, would sort the men from the boys. It was, however, an old-fashioned mode of selection that was now unsuited to the needs of the time. There was no doubting the need for men of strong character and intellect to command the nuclear boats, but leadership came in many forms, which embraced elements that Rickover himself did not recognise, even down to the quirks and occasional bursts of eccentricity of men who in every other respect were determined leaders. In their book *Submarine Warfare*, authors Captain

J.E. Moore and Commander R. Compton-Hall recall that Rickover was once described as a banyan tree under whose shade nothing else could grow, and under his personality cult innovation was not encouraged. The authors noted: 'It was arguably this conservatism in the United States Navy, which only began to break following the late Admiral's retirement, that allowed the Soviet Navy to leapfrog in a number of disquieting areas over Western submarines.'

Britain's somewhat modest entry level into the control and management of nuclear submarines meant a clean slate and the potential to develop new operational and man-management systems. Those involved in the nuclear programme stood slightly aloof from HMS *Dolphin*, the Portsmouth home of British submarines, and while further cuts in manpower around the conventional force were carried out in line with a general reduction in Royal Navy numbers, not a few stalwarts were apprehensive about the future.

Meanwhile, substantial specialist shore support facilities were required for the planned arrival of the British nuclear flotilla. The infrastructure had to cover a range of disciplines, including communications and control, intelligence, weather reports, secure berthing and maintenance facilities, weapons systems analysis, general stores and training – all geared exclusively to the needs of the nuclear boats. In addition, housing was needed for crews and their families. The Ministry of Defence Research Station at Dounreay, Caithness, Scotland, provided the initial home, and there Rolls-Royce and Associates won the contract to build the reactor plant alongside the support and control centre, which included a replica of the submarine hull for complete simulation for the training of crews. Naturally enough, this great revolution in submarine capability caused great interest and fascination among the media and the public at large, not least from the increasingly vocal Campaign for Nuclear Disarmament. A colleague of the author went aboard *Dreadnought* not long after she was commissioned and provides a view, written at the time, that gives an indication of the surprising features of vessels which eventually became the norm for British submarines:

The hatch that went down into the secret world of *Dreadnought* looked the size of a pavement coal hole. Five men can stand in the top of the conning tower – or sail, as it is properly called. Behind are the eyes, nose and some of the ears of the boat. Two periscopes to see, the snort tube for taking fresh air aboard, and an assortment of aerial devices for listening. Below, ropes are being coiled into hatches and a tug is pulling *Dreadnought* away from the trot (the dockside in submarine talk). Then, under her own steam, there is no shudder or noise, but a great thrashing wake begins to carve its pattern astern and soon that blunt bow digs a deep furrow in the Clyde.

It is time to go below. The control room of a nuclear submarine is like the cockpit of a jet airliner – a complex of switches, dials, lights, knobs and consoles of instruments. Two men steer the boat with aircraft-type joysticks. There is also an automatic system doing the job. Dominating the control room is the main search periscope, where the captain sits astride, manoeuvring it round with his right foot on an accelerator. Even while *Dreadnought* is on the surface, the captain is now watching from below, telephoning the men remaining in the conning tower as he sees what they see, changing course, enquiring, ordering, requesting, chatting, establishing the pattern of watchful caution that is to last for many long hours.

The captain calls his instructions in a clipped tone. Replies come in a babble of accents – Scottish, cockney, southern and northern town and country – but not a sound is missed at the periscope. In the early minutes it is obvious that this boat runs on a two-way principle of confidence. Confidence of officers that every rating can do his job and confidence returned. Twenty million pounds are in good hands. Now it is time for a wardroom lunch. Soup, a choice of pork chop or shepherd's pie, rice pudding, and cheese. Everybody aboard eats from the same galley. There is no room for favoured treatment. First Lieutenant Richard Heaslip remarks: 'We all get fat on a long cruise; you eat a lot of stodge and do no exercise.' From a hatch the steward produces cans of beer, but these men drink only to quench thirst. There is work to be done, machinery of devastating power to be looked after. The captain laughs: 'You could call this a Cambridge boat – five officers got degrees there.'

In this space about ten feet across and sixteen feet wide – ceiling six feet six inches – sits a concentration of modern technology, men with understanding of nuclear physics, computers, electronics, all apart from being naval officers. 'We will dive at 1430,' the captain tells his crew over the intercom. The rising wind has given the boat a slight roll. Apart from the hum of air-conditioning vital to keep the marvel machines of modern science as efficient as the men, there is no noise, no vibration from the boat's engine. Before diving, a group of men check every hatch and valve. Then they are checked again with an officer. No chances are taken.

Instruments can check it all again. In the control room there is now an atmosphere of purpose, but no fuss. The captain is astride his periscope searching for surface peril. Sunlight gleams on the iris of eyes. 'The big tankers draw fifty feet under water,' he says. 'We have to make damned sure there aren't any around.' Commands are given. A klaxon sounds. There is a noise of water filling the tanks in that bulky waist.

There is no sensation of sinking or going down – it is so slow and simple; a leading seaman flicks switches and reports, the captain asks his navigator for a fix, a seaman reads off the compass bearings. It is an effort of will to imagine any disaster, such is the atmosphere of order and calm. And so *Dreadnought* is now in her element under the sea where waves have no effect, where her bull-nosed shape makes her as efficient as a porpoise at twisting and turning, where that silent nuclear engine can build up speed, where know-how and science have made a curiously comforting world for those of us privileged to share it.

The first lieutenant is an enthusiast about this boat. We go from the control room to look around. First stop is at a sign by a formidably locked hatch: STRICTLY FORBIDDEN UNLESS TO AUTHORISED PERSONNEL. He turns it round from the side usually shown when VIPs are aboard and now it reads: CHECKPOINT CHARLIE: YOU ARE NOW ENTERING THE AMERICAN ZONE. Behind the hatch lies the nuclear-propulsion unit bought from America. Nobody can pass that door without supreme authority. Before I could go on operations with *Dreadnought* the Defence Ministry had to assure the Pentagon that this rule would be observed. This much I can tell about the engine. It heats steam to propel the boat, provides electricity for lighting, running the computers and electronic devices that fill every spare cranny, heat for cooking and warm showers for every mess, the juice for a miniature launderette.

Dreadnought touched more than 20 knots while I was aboard. Her true top speed is reserved for occasions when the crew are alone in mid-ocean. 'Then,' said the first lieutenant, 'it is like handling a sports car. She banks as she turns and a dive, even at one degree, is like going down a steep hill.' We were going through narrow, often crowded gangways, looking in radio rooms, the galley, the messes where forty men find comfort in a relatively small space. But the men who eat, sleep and relax in these areas are not moaners. Firstly, they are bound by mutual respect for each other. Secondly, they are well paid for their duties, and life aboard the submarine spares them at least the ordeal of facing storms and dirty weather half the year. Thirdly, they are sensibly given every comfort and privilege. Nobody folds blankets. Everybody has a sleeping bag. They have their rum, a canteen ration of two cans of beer a day, which has to be paid for, good solid food, a library, film shows, a shop that opens daily, framed pin-ups, from *Playboy* magazine around the mess. It is a life that 40 per cent volunteer for at first, and after five years 95 per cent decide to sign on again for another spell. Back in the control room the captain prepares to fire some practice torpedoes, followed by high-speed runs to test whether a helicopter can detect us with new equipment. The crew know because he has told them all over the intercom, just as they know I am aboard or what time we will moor off Rothesay. Information pours out all the time.

Now all the sounds of the deep are in symphony.

Echo sounders, radar, sonar are pinging and chirping and pulsing. Lights are dimmed and the vital dials are a deep luminous red, the radar screens luminous green, the sonar scanner pale orange. This kind of day with testing the helping coastal command is all too routine. The crew look forward to a long cruise. Perhaps under water to Gibraltar or the West Indies. But one privilege they lose is calling on foreign ports. Hardly any port in Europe will allow a nuclear ship to enter for fear of radiation or accident. To the men aboard *Dreadnought*, living only yards from radiation, this is nonsense. Each of them carries a film sensitised to record a change in radioactivity, and the air aboard the boat is checked regularly for any change. They are all confident that they face less radiation than a civilian walking through Piccadilly Circus wearing a luminous wristwatch. Doctors and radiologists have constantly checked this view and found it correct.

Night-time off Rothesay and we have surfaced. The sea is too lumpy to allow a tender to take men ashore so we have supper and watch a film. Then, apart from the duty watch, the crew settle to sleep. All around the wardroom are cabins sleeping from two to four men. Only the captain has his own seven-foot-square area. In the first lieutenant's cabin a bunk is pulled from the bulkhead, a sleeping bag laid, and soon there is only the sound of the sea to be heard slapping on the black hull.

Dreadnought went on to score many British firsts in terms of speed and endurance and in March 1971 became the first British submarine to surface at the North Pole, a feat by now already performed by several American nuclear boats. For seven days, *Dreadnought* travelled 1,800 miles under the polar icecap before her then captain, 36-year-old Commander Alan Kennedy, brought her up with much crashing and creaking at the pole as the conning tower pushed upwards through 4.5 metres of ice. There, while members of the crew stood guard with rifles to ward off polar bears, others got out to take photographs of the extraordinary sight of their ship's conning tower protruding through the ice. Kennedy, pleased that his boat suffered only two dents in the process, said on his return: 'This is an area in which we must be fully operational. Only now, with more nuclear submarines coming into service, can we devote the time for this sort of experimental work.' He was right, and the Americans and the Russians had already shown the way – USS *Triton*, for example, had circumnavigated the world in 60 days as early as 1960 without once breaking the surface. Britain was indeed lagging well behind in what had essentially become a two-horse race.

However, although derived from *Dreadnought* in most respects, the new British Valiant-class boats had a completely new propulsion system and near-perfect streamlining with a fin-like conning tower that was intended to reduce drag. This proved to be entirely successful with the first of the class, *Valiant*, leading the way. Commissioned in July 1966, she was soon to set a record 28-day non-stop submerged journey of 12,000 miles from Singapore. Soon month-long submerged patrols became commonplace.

She was to be followed by *Warspite*, *Churchill*, *Conqueror* and *Courageous* – all with an expected operational lifespan of 20 years. They were commissioned between 1966 and 1972, and were slightly larger than *Dreadnought* with an overall length of 86.8 metres and a submerged displacement of 4,500 tonnes.

Petty Officer Bryan Tilley, the sonar specialist whom we

met earlier recounting experiences about the new Porpoise class, was among those who retrained for the nuclear boats and found the switch from conventional submarines to nuclear power an incredible experience:

I joined *Warspite* in 1965 fresh from the yard at Barrow, where she was commissioned by the then prime minister's wife, Mrs Mary Wilson. We moved up to Scotland, to Faslane, the Clyde nuclear submarine base from where we did our work-up. That's where we preyed from, and we had to adjust very quickly to our new long trips submerged – and for me the longest I ever made. We dived just outside Faslane and surfaced in the Malacca Strait just over four weeks later. We travelled at around 60 metres around the Cape of Good Hope and spent Christmas in the Indian Ocean.

The living on board was good. There were only three messes: senior rates, junior rates and the wardroom. All the senior rates of the submarine were together. We had a separate bunk space for both rates. Any visitors slept in special bunks in the torpedo compartment. The biggest luxury of all was a bathroom, decent showers and decent toilets. We could also smoke on board, which was always up to the captain. On *Warspite*, we smoked all the time.

We began by going out on exercises, which were always in strategic places in, for example, the Icelandic gap. The sonar equipment was much more sophisticated. The whole bow of the submarine was a sonar dome and you had to do an awful lot of work. In a war situation, the equipment was designed to detect and sink enemy submarines. For us, then, surveillance was the name of the game. The Russians were doing the same.

Warspite was a very fast boat and, of course, moving around at speed under water you always had to face the possibility of a collision. Salt water is a terrible medium to play in. You don't take anything for granted and, unlike sight or even radar, you don't have much chance of knowing what you're coming into. You could even collide with your quarry. One of my young lads on *Warspite* asked me: 'What happens, PO, if we hit something?' I had to tell him that he wouldn't know anything about it because it would be too late then. You might hit anything, anything that's submerged, even a whale. A school of whales could be a real problem particularly if you're trying to pick up something ahead of you. You haven't got a hope of hearing what's the other side of them because of the noise they make, talking to each other. They weighed perhaps as much as 60 tonnes each and could be down at 60 metres or more. Dolphins are another problem. They issue a shrieking whistle that kills your sonar. The *Warspite* gave us no problems, other than changes of skipper. So much depends on the man at the top.

The skipper, on the other hand, might say the same about the crew, especially on long patrols. *Warspite* went on to log what was at the time the longest-ever submarine running period; it lasted 112 days. Longer ones would follow. False decking had to be built to store boxes of tinned food and general supplies. The length of the running period was seen as a major innovation, not just for the boat but for the crew, and there is no doubt that it was a testing time that ran through every aspect of life inside the vessel. Coxswain Fulton famously wrote in his diary on the last day: 'Thank God that's over.'

The feelings were entirely mutual among everyone aboard

because, after almost a third of a year in such a confined space together, certain personality quirks that every one of them possessed in some form or other might have become incredibly irritating. But then what did they do when they got off the boat? As another *Warspite* veteran, Lieutenant-Commander Bob Harboe Bush, pointed out:

> We went to the nearest pub for a last drink before going home, and stood around in a group talking about submarines. Going home is not easy after a long trip away. No one knows how difficult it is, and there were more rows when we got back than there were on the boat, and you never seem to know what they are about. You end up saying, 'I wish I was back at sea', and she says, 'Well, bloody well go, then'. Partly, what it is after being jammed together in the boat, you need to be alone. Unforgivable though it seemed at first, my wife and I came to understand that, and I would go off and do a bit of mountain-climbing. It was not at all an uncommon phenomenon among submariners and quite different, I think, from the wartime experience of being away from home for far longer.

Although understanding and helpful in special cases of personal trauma or emergencies, the Royal Navy has never been known for mollycoddling its men. But beginning with *Dreadnought* and on through the first decade of nuclear-powered submarines, COs and welfare officers alike found themselves on a major learning curve in handling what were termed as the external effects of longer patrols on the men themselves, their wives and families. Problems of not being there, which all submariners had faced, were now to be amplified by the simple fact of not seeing daylight for possibly weeks on end. Unlike sailors on the surface, who had general access to the airwaves, newspapers, the telephone and a mail delivery system, nuclear submariners had none. Their only link with the outside world was described by one rating as little news flashes:

> We would very likely be out to sea for two months, and every so often they would copy radio broadcasts just for general information. Huge headlines of maybe national importance and stories of great import would get reduced to 25 words, and you could hardly make judgements from that kind of brevity. But that's it in a nutshell . . . as soon as the hatch shuts, you know you are divorced from the real world. For the next two months or more, what is going on out there has nothing more to do with you, unless, of course, there's a war or some other rumpus that we as a submarine might become involved in. If you are not a worrier – and I can tell you, it isn't good to be a worrier on a nuclear submarine – it is strangely liberating not to know. Your car may have been stolen, your house may have burned down, the wife may have run off with the guy next door, but you don't know about it, and even if you did there is absolutely nothing you can do, so why worry? It's an odd thing.

A weekly familygram from wives and relatives was limited then to 40 words, except under special circumstances. To say the text was censored might be overstating the issue. The messages were, however, read at the shore base before they were forwarded on to the submarine and might be held back if it was felt the content could cause the recipient to become depressed or unstable. As patrols became longer, routinely extending to 70 days and more, difficulties experienced at home were wide and varied and eventually might require the specialist attention of family welfare officers, although a fairly tight and self-protecting onshore community was built up around the submarine bases.

The wives and partners all knew the problems. As earlier testimony shows, a fairly common situation arising among submariners returning from patrol was that they were often quiet and introspective for several days, unable to communicate very well with the families they had not seen for so long. Wives became very independent, by necessity having to run the household, handling everything from paying the bills to seeing the children through ailments. They never had the luxury of being able to talk any immediate crisis through with their husbands, because they were simply not able to be contacted, except through a little-used, and secret, process for extreme emergencies. Wives with three or four children might find the task of running the family home daunting, while returning husbands, on the other hand, might discover that their children were resentful of them, suddenly getting all their mother's attention, which had previously been showered on themselves. 'Perhaps that was the most daunting thing of all,' said *Warspite* steward Paul O'Brien, 'missing whole chunks of your children's lives.'

Other peculiarities surfaced with the homecomings. Some members of crew found it an unpleasant experience when they came out of the hatch to smell the fresh Scottish air in their nostrils instead of the ship's air-conditioned atmosphere to which their senses had become attuned. Their eyes were also affected, unable to focus immediately on bright colours, long distances and panoramic views, which had been absent from their grey, enclosed world for so long. For some, their eyesight was so unused to distances beyond 2 metres or so that sailors were warned not to drive their cars until they had acclimatised after a number of crashes occurred after the patrols. All these things cropped up during the first years of nuclear boats, and a resolution to those that were solvable was vital to the smooth running of the entire operation, especially as the Royal Navy moved towards the next major step in its accumulation of nuclear power.

With the nuclear submarines came a clear distinction in the role that submarines were to play in the overall scheme of things. The craft of the Valiant class were designated fleet submarines, or, as they became more commonly known, hunter-killers. A hunter-killer could both operate with the fleet and act alone against surface ships. It could join forces with aircraft in anti-submarine operations: air observers locating targets and the submarine hunting them down. It was capable of firing a variety of weapons from its torpedo tubes in support of a naval task force, and in peacetime roles the primary work of the Valiant submarine was to join various fleet and NATO exercises, perform a fairly rigid programme of simulated attacks to keep the crew on top form, shadow submarines from potentially hostile nations, reconnaissance and intelligence-gathering.

But even as the first Valiant submarines were going into production, the next stage of nuclear development was already signalled. Strategic submarines were introduced in the USA when the George Washington class became operational in 1959. They were huge 5,900-tonne, 116.4-metre vessels carrying 16 Polaris missiles with a range of 1,200 nautical miles. They were to be matched by the Soviet Union's bigger and better missile carrier, the 8,000-tonne Yankee-class submarines, which carried 16 SS-N-6 missiles of 1,300-nautical-mile range. Strategic submarines of the Polaris-carrying variety were to be the 'bombers' of the

The crew of *Truculent*, which came into service in September 1942, earned its Jolly Roger flag with a number of successes, including the sinking of German U-boat *U308* north of the Faeroes in June 1943. The wartime crew was paid off and later the boat went into refit. The new crew, including some old hands, joined for post-refit trials in January 1950 when, as well as the full complement, a number of dockyard workers were on board. Tragedy struck as the boat returned from the first day's manoeuvres. She was in collision with a tanker and sank in the Medway estuary. Sixty-seven men made a near perfect escape from the stricken submarine, but only eleven survived – the rest perished in the freezing waters or were swept away by strong currents and drowned.

Left: The Chariot, one of a number of special craft linked to the Submarine Service introduced during the Second World War and used on specially targeted, and usually exceedingly hazardous, missions.

The Sleeping Beauty, or Motorised Submersible Canoe, carried by submarines for attacks against Japanese shipping around Singapore.

The German battleship *Tirpitz* which became the object of numerous Allied attacks, especially by the newly created X-craft force of midget submarines (see facing page).

Left: The precarious management of X-craft midget submarines used for heroic attacks on German and Japanese shipping. Above: Inside the control room of the tiny craft.

X-craft officers who took part in major raids including an all-out attack on the *Tirpitz* behind her anti-submarine defences, from left to right T.L. Martin, RN, K. Hudspeth, RANVR, B.M. McFarlane, RAN, B.C. Place, RN, D. Cameron, RNR. Cameron and Place were awarded the Victoria Cross, as were Lieutenant Ian Fraser and Leading Seaman James Magennis for a later attack on Singapore harbour.

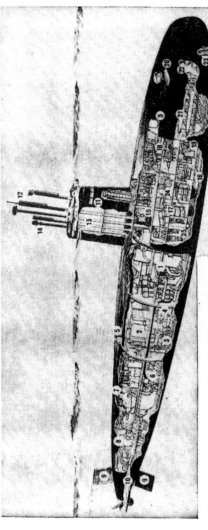

1 Reactor Compartment.	8 Electric Propulsion Motor (Alternative drive).	15 Control Room.	21 Torpedo Space.
2 Reactor Control Compartment.	9 Rudders.	16 Electric Batteries.	22 Torpedo Tubes.
3 Auxiliary Machinery.	10 After Hydroplane.	17 Crew's Quarters.	23 Stowed Anchor.
4 Diesel Generator.	11 Surface Navigating Bridge.	18 Officers' Quarters.	24 Galley.
5 Escape Hatch.	12 Periscope.	19 Electrical Space.	25 Store Rooms & Refrigeration Space.
6 Main Condenser.	13 Radar & Radio Aerials.	20 Forward Hydroplane.	
7 Main Turbines.	14 Snort.		

An Admiralty cut-away diagram of the interior of *Dreadnought*, Britain's first nuclear- powered submarine.

The Queen launched *Dreadnought* in October 1960. Below: A decade later, the submarine surfaced at the North Pole.

Modern times – life on board the Trafalgar class hunter-killer submarines:

Top left: 'chef' prepares for one of the several mealtime sittings on a boat that is operational 24-hours a day.

Top right: at the chart table in the control room.

Bottom left: Running maintenance on electrical circuit boards, one of the many tasks that today require specialist skills. (*British Crown copyright/MOD*)

The Trafalgar class periscope action (above) and, below, the clean-as-a-whistle engine room, a place that once clanked and clanged and was covered in grease. (*British Crown copyright/MOD*)

The Polaris missile compartment and control panel (left) of *Resolution*, Britain's first nuclear-armed submarine class which was retired in the 1990s to be replaced with the *Trident* nuclear missiles (above) carried aboard the hugely powerful *Vigilant* (below).

future, as opposed to the hunter-killer role of the fleet submarines. They were the second-strike deterrent in the event of a nuclear attack, and Mountbatten's dream of achieving this capability for the Royal Navy was now not far off.

CHAPTER FOURTEEN

More Power Than all the Bombs Dropped in the Second World War

The need for a 'hidden' second-strike nuclear force arose from the continuing post-war debate over what might happen in the event of a nuclear conflict. There had been, under Eisenhower, a policy of avowed 'massive retaliation' by the USA in the event of any trouble with the Soviet Union, nuclear or not. Then came Mutually Assured Destruction, known as MAD, which was criticised by the hawks because if such a threat was used to deter only a nuclear attack, the threat of retaliation against conventional warfare would be devalued and also might undermine the promise America had given to her allies to use nuclear weapons on their behalf if they faced aggression. More often than not, the debate reverted back to the 'ultimate deterrent' principle, that if a certain level of destructive capability was reached by both sides, an effective stalemate would be established and extra weapons, as Winston Churchill put it, would merely 'make the rubble bounce'.

Then, in the late 1950s, a high-powered American think-tank came up with another disconcerting theory – demonstrating that all Allied nuclear installations were vulnerable to a surprise attack, after which retaliation would be impossible. A devastating attack was considered possible in the wake of Russia's considerable advances in guidance systems. Their successful delivery of Sputnik 1 into orbit around the earth also scared the Americans half to death. A successful 'first-strike' attack that rendered retaliation impossible would be decisive: he who struck first would win. If, however, the attacked nation had already taken steps to ensure that hugely destructive retaliatory weapons would survive the first strike, it would have what became known as a second-strike capability.

Until the late 1950s, America took the precaution of keeping its Strategic Air Command on constant alert and had fully loaded planes permanently in the skies because military analysts remained convinced that all NATO and Allied bases, missile sites, airfields and dockyards were targeted by the lines of Russian land-based missiles pointing in the direction of the British Isles and Europe. And so the strategic submarine was born when the arrival of inertial guidance systems meant that long-range submarine-launched ballistic missiles could supposedly be delivered with incredible accuracy to targets initially up to 1,300 miles away.

The idea of strategic submarines had been around for a long time but became truly effective only with the arrival of nuclear propulsion, which allowed them to operate continuously submerged without having to surface or reveal their whereabouts. The power of the missiles that the submarines were capable of carrying totally negated the pre-emptive attack and, as America discovered, it was a cheaper system in the long term than the proposed second-strike alternative, the Skybolt project. This was an air-to-surface missile system to be carried by a new V-bomber force which would have cost the British taxpayer £100 million. But after successful trials with Polaris, America cancelled Skybolt in 1961.

This left Britain high and dry. The Macmillan government had opted to take the Skybolt from America to honour its second-strike commitment to NATO, and now they had none. Worse, it came at a time when the world had just stepped back from the brink of nuclear war over the Cuban missile crisis. Soviet leader Khrushchev had promised to dismantle missiles in Cuban bases if President Kennedy would lift the American blockade of the island. Neither promise was fully adhered to, but at least the world was saved from what had threatened to become the first exchange of nuclear missiles, and from there who knew what?

Some hasty diplomatic exchanges followed, and Lord Mountbatten, by then Chief of Defence Staff, was quietly delighted with the collapse of the Skybolt deal and was back in the fray campaigning for the government to try to persuade the Americans to sell them Polaris and thus pass control of Britain's nuclear deterrent from the RAF to the Royal Navy. In December 1962 Prime Minister Macmillan flew to Nassau, in the Bahamas, to meet President Kennedy. There was only one major item on the agenda for this crucial meeting: submarine-launched ballistic missiles. They hammered out a vital deal that became known as the Nassau Agreement, under which Britain would get the latest Polaris A3P SLBMs to maintain the UK's deterrent potential during the years ahead.

Britain would buy the complete weapon system but would design and build her own submarines and nuclear warheads for the missiles. The deal was also secretly linked to the further expansion of the global signals intelligence-gathering and listening operations under the UK–US agreement forged during the Second World War between the two countries, along with their Commonwealth allies Canada, Australia and New Zealand. Henceforth, British submarines became an integral part of a global intelligence-gathering network that operated from land, air and sea established principally by America but with considerable input from its partners in the UK–USA alliance. Quite apart from taking prime responsibility for the second-strike capability, the British submarine service moved to the very front line of the Allies' intelligence war, and for the rest of the twentieth century remained at the forefront of a watching brief against Russia, to which the latter reciprocated in fulsome manner.

When Kennedy and Macmillan had concluded their talks, a British Admiralty negotiating team was sent to the USA to finalise a detailed UK–US agreement, signed on 6 April 1963. By then, a massive building operation was already under way, with approval for four Resolution-class Polaris submarines having been formally authorised in February.

The submarines were to be constructed in pairs at maximum speed, two at Vickers' Leaf Yard at Barrow-in-Furness and two at Cammell Laird's Birkenhead yard. They were to take the names of ships Mountbatten had served on:

Resolution, built by Vickers Armstrong at Barrow-in-Furness, laid down on 26 February 1964 and launched on 15 September 1966 by the Queen Mother. Commissioned on 10 February 1967. Cost £40.2 million. Launched first UK Polaris missile on the US test firing range on 15 February 1968.

Repulse built by Vickers at Barrow. Launched on 4 November 1967 by Joan Zuckerman, wife of

Mountbatten's close friend Sir Solly Zuckerman, chief scientific adviser to the government, with a bottle of her home-made elderberry wine. Commissioned on 28 September 1968. Cost £37.5 million.

Renown, built by Cammell Laird, Birkenhead. Launched on 25 February 1967 by the wife of Defence Secretary Denis Healey. Commissioned on 15 November 1968. Cost £39.5 million.

Revenge, built by Cammell Laird, Birkenhead. Laid down on 8 May 1963. Launched on 19 May 1965 by Lady Law, wife of Vice-Admiral Sir Horace Law. Commissioned on 4 December 1969. Cost £38.6 million.

The awesome size and capability of these four boats are again demonstrated by the statistics that emerged as each new class reached the starting blocks: 129.5 metres long, a beam of 10 metres, a surface displacement of 7,400 tonnes, a speed of 25 knots submerged and a diving depth in excess of 300 metres. In terms of space, the boats were palatial even compared with the Valiant class, which was 42 metres shorter. They carried 14 officers and 129 ratings, each of whom had his own bunk – the first submarine in the Royal Navy to provide such a facility; previously, most of the ratings used the 'hot-bunking' system – sharing with a colleague on a different shift.

The missile compartment housing the 16 Polaris missiles was nicknamed Sherwood Forest, each missile being 9.5 metres in length, 1.4 metres in diameter and weighing 1,270 kilogrammes. Fired from a submerged submarine, the missiles would soar into the stratosphere and devastate a target 2,500 nautical miles away. The boats were each assigned two crews of 143 men, turn and turn about, so that at any given time there was at least one, and hopefully two, boats on patrol. The average length of the patrols was generally two months, though in practice often longer.

The most significant feature illustrated the submarines' power and potential: one Polaris submarine carried more destructive capability than the total amount of explosives expended by all sides in the Second World War – including the atomic bombs dropped on Japan.

As work on the four submarines began, the creation of a massive shore-based operation swung into action to build from scratch and complete within four years the support and command centres that would control Britain's first submarine-launched ballistic-missile programme. A special Polaris Executive was set up immediately to mastermind the formation of the second-strike force with an overall budget of £325 million. Flag Officer (submarines) Rear-Admiral Hugh Mackenzie, of *Thrasher* and *Tantalus* fame in the Second World War, was appointed Chief Polaris Executive and given the task of making Polaris operational within five years. Mackenzie was given carte blanche to pick his staff and soon gathered a nucleus of very able officers, by no means all submariners, but Polaris was still an undertaking of immense complexity. The Americans, without whom the Polaris project would have been impossible, were quickly charmed and impressed by Mackenzie's manner and energy. He also had to overcome considerable manpower difficulties and problems obtaining materials, coming at a time of the abolition of the Admiralty as a separate organisation and an incoming Labour government, many of whose members were hostile to Polaris.

Mackenzie's task was, quite naturally, of supreme importance and incredible magnitude, given that he was to form an entirely new structure of command and control disciplines which provided the chain-link of procedures and checks, leading ultimately to 10 Downing Street in the event of having to fire the missiles for real.

Working against the clock, Mackenzie pulled together a vast network of scientists, mathematicians, nuclear development teams, specialist organisations, shipbuilders and general building work contractors on a scale unprecedented in British naval history. Substantial quantities of detailed documentation had to be prepared for the building, operation and maintenance of the submarines and their support establishment. The planning and design that went into the submarines themselves, for example, accounted for a colossal 500,000 man-hours and the creation of more than 10,000 detailed documents that translated into the physical effort of building the vessels. A full-scale wooden mock-up of the submarine was built at the Resolution assembly shed to provide a guide for the exact positioning of the miles of pipes, cables and trunking and the hundreds of thousands of pieces of equipment that were to be installed in each boat.

The Atomic Energy Authority had to set to work on designing Britain's own warheads for the missiles at the Aldermaston Atomic Weapons Research Establishment, working closely with a joint US–UK steering group. The submarine nuclear power plants were in the hands of Rolls-Royce and Associates, and this programme was linked to the construction of shore facilities necessary to train crews and the land-based workforce, in addition to general maintenance once the submarines were operational.

The navy's technical establishment at Bath worked on problems of design, maintenance, technical support and logistics. They were linked to a Washington team concerned with the supply of Polaris and ancillary services. The Faslane base and refit dockyard had to be built and equipped, along with 2,000 houses to accommodate staff and naval personnel. Submarine crews and naval and civilian maintenance staff all had to receive specialist training. The whole undertaking was such that day-to-day communications were vital, and the navy built its own network linking London, Washington, Bath, Barrow-in-Furness, Birkenhead, Rosyth, Faslane and other centres. The submarine service also extended its own nuclear training school at Greenwich to cope with the extra intake of men necessary to man the project, involving more than 1,000 personnel for the Polaris boats alone, all this running in parallel to the ongoing work and training for the Valiant-class submarines that were coming off the slips progressively over the same time-frame.

Training for Polaris crews was necessarily substantially upgraded to cover the additional disciplines, and not merely the physical technicalities of working in a nuclear-armed boat were included in the curriculum. The psychological elements were equally important, given that the men involved would be manning a delivery system for the most potentially destructive force the world had ever known. This aspect had to be discussed and explored at length because it was no longer confined to military issues or doing your duty in the event of war. There were much deeper implications. Anyone who was judged to have the slightest reservations or who themselves felt that when the time came they would be unable to contend with the probability of being the instrument of death to perhaps millions of innocent people were invited to transfer elsewhere. The navy was quite blunt about issues, and had to be. Anyone who could not make that decision, or felt in his heart of hearts he could not face it or be party to it, was in the wrong business. Those who stayed were taught to appreciate that Polaris was strictly a retaliatory system and that in the unlikely event that they ever did have to fire missiles, it would be because their own homes were already in ashes.

For new would-be commanders, the Perisher course had become a tremendous challenge, not just for potential Polaris commanders but across the board. The course had always been tough; now it was tougher. It was designed progressively to test to the utmost, almost to breaking point, the resilience of the senior officers. Apart from technical skills and leadership qualities, it took officers down the road of exploring, and accepting, their personal limitations. The point was made quite firmly: if the officer did not appreciate the boundaries of his own ability, he was a dangerous man to have around. That was one of the principal challenges on the Perisher, and the teacher's task was gradually to bring those who were not too successful on the course to the realisation that they were not good enough for it. In other words, no one was failed; they failed themselves, in which case they left the submarine service and returned to general naval duties. If successful, they were handed the controls of some of the most powerful machines on earth.

Finally, when all the work was done and the submarines built and trialled, it came down to stocking the boat for the essentials of life under the waves, for weeks on end, with enough food to give 143 men three good meals a day and a few treats in between. Someone somewhere worked out, as they do, a piece of useless information that the amount of supplies taken on board for a typical patrol would have kept a family of four happily fed for five years. For a typical patrol, the basic commodities included 1,587 kilogrammes of beef, 2,268 kilogrammes of potatoes, 5,000 eggs, 1,000 chickens, 2 miles of sausages, a tonne of baked beans and so on. A young officer, fresh from Greenwich, admitted:

When I came into the Polaris team, I was told I was being given the supply officer's job, which I wasn't very happy about. But in fact it gave you a wonderful insight into the things you hadn't been trained for. I was running not only the public accounts for food and stores but also the non-public funds, such as the welfare fund, the wardroom wine and so on. There was a great deal of organising to be done, and I look back on that period as one of learning how to prioritise, how to get things done. You had to get it right. You couldn't go on a Polaris patrol and run out of bread! Planning had to be meticulous.

Captain Geoffrey Jacques was 30 when he learned he was to go forward for training to command a nuclear boat and at that point had no idea of the responsibility that would fall into his hands. He had joined the navy straight from school and made the decision to volunteer for submarines fairly early in his career. After initial training both at Dartmouth and then as midshipman in the fleet, he joined the 'big ships' and remained until he was promoted to sub-lieutenant and moved on to what was called a 'small ship time'. It was the only time during training in which young officers could get a look at submarines. Those who liked them volunteered to do their small ship training in submarines. In 1956 he spent three months in *Tiptoe*. Ten years later, having spent time in Australia, where he completed his Perisher course to qualify as a commanding officer, he returned to England expecting to be sent back into general service in the navy:

My return coincided with the start of the Polaris programme, and in fact no officers in the submarine service were freed at that time to go back. We were all sucked into the system, and I was sent off to stand by for the completion of *Revenge* at Cammell Laird. We moved up to Chester for the finishing off of the build at Birkenhead and then taking her through sea trials, demonstration firings and the first three patrols. There were two crews on standby for each of the Polaris submarines, and so we had four crews all living in local accommodation and attending training programmes and familiarisation. That phase in itself was demanding and exciting because the knowledge of these boats was very limited. We had to set up all our own training programmes and take this beast off to sea, none of us with any depth of experience in the equipment we were about to use.

The first thing that hits you is the size, and, if you look at the domestic situation first, there is simply no comparison with what I had experienced so far. In the T-boat the captain had his own little cabin while the other officers still had bunks in the wardroom, where the seats turned into bunks at night; it was also their dining room and general living space – about six feet by eight feet, not much more. On *Revenge* we had a wardroom which could seat twelve to fifteen people at a long table and still had a sitting area with armchairs for another six to eight people. All of those people shared double cabins and there were bathrooms and proper showers that could be used virtually without limit.

The sailors had their own mess-decks, bathrooms and sleeping quarters, and quite simply we were in a completely different world. We had real air-conditioning and real control of the air and were able to maintain a pleasant temperature. The air was still recycled, but pushed through great banks of carbon filters and other equipment to cleanse the air and then replenish the oxygen. In the old days they used to burn oxygen candles to generate oxygen. Now they had electrolysers, which rely on the electrolysis of water and splitting the hydrogen and oxygen, and the oxygen is made available to come back into the air and the hydrogen gets discharged overboard. There was now unlimited power, unlimited supplies of virtually everything we needed to make life comfortable.

But the most significant factor of all was we had a true submersible and one that was virtually silent in every respect when under way. Instead of having submarines which generally moved about on the surface, and had a limited period for endurance dived, suddenly there was a submarine that could stay dived, travelling as fast as it could for as long as was necessary, limited only by human nature.

Initially, the average patrol lasted six to eight weeks, although there was no specific pattern because others might recognise it. Indeed, our first challenge was to get out of the Clyde and into deep water without being detected by the Russian ships which were waiting for just that purpose. They were surveillance boats, converted fishing vessels, which were run by Soviet naval intelligence. There was always one on station off Malin Head, and there were others about. One of their primary roles was to try to detect you coming out and ideally pass you over to a Russian nuclear submarine that would then stay on your trail.

So the whole essence was one of cloak and dagger and cat and mouse. You'd never go out at set times or set dates. All sorts of measures were taken to avoid being pinpointed by the Soviets, and the whole point of the exercise was to get out there into the ocean undetected by anybody. Safe cruising depths were about 100 feet, so that any ship passing over the top would not cause a problem. Then you would choose your depth according to water conditions and what exactly you are trying to do, such as hiding, or you may take the view that you want to be able to hear and pick up someone else. So you have lots of priorities to weigh up in accordance with intelligence on who else might be in your area. You also have to balance this with communications.

The Polaris boats never spoke to anyone but were always constantly listening, and thus you had to make sure that you could hear all the time and receive any signals that might have been sent to you. These were sent on a variety of broadcasts; submarine broadcasts traditionally have been on a very low frequency and you have a number of aerials you can use. Among the more recent ones was a trailing wire with which you had to be careful. Once you were out in the open ocean, but in flat, calm waters, an alert aviator could pick up a wire, and thus all the time you had to be aware of the conditions in which you were operating and what your priorities were. We were given very large areas for our patrols, and no one would know where you were in that area so that everything was done to make sure you could remain undetected, and one of the best ways of achieving that was the freedom to operate in a large area and go where you liked.

The ship's navigational management people and senior officers were the only ones who knew where we were. North Norwegian Sea, right round the western Atlantic, the Mediterranean . . . if one assumes we were looking towards Russia, you just take your compass and take the range of the missiles and choose where you want to put people. Northwood headquarters [the submarine control and command centre] gave you your water in which to operate and made it as large as possible so you had complete freedom. You would have intelligence and knowledge of national, European and NATO naval activities because you would want to avoid getting involved in those areas, and we were fed as much intelligence on the movement of other people as they had available so that you could keep out of everybody's way. In a sense, everyone else was the enemy, because the object of the patrols was to remain undetected. As far as I am aware, none of the patrols was ever compromised.

In regard to the missiles, target information came in sealed tapes. They were loaded into the computer that had various verification functions which said it had accepted the tape and recognised it, but the coordinates of possible targets were never displayed anywhere. I suppose it was possible for the weapons officer to work them out, but it would have taken a long time. I certainly didn't know what was targeted, but whether or not I would have found out if there had been a bun fight and I received instructions to open other documents, I don't know.

There was a procedure to follow if that had happened. The missiles themselves were connected to the inertial navigator so that they knew where they were starting from. The missiles were given the target coordinates, and when you fired them on-board computers did the rest. It was a wonderful system, and whenever we had to fire the missiles on the test range in the USA the system always worked. Of all the gunnery systems one has had throughout one's time in the service, there were good days and bad days, but in my experience this one never had bad days. It was an incredible piece of engineering. It was a solid-fuel rocket, no nasty gases or liquids to handle, a very impressive system.

There were various tests and functions carried out daily or periodically, and the system itself was self-checking and self-diagnostic. There were also periodic dummy launches, which you ran for your own benefit or externally originated by signal from headquarters. Everything done on board was logged and the data went back to control. They crawled all over the data, rather like the black box procedure in aircraft. At the end of each patrol, there were vanloads of data recording everything that had been done on board. It was all analysed in minute detail. They were able to check how everything was running and whether all the parameters were correct.

We were at the absolute sharp end of the Cold War, although it was never set up as a first-strike weapon, and we were all made aware of that. It was always there as a deterrent. As to our own feelings about being the deliverer of such a powerful force, one always felt that in the scenario that you might have to press this button, there would be so much chaos and mayhem going on, everything you'd ever stood and lived for was probably in smithereens, you would have wanted to hit the button anyway. The scenario would have been filled with such doom and gloom that I don't think you'd have a problem if you received the signal to go, to get on with it. Also, I always had the feeling that it was a deterrent, and it was going to work, and because we had got it and because it was so awful, we were most unlikely ever to be faced with the problem. The system itself seemed to be so good, you felt confident that you had a system that was going to work and was recognised as such worldwide.

If you are going to have an effective deterrent, a) you must be able to deliver a system to the other side that does work, b) they have to know it is going to work, and c) that you'll certainly use it. I really do believe that deterrents work, and it really did work. It was capable of enormous damage and therefore, providing you had a sane adversary who would not want this inflicted on him, then you did have a very nice big system. I don't think any of the COs had any hang-ups about what on earth we would do if we got a firing signal. I certainly didn't. I think in advance we would have already heard of how things were deteriorating, that there had been exchanges and that nuclear weapons had already fallen on London, Birmingham and the like. The firing signals, as far as we were concerned, had all kinds of built-in checks and balances which started in 10 Downing Street and ended up in the CO's cabin. There were keys involved, and there was a set of procedures that had to be gone through in stages, with two people checking each stage and each other. It would have been impossible to have a nutter who decided we'd have bonfire night tonight. It was a very elaborate system, and if it had ever come about there would have been no misunderstanding; you would be absolutely confident that you had the right instructions.

Turning to the domestic arrangements on board during what might be a long patrol, dived for most of the time, there would be no daylight and the human consciousness needed some sort of pattern to recognise night and day. We were in the normal naval watch-keeping system of three watches, although more recently the SSNs [ships submersible, nuclear] run a two-watch system. In the early days we used to put all the accommodation areas into red lighting at sunset so that you did have some semblance of night and day. It was done for the very good reason that if you did have to look up the periscope, you would have your night vision.

Food was always an important factor when there was not a lot going on. The feeding arrangements were very good. A lot of effort was put into making sure you got good chefs. It had patterns that were quite strange. When you started off, people were eating quite a lot, and then suddenly they would go down and they wouldn't eat much, perhaps linked to periods when activity was low. Then, they would get interested in eating again and there were some interesting eating profiles. We also had facilities for exercise, such as rowing machines, bicycle machines and a doctor who would carry out medical research on pulse rates. He usually had a number of tasks set for him by the medical world. On one patrol, for example, he wanted a list of candidates who would do a certain amount of exercise and he would measure their pulse rate in week one, week two and so on.

Probably the most important recreation was the film which ships have traditionally shown in the evening, and again Polaris had priority to get the most recent releases. In the early days, certainly, there was always a film show every night in the sailors' mess. Things have changed again now because of television and videos.

So in terms of daily routine, the pattern emerged whereby they had their watch-keeping, their feeding times, recreation times and sleeping. There was also a good deal of training for general duties, emergency exercises and routine procedures, and you also had a general level of 15 or 20 per cent of trainees on board who all had to qualify, so there was quite a lot to do. Then, of course, the ship's systems did not always work beautifully all the time. So there were repairs going on, different situations, and there was always a large number of things that interrupted the routine. Occasionally, some of the dramas of real life intercede. The one and only time I can remember a medical emergency occurring was, as luck would have it, during the first patrol of a new doctor. One of the men had appendicitis. We had him on a saline drip at one stage. The doctor was sweating quite a bit, not because there was any real danger, but he was so used to being able to do something straight away and was now having to take a slightly different view. We did have operating facilities on board, but I don't know whether anyone ever had to make use of them. There were various guidelines, again, that depended on various states of emergency that existed at the time. There were guidelines under which the patrol might be broken and the man brought back for treatment, but if for example a state of emergency existed, then that would not be permitted. In this instance, I'm glad to say that the chap's appendicitis calmed down, but it caused the patient, doctor and myself a certain amount of sweat for a while.

As far as alcohol was concerned, the wardroom didn't serve spirits at sea and we had an unwritten rule of half a pint of beer or a glass of wine. The senior rates had the same, and the sailors had a can of beer a day, which had to be opened at the time, rather than stocking it up and having five, say, on Friday. There was a lot of discussion about it so we didn't touch our duty-free alcohol supplies. This often caused some discussion with Customs and Excise because when we were in harbour, we used to entertain and do other things. Customs, would you believe, used to insist on boarding the ship when she came back because the MoD wouldn't tell them where she had been and would not confirm that she had not called at another port, which, of course, we hadn't if we had been on patrol.

When we went across to America to fire our missiles, the one thing that gave me great satisfaction was when we left we dived about an hour out of Port Canaveral and we didn't come up for anything or anybody until we were just off Northern Ireland. In fact, we came up spot-on to our position, and we had travelled throughout the entire journey without seeing daylight.

When the Polaris project was launched in 1963, Chief Executive Hugh Mackenzie made a diary note: that the first missile from a British submarine would be fired at 11.15 Eastern Standard Time on 15 February 1968. *Resolution* was indeed in position off Cape Kennedy, Florida, on that day to fire a missile down the US Air Force Eastern Test Range, but she failed to meet the designated firing time by 15 milliseconds. Otherwise all went well. The remaining three Polaris boats were all in service within a year, and in 1969 the RAF Strike Command formally handed over responsibility for the strategic nuclear deterrent to Flag Officer (Submarines). They remained in service until the mid-1990s, having had several refits and their weapons systems upgraded to take the new British warhead Chevaline, and the A3T missiles were replaced by the more powerful A3TK. They were taken out of service progressively from 1993 to 1996, having completed 229 patrols thankfully without having to disturb their slumbering, deadly cargoes in Sherwood Forest. Their role, as we will see, was already in new hands . . . twice as big and more much powerful.

CHAPTER FIFTEEN

Murder, Intrigue and the Sinking of *Belgrano*

The decade of the 1970s brought impressive additions to the British submarine force and, in terms of the workload that now surrounded the nuclear flotillas, they were badly needed. The arrival of the Polaris boats had added to the pressure. The 'bombers' of the fleet which now had prime responsibility for providing Britain's second-strike capability themselves needed bodyguards, and that meant more or less round-the-clock protection supplied by the hunter-killer group. Although the most powerful machines in both size and weaponry, the Polaris submarines were no less vulnerable to attack from enemy hunter-killers, or from any of the increasingly sophisticated anti-submarine systems in the air and on the surface. Because of that, something of a revolution was under way in anti-submarine warfare, with attack submarines also becoming the primary anti-submarine weapons. They were armed with torpedoes and, increasingly, with anti-ship missiles capable of hitting targets 35 to 50 miles away. Strategic submarines carried similar weapons, but as their primary weapons were ballistic missiles with nuclear warheads, it was obviously not advisable that they got into a scrap.

The British submarine service as a whole – conventional and nuclear boats – was kept at full stretch in meeting these demands, juggling the nation's own requirement with attendance to the Cold War and commitments to NATO, including regular major exercises as the tension between East and West ebbed and flowed. After delays during the building of the Polaris boats, the hunter-killer fleet submarines derived from *Dreadnought* in the Valiant and Churchill classes were fully operational by 1972 but, long before the building programme was complete, five more attack submarines were ordered for delivery at regular intervals between 1973 and 1979. They were to be the Swiftsure class, starting with *Swiftsure* (completed in 1973), *Sovereign* (1974), *Superb* (1976), *Sceptre* (1978), *Spartan* and *Splendid* (both 1979). They were all slightly shorter in length than the Valiants, although the beam and depth remained the same. The crews, however, were larger, with 13 officers and 103 ratings.

The work-ups for the new boats were long and arduous, with a variety of new tasks now in view, and throughout these years of building, many of the major systems were being updated. Since only other nuclear boats could keep up with the strategic submarines, the navy was forced to adopt a dual role for their modern nuclear-attack submarines: to attack enemy surface ships and to destroy enemy submarines, if it ever came to it. A daily head-to-head in this tense war of nerves was, however, with the main enemy, the Soviet Union. That put British submarines principally against the three talented Russian Victor classes in the coming decade. The Victor I vessels entered service in 1968, around the time of the first Polaris launch. These and the 6,000-tonne Victor II and III classes of the following decades were fitted with rocket-launched torpedoes or nuclear depth bombs, giving them a battle range extending to 50 nautical miles. China also had strategic submarines on the stocks for 1980, and the French were lining up a flotilla of six. And, of course, submariners in the nuclear age would have the constant worry about the diesel submarine, especially from the Third World, of which there were signs even then of proliferation. Thus, the major fleets were all having to revise their anti-submarine warfare (ASW) strategy. Surface ships engaged in anti-submarine operations suffered the handicap of having sonars that could not operate as freely as those of a submarine. This was overcome to some extent when surface vessels began to tow passive sonar arrays at submarine-like depths. But only submarines could operate near enemy bases and only they could lie in ambush with little chance of being detected.

This was vividly demonstrated in January 1972 while one of Britain's newest frontline SSNs, *Conqueror*, was on patrol in the Atlantic, attempting to locate a possible IRA gunrunning ship. The submarine was scrambled after reports that a Victor-class Russian submarine had penetrated the inner Clyde areas. It turned out to be true and *Conqueror* found the intruder. It was, in the words of an officer, 'pretty exciting stuff . . . We had close passes of less than 1,000 yards with the Russian submarine doing 28 knots and us going in the opposite direction.' This was by no means an isolated incident. Getting up close and personal to each other's submarines was one of the major preoccupations for both sides during much of the Cold War. They were listening to each other's movements, tapping into their signals, tracking the strategic vessels, taking a good look at their exercises and generally playing a deadly cat-and-mouse game.

Britain, meanwhile, had quite a few problems closer to home which entailed the use of submarines in intelligence and surveillance. Operations around Ireland, extending from 1969 until the early 1990s, were mostly in connection with attempting to track possible gunrunning ships, which provided diversions for both nuclear and conventional submarines. Submarines were also used on a regular basis for landing special forces units. Once again, these special operations were becoming a regular feature of submarine work, usually with the Special Boat Service and the Royal Marines. General anti-terrorist activities, other than Northern Ireland, included the new phenomenon of protecting oil and gas installations around Britain's North Sea coastline. Major contingency plans against terrorist attacks, which burgeoned internationally in the 1970s, were drawn up to combat all possible scenarios, such as the capture of one of the installations so that it could be held to ransom.

At the same time, there were also progressive cutbacks in the government's overall defence budget, and although Britain was spending substantially more on fewer submarines it was also quite clear that the country was operating on the basis of bare minimum requirement. By the mid-1970s the submarine service was down to the lowest number of boats since before the First World War. Virtually all remaining Second World War-vintage submarines had been sold, scrapped or used for target practice by the end of the 1960s. The A-class boats, which were first introduced from 1944, were next to go. The remaining 13 had all been taken out of service by 1975, including *Andrew*, the last submarine in the Royal Navy to carry a gun-deck, and *Alliance*, which was preserved at the Royal Navy Submarine Museum at Gosport, Hampshire.

The main conventional thrust was left with 13 Oberon-class boats, which remained on call until the early 1990s, and 8 second Porpoise class, which were also soon to face the axe. That left 11 nuclear boats in 1976 with 3 more due in the second half of the decade. In real terms, annual submarine production by the three main powers was already beginning to peak as conventional submarines dropped out of the budgets. But Britain's number was still on the low side whichever way it was viewed.

The Soviet Union possessed around 246 attack submarines in 1980, of which 87 were nuclear powered and 77 were capable of launching nuclear missiles. They also had 89 SSBNs (ships submersible, ballistic nuclear), which were the equivalent of British Polaris boats. The Americans fielded far fewer than the Soviets: 41 Polaris boats and 89 nuclear-attack submarines. The French later came in with six SSBNs, but it was the British who were logistically in the NATO front line, along with the US boats based at Holy Loch.

British boats were more or less at full stretch throughout these years, and several major refits were scheduled to take some of them temporarily out of commission. There was virtually no scope for mishap or long-term absences through defects. The case for a further increase in the complement of attack submarines was put to Harold Wilson's Labour government and was finally, and somewhat grudgingly, approved. The first of a new and more sophisticated version of the Swiftsure group, to be called the Trafalgar class, was ordered in 1977. *Trafalgar* was scheduled for delivery in 1983, with a second, *Turbulent*, approved to begin building in 1978 for delivery in 1984. Five more would be added to the class – *Tireless, Torbay, Trenchant, Talent* and *Triumph* – between 1985 and 1991. The price had also gone up. Over the decade, the seven Trafalgars would cost a total of £4 billion. This, in turn, led to a major overhaul of the way in which the submarine service was run.

Many British commanders at the sharp end of operations felt that a centralised command and control for all their boats was long overdue, although there was opposition from some of the traditionalists in the naval hierarchy. The British submarines were being sent far and wide by a navy, and submarine service in particular, that was totally preoccupied with the Russians. In addition, they were protecting the deterrent, they were heavily into intelligence-gathering, they were becoming more actively involved in anti-submarine warfare exercises and generally doing everything they could to keep track of what the other side was up to. But because there was only one main adversary, it dictated the way the British command operated.

There were significant additional responsibilities, too. The 1970s were the formative years for a considerable expansion in undersea monitoring activity that went well beyond merely watching and listening to the Russians. While much of the intelligence-gathering and operational tactics for submarines were designed to counter the Russians, this work was locked in to the overall Allied surveillance and intelligence effort first established in the early 1960s but which had grown massively in ten years. The network was a global one, and intelligence, surveillance and reconnaissance (ISR) would involve submarines on an increasing scale.

Submarines were able to intercept signals of critical importance for a wide array of surveillance operations for military or state security. Their ability to remain covertly hidden in sensitive areas for extended periods made it possible to tap into satellites, undersea cables and other sensors without discovery. Submarines operating in the coastal regions were also able to intercept signal formats that were inaccessible to reconnaissance satellites or other forms of surveillance such as spy planes. From this starting point, the use of the submarine force in ISR work more than doubled in the forthcoming decade of the 1980s and, even as the threat posed by the Cold War began to subside in the 1990s, ISR continued to increase against a backdrop of technological revolution, with submarines even more uniquely equipped to keep a watching brief on a variety of opportunities.

A snapshot has emerged of the general level of surveillance, but by and large it remains in the top-secret drawer, especially in Britain. Clues have emerged from the USA, as from nuclear-submarine commander Whitney Mack, who knew only too well the risks of getting in close – and the rewards. Back in 1969, Mack slipped in behind one of the newest Soviet missile submarines and followed her every move for 47 days:

Every 90 minutes, he changed course. It wasn't 89 minutes or 91 minutes; it was exactly 90 minutes. And that's the longest I slept for the whole time. He'd go up, we'd go up, he'd come down, we'd go down. And sometimes we'd go pretty deep. We just did the merry old dance, two 6,000-tonne ships circling each other. I think that probably the most important thing is that when we came back ... we had a tremendous insight into the method of his operations. We could actually separate the different officers of the deck. We knew which guy had the deck just by the way he handled the ship, the way things ran. When you live next door to somebody, you learn a lot about him, and we did. And we brought all that information back. This business of surveillance against the Russians and finding out what they were doing was just like cowboys and Indians. And naturally, as it got more sophisticated, it was a bit more like three-dimensional chess but with the added spur to it, knowing that somebody might be nudging up your backside any minute, and really being quite nasty about it.

American submarines, some operating out of the Scottish base at Holy Loch, and dedicated spy submarines began to push the boundaries of surveillance to a dangerous degree. In a 25,000-word document commissioned by the Scientific and Technical Options Assessment Department of the European Parliament, British investigative journalist Duncan Campbell pinpoints significant developments in the use of submarines for intelligence-gathering:

In October 1971 . . . a US submarine, *Halibut*, visited the Sea of Okhotsk off the eastern USSR and recorded communications passing on a military cable to the Kamchatka Peninsula. *Halibut* was equipped with a deep-diving chamber, fully in view on the submarine's stern. The chamber was described by the US navy as a 'deep submergence rescue vehicle'. The truth was that the 'rescue vehicle' was welded immovably to the submarine. Once submerged, deep-sea divers exited the submarine and wrapped tapping coils around the cable. Having proven the principle, USS *Halibut* returned in 1972 and laid a high-capacity recording pod next to the cable. The technique involved no physical damage and was unlikely to have been readily detectable. The Okhotsk cable-tapping operation continued for ten years . . . new targets were added in 1979. That summer, a newly converted submarine called USS *Parche* travelled from San Francisco under the North Pole to the

Barents Sea and laid a new cable tap near Murmansk. Its crew received a presidential citation for their achievement.

The technology was considerably improved as the decade wore on, and was substantially upgraded during Ronald Reagan's presidency, as reported in a 1999 investigation in America, in which a Nova PBS broadcast revealed:

They [American surveillance specialists] used a specially designed submarine to bury a listening device in the seabed underneath the main Soviet communications cable of the Russian Northern Fleet. They could lift up their cable and inspect it; it would be clean as a whistle. They would lay it down again, right back down on our listening device. From this tap, you'd run a cable off, over 1,200 miles of the seabed to Greenland, where that information would then be up-linked to satellite and down-linked to Washington, and you'd be listening to the Northern Fleet activity as it happened and, in effect, have advance notice for Armageddon. This involved the development of massive amounts of new technology, and, of course, the expenditure of massive amounts of money. The whole thing would have come to about $3 billion. Cheap. For the results that were envisioned, this was going to be cheap. It was the highest-priority and the biggest-budget item in the intelligence budget in the Reagan administration. Then it was stopped because of one guy. Ronald Pelton was an analyst working for the National Security Agency. He was convicted of spying for the KGB, and it was discovered the on-line tap was one of the operations he compromised. But the technology had been developed, and we needed it to get the intelligence that we desperately needed. And that was important. That gave us a lot of confidence. It made us probably a lot calmer than we would have been otherwise, probably a lot less paranoid than we would have been.

All these elements had been bubbling to the surface when the soul-searching that followed the Russian Victor penetrating the inner Clyde brought matters to a head and led to a significant change. A new command and control of all submarine operations was formed at Northwood, outside London. At the end of 1977, Rear-Admiral John Fieldhouse was appointed to take charge and in six weeks had pulled in his team from various submarines and shore bases. He established a centralised operational control centre which became a model for other services. The navy's air and surface commands followed, and eventually they were all brought together, all working in the same operations room.

By September 1980 the last of the Swiftsure class, *Splendid*, completed her contractor's trials to join the force and settled into the patrol routine for what was a fairly busy year. Tension between the West and the Soviet Union was on the rise again. On 17 June Margaret Thatcher's government announced that it would be allowing 160 American-owned cruise missiles to be based in Britain. They would be sited at the US Air Force bases of Greenham Common in Berkshire and Molesworth, Cambridgeshire. This followed the positioning of a large number of Soviet SS-20 rockets in Eastern Europe. The anti-nuclear groups rose up in anger and the Greenham women's peace camp opened up for business. Before the year was out, the demonstrations that were to become a feature of the area for the next 15 years began.

In November Ronald Reagan began his angry tirade

against the Evil Empire. Things were hotting up, and as the Admiralty forked out a downpayment on *Torbay*, to put the fourth member of the Trafalgar class into production, Defence Secretary John Nott produced his controversial plan to prune defence spending elsewhere. Among the navy cuts was the sole bearer of the White Ensign in the southern hemisphere, the ice patrol vessel HMS *Endurance*, to save £3 million a year. Something of a national debate opened up, with letters to *The Times*. The Argentinians were listening. General Leopoldo Fortunato Galtieri, head of the Argentine military junta, decided the moment was right for him to reclaim the Malvinas, as he insisted on calling the Falkland Islands.

The British government and its ministerial team at the Foreign Office had shown a remarkable reluctance to accept that he would even try. Due notice had been served, well in advance. A British embassy naval attaché in Buenos Aires made a report to Whitehall in January predicting almost to the very day an invasion by Argentina. No one paid much heed, even though *Endurance*'s commanding officer, Captain Nick Barker, had been warning of increasing Argentine radio traffic since the beginning of the year. He and others had correctly read the signs, but Foreign Secretary Lord Carrington's late-in-the-day request to keep *Endurance* on station, along with her own detachment of 12 Royal Marines and 42 others in the token garrison at Port Stanley, was turned down by the Cabinet. Minds were only changed at the very last minute when a gang of Argentine scrap dealers landed on South Georgia – not part of the Falklands – and upset the locals.

The submarine service was the first to get the alert. *Splendid*, for example, was chasing a Russian submarine when she was called off by Northwood and ordered to go quickly to Faslane and fill the boat with stores and torpedoes. The order came on 30 March 1982, two days before the invasion. A top-secret classification was slapped on the 'Going South' order, and no telephone calls could be made to relatives by the crew in spite of the fact that *Splendid* had already been at sea for ten weeks. At that point, the crew had no idea of the plan of action, and the politicians probably didn't either. Submarines had been turning up to provide a spot of old-fashioned gunboat diplomacy in British-linked hot spots for years, and they would be there again, three of the best shots in the business, long before the task force was anywhere near ready to sail.

Nuclear power enabled the UK task force commander and former submariner Rear-Admiral Sandy Woodward to have three of his allocated attack submarines on station to enforce the 200-mile Maritime Exclusion Zone around the Falklands by 12 April 1982, ten days after the Argentine invasion. *Spartan* was first to arrive. Having left Gibraltar, she completed the 6,500-mile journey to her designated patrol area in less than ten days, a speed of advance of around 26 knots, which, allowing for navigational checks and going to shallow depth to receive messages, was virtually flat out. *Splendid* and *Conqueror* were not far behind, although a long way back came the diesel-engined *Onyx*, which had a submerged speed of 8 knots. She arrived three weeks after the nuclear boats.

Galtieri's troops had been pouring into the Falklands by then and had taken the token British force of Royal Marines prisoner. Argentinian photographers flashed around the world a photograph of them being marched away with hands over their heads. Margaret Thatcher was furious, and so she might be. In the words of Denis Healey, it had been 'an almighty cockup'. Lord Carrington resigned, accepting full responsibility for 'this national humiliation', along with two other ministers. John Nott offered to go too, but his resignation was rejected. He would, however, depart later. Thatcher responded on the day of the invasion by announcing she was sending a task force of 40 warships and a very large contingent of her finest soldiers, including commandos, Gurkhas and paras with some side action from the SBS and SAS, to get the islands back.

Suddenly, money was no object. First, 2SBS, plus a strong command team, set off by air to Ascension Island to catch either *Spartan* or *Splendid* for a quick route south. That plan was aborted by operational headquarters, CINCFLEET, even as they were en route. Neither submarine was to stop at Ascension and was to make speed to the Falklands. However, 6SBS travelled to Faslane, Scotland, to get a lift with *Conqueror* and set off for the South Atlantic. They were subsequently cross-decked to other transport as politics ruled over military planning and instructions came from on high that *Conqueror* was to go direct to join *Splendid* and *Spartan* patrolling the waters between the Falklands and Argentina.

Information on Argentina for the submarine commander was sparse, to say the least. *Jane's* provided the best intelligence. Whitehall and the Ministry of Defence had little to offer in the way of up-to-date information about the Argentine fleet and what kind of opposition or anti-submarine operations the British boats might expect.

Splendid, commanded by Commander Roger Lane-Nott, arrived on station 11 days after leaving Faslane, her journey down utilised for a heavy training programme that involved a great deal of effort on the part of every member of the crew. Commander Jim Taylor in *Spartan* had already begun his patrol, but both commanders were short of information. They were eventually tasked by submarine HQ to locate and observe a suspected movement of Argentine ships towards the Falkland Islands, including the aircraft carrier *25th May* and the cruiser *General Belgrano*. The British submarines moved in to find them. *Spartan* would cover the east, off Port Stanley, and *Splendid* was first positioned to the west, between the islands and the Argentine coast. It was a slow process because they had no idea where they were. They did know, however, that the Argentinians had a US-built Guppy-class diesel submarine transmitting somewhere around the Falklands.

Splendid was then moved to patrol the northern end of the Falkland Sound, since there was a great fear that the *25th May* would get into that area before the British task force arrived so that she could extend the range of her aircraft armed with Exocet missiles. The submarine hung around for a couple of days, but the carrier did not arrive and *Splendid* was assigned to intercept anything between the islands and the Argentine bases. Diplomatic efforts were still proceeding, and the rules of engagement were still changing from 'sink' to 'do not sink Argentinian ships'. On 26 April *Splendid* reported to Northwood that she had sighted an Argentine task group composed of two type-42 destroyers together with Exocet frigates moving south along the coast. It was possible they were going to escort the carrier in, but once again there was no sign of the carrier. *Splendid's* commander had had the destroyers in his periscope sights but did not have rules of engagement and could not fire. Instead, he was ordered to break off and join the hunt elsewhere. In the absence of *25th May*, the principal target in this operation by the British submarines, concern switched to the cruiser *General Belgrano*, now thought to be moving towards the exclusion zone. *Splendid* went north with *Spartan* between Argentina and the task force, while *Conqueror* searched to the south.

The rules of engagement had started to become specific, and the British made known her intention to order the sinking of anything within the 200-mile exclusion zone. The Argentinians would also be aware that nuclear submarines were prowling the area.

On 1 May, however, *Conqueror*'s CO, Chris Wreford-Brown, found *General Belgrano* in his sights. His submarine's nuclear power allowed him to track the cruiser for 30 hours and choose the moment for attack when authorised to do so. The 'sink her' command came from London, and he fired a salvo of three ancient Mark VIII torpedoes from 1,100 metres. They were straight-running, non-homing torpedoes of 1940s vintage, travelling at 45 knots, and two of them struck on a right-angle track. GOTCHA! trumpeted Kelvin Mackenzie, editor of the *Sun* newspaper, in his headline over a photograph of the stricken cruiser, which sank fast with the loss of 362 lives. The question arose immediately as to whether the ship was inside or outside the exclusion zone. As it transpired, it was outside and had been for six hours. The question, as far as the three submarine commanders were concerned, was immaterial, and indeed Northwood and the naval high command could, and probably did, advise that ships engaged in anti-submarine warfare were frequently pointing away from the direction they intended to go. They were at one in concluding that just because *Belgrano* happened to be pointing in the wrong direction when she was sunk did not mean the ship was not a threat to the task force. If, possibly as part of an Argentine pincer movement, the cruiser had been allowed to get through, the submariners would have been castigated because the ship would have posed an immediate threat to the British ships.

The situation would get bad enough as it was. Argentine aircraft, flying low to avoid radar, fired deadly French-built

Exocet missiles from a range of about 20 miles, causing much grief to the task force. HMS *Sheffield* and her sister ship *Coventry* were both sunk, with 46 men killed. Two others, *Ardent* and *Antelope*, were sunk in what became known to the sailors as bomb alley. The supply ship *Atlantic Conveyor* and troop carriers *Sir Galahad* and *Sir Tristram* were also hit.

The age-old British pastime of crucifying men whose colleagues see them as heroes soon came into play, caught up in the politics of the affair. Why had the submarine fired when *Belgrano* was turning away? That was the nub of the ensuing debate, and critics, helped by the disclosures of civil servant Clive Ponting, eventually drew admissions from the government on the timing of the sighting of *Belgrano* and the direction in which she was sailing. Mrs Thatcher, however, refused to back down from her stance that the sinking of *Belgrano* was a necessity of war and probably saved many British lives. The commanders of the three nuclear submarines had no doubt about that.

The affair was not done with yet. Labour MP Tam Dalyell and *Mirror* columnist Paul Foot saw a conspiracy coming on. Already dissecting, minute by minute, the last journey of the *Belgrano*, a new development brought a murder into their theories. The victim was Miss Hilda Murrell, a vociferous anti-nuclear campaigner and the aunt of Commander Robert Green, staff officer (intelligence) to CINCFLEET at Northwood at the time the order to fire was relayed to Wreford-Brown. Her body was found some distance from her house, and soon a flurry of articles and later a couple of books purported to show that Miss Murrell had been murdered by MI5. They were disturbed, so the story went, when they broke into her house to retrieve secret documents left there by Green, panicked and killed her, then removed her body to cover their tracks. Some newspapers even managed to have

Green aboard the *Conqueror* at the time *Belgrano* was sunk, and the documents were his log of events on the submarine. But Green was at Northwood. Although some suspicious circumstances surrounding the death were never fully investigated (thus leaving room for further speculation), the remainder of the saga, which dragged on for a decade or more, is barely worth repeating now: suffice to say that Dalyell eventually conceded that Hilda Murrell's murder had nothing to do with the sinking of *Belgrano*. Green himself had said it all along.

Captain Wreford-Brown, meanwhile, was caught up in the politics, the intrigue and the conspiracy theories. He was pilloried in the media, and his colleagues were, as one put it, 'absolutely disgusted at the way he was hounded by Tam Dalyell . . . it showed a complete lack of understanding of what had actually gone on. If he had just read the reports and tried to understand what was happening, instead of the nonsense he spoke, it would have been better for everyone. His personal abuse and insults directed at Wreford-Brown in particular were nothing short of disgraceful.'

The reports referred to came from the submarine logs at the time, which showed that the three commanders were pursuing both the Argentine cruiser and an aircraft carrier simultaneously, and they appeared to be working towards a pincer movement that would have put British ships at risk, including the aircraft carriers *Hermes* and *Invincible*. Wreford-Brown himself waited ten years before commenting publicly, in an interview with the *Guardian*. 'I knew exactly what happened,' he said. 'I suppose to me things were pretty cut and dried so I probably don't know why they weren't so cut and dried in other people's minds.'

He believed the controversy surrounding the sinking was unnecessary and the fact that *Belgrano* changed course and was sailing away from the British task force when she was hit was 'in military thinking a red herring'. He strongly supported the change in the rules of engagement, passed by the War Cabinet at the request of the military on the morning of 2 May, which allowed him to launch the attack, because the cruiser still could have been a threat to the British task force. In his opinion, the change of direction meant little. 'Although, where it was at the time, the rules of engagement were explicit that we couldn't attack it, we felt from the military point of view, as opposed to the political point of view, that those rules ought to be changed and indeed that the force ought to be neutralised,' said Wreford-Brown. He had signalled naval fleet headquarters regarding the change of course on the morning of 2 May. The authorisation to attack came that afternoon. He described the attack as an unemotional moment, like a well-rehearsed drill, and having given the order to fire and having heard the torpedoes run out, having heard and seen them hit, the first emotion was one of having achieved something successful. There was a sense of relief that they had hit the target. 'We might have been more controversial among the military if we had missed,' he said. 'Any loss of life is unfortunate, but I don't dwell on it. I think the reason it doesn't affect me is that at the end of the day those who join the armed forces have to accept that they have joined to kill, if necessary. We were in a submarine attacking a ship as against attacking men. You don't actually see the men or hear them or anything like that. It is conducted at a distance which removes the thought processes you're suggesting I might have had.'

After the attack, the submarine took evasive measures on the assumption, at first, that they were being pursued by *Belgrano*'s escort destroyers, although that proved not to be the case. Wreford-Brown was proud of his ship's company. It was a team operation, and if any submarine was going to carry out the attack he was delighted it was *Conqueror*, although he admitted that the political furore over the government's handling of the *Belgrano* affair brought a few cynical smiles to his lips.

Interestingly, a slightly different perspective is given by a junior officer on *Conqueror*, in extracts from his diary also published in the *Guardian*. Lieutenant Narendra Sethia wrote:

> This afternoon I knew what fear was. At 1400 we received a signal, authorising us to sink the *Belgrano*, even though it was outside our exclusion zone. We had been trailing her for more than 25 hours and held her usually at PO [periscope observation]. After tracking her for a while we went to action stations around 1500 and shut off for attack. The tension in the control room was mounting steadily. At about 1600, we fired three Mark VIII torpedoes. The atmosphere was electric . . . forty-three seconds after discharge, we heard the first explosion, followed by two more . . . the control room was in an uproar, 30 people shouting and cheering.

Sethia said that the skipper ordered shut-off for counter-attack and took drastic evasive measures, plummeting down to 150 metres. For an hour, the boat hurtled along at full speed, and suddenly it seemed that they were the hunted:

> I felt scared, almost trembling, sweating and nauseated. I thought of what we had done – of the men we had killed; although we may not have sunk the cruiser, the captain said he had seen flashes of orange flame as the

weapons hit . . . We thus became the first British submarine to fire a weapon in anger since the Second World War. As I write, I am still a bit overwhelmed by it all and can hardly believe the enormity of what we have done. I wonder how many died? I wonder, even more, what the reaction will be? The lads have all taken it very well – a couple were very frightened outwardly and the rest of us made do with being frightened inwardly. We had a glass of wine in the wardroom and spent the evening discussing what had happened.

After the sinking, it became clear that the submarines would not see much more action. The message had gone out loud and clear. The Argentinians knew the nuclear submarines were down there and their ships retreated (although Argentine submarines were thought to be operating). *Splendid* had had technical problems with one of the two turbogenerators. A spare part was sent from her home base by Hercules aircraft, packed in a timber case, and was parachuted to the boat at a rendezvous position. It was so heavy, however, that when the crate hit the water the box splayed open and the machinery sank. A replacement was sent a week later, but that became contaminated with sea water. By then, repairs were critical, and the submarine engineers devised a way of carrying out the repairs. The work had to be done at a time of mountainous seas and winds blowing at Storm Force 12, which made it impossible to stay at periscope depth. The commander had to go to 106 metres and shut down while the repairs were being carried out. It was touch and go whether the battery would last. Fortunately, the engineers managed to do the work in time, and it was the only significant defect that occurred during the 12 weeks they were away.

So that was that, the task completed, and all that remained was to record the irony of the situation – that a whole generation of submariners had been trained to perfection in their hi-tech world and spent their entire careers focused on one potential enemy: the Soviet Union. Yet the first nuclear submarine ever to fire a weapon in anger anywhere in the world did so using torpedoes of a type first produced in 1928 to sink a ship, *General Belgrano*, of Second World War vintage.

CHAPTER SIXTEEN

Trident, the £12 Billion
Insurance Policy

The use of nuclear-powered submarines during the Falklands War provided a vision for the future that captured the imagination of some politicians. Others, of course, remained firmly against them and all forms of weapons of mass destruction. Many in Whitehall saw nothing else but big, fast, heavily armed submarines that could reach out to anywhere on the earth's surface in relatively short order. They could see no point in having any other vessels, and pointed out that America had long since ditched her conventional boats. As *Conqueror* discovered in operations delivering the special forces to covert operations in the Falklands, nuclear-powered boats were not always suited to close inshore work, especially around relatively uncharted coastlines when, in any event, the dangers of attack were always greater.

A detailed study was ordered to discover if it was feasible to gather up some of the technology and features of the hunter-killer nuclear group and amalgamate them as a workable package inside a conventional diesel-powered submarine. The aim was to build a boat with enhanced electronics and weaponry while at the same time being available to mount coastal operations in support of the special forces.

Out of this study came a proposal for a new Upholder class. The boats would be fitted with all the computer power and the sensors of a nuclear boat and were described at the time as a substantial leap forward in technology for the Royal Navy. Eighteen were planned, and there were high hopes that they would attract a worthwhile volume of export orders. Vickers, who won the contract for building the first four, were charged with integrating the construction features of the Trafalgar-class SSNs into the new design. The boat was 70.25 metres in length with a submerged displacement of 2,400 tonnes. The class was named after the boat commanded by Lieutenant-Commander Wanklyn, VC, during his exploits in the Mediterranean, and indeed carried his crest. Upholder was packed with exclusive technology in sonar, intercept sonar, navigation radar and a significant array of weaponry capable of discharging heavyweight torpedoes, anti-ship missiles and submarine mines.

The command system, according to Vickers' sales sheet, was 'a fully integrated computerised suite which provided long-range detection and attack capabilities . . . and also processes visual data from the periscope, information from the radar and manual inputs such as navigational data'. In other words, they were probably the best conventional submarines ever built, certainly in terms of technology. There was another advantage: they came with automatic surveillance systems, which meant that the crew was cut to the bare minimum – 47 men, compared with 120 for a similar SSN or

75 for the conventional Oberon class which the Upholder was replacing.

After such a build-up, submariners could not wait to get their hands on the Upholder squadron, especially those who still had a great affection for the conventional boats. They were set down for immediate construction, and work on the first one, *Upholder*, began in 1985. Given that the building time was around four years, she was eventually commissioned in 1990, although there was a further delay in getting her into service because of a design problem with the torpedo tubes. Meanwhile, the remainder of the squadron, *Unseen*, *Ursula* and *Unicorn*, were produced by 1992, two of them at the Cammell Laird yard. But a lot happened between the time of approval and final delivery in the early 1990s. When the time came, the Upholder squadron barely had time to get out into open seas before they were pulled back, mothballed, put up for sale and then lay idle for the rest of the century.

Three developments brought about that decision. First, Britain's much-vaunted Trident programme to build four massive strategic submarines to replace the Polaris squadron was given the go-ahead by the government in 1982 for completion in 1994, when Polaris would be almost 20 years old. The cost: an estimated £14 billion (in fact it came in £2 billion under budget), plus £200 million a year running costs for 30 years – the largest single item of expenditure by the Ministry of Defence in British history. It caused major controversy, given the mood of the nation at the time, with increasing unemployment and factory closures, rioting in the streets, IRA bombings and the upcoming miners' strike. Thatcher pressed on regardless.

When Upholder and Trident were ordered, Ronald Reagan was in the first half of his presidency, and the Cold War was still in deep freeze. The Russians were as busy as ever, and so the game of cat and mouse went on. But then in 1989, as one optimist put it, 'the Communists came out with their hands up'. The need for 18 new Upholder-class submarines no longer seemed pressing – nor, indeed, did a number of other things as the politicians peered through their rose-tinted spectacles at the state of the world and the prospects of a modern equivalent of 'peace in our time'. And so the third, and defining, development that affected the future of the Upholder class came in 1992. The Soviet Union, which then had 62 submarines carrying ballistic missiles – more than the number all the Allies had put together – had pretty well packed up and gone home, for the time being at least. John Major's government saw this as an opportunity to make swingeing cuts in the defence budgets, across the board and affecting all three services. The result, for the submarine service, was that the four Upholder boats were mothballed and remained idle until a lease-purchase agreement was made with Canada, after a good deal of toing and froing, for delivery in 2000. That was a disappointment to many, and especially to those who had built them. They had proved to be everything that was expected of them, except that they failed to attract any other export orders. So the Upholders sailed off into the sunset towards Canada, where they would be renamed.

In the event, the collapse of communism and the retreat of Russian submarines more or less signalled the end for conventional diesel/electric submarines in a modern British force on the grounds that only nuclear boats met the requirements of speed and mobility for the global role now envisaged. At the same time, the submarine service found itself moving away from independent, covert operations to become more closely integrated with the various joint task groups in both national and NATO operations. Submarines remained a favourite for inserting special forces into littorals. There was no other mode of transport that combined stealth and endurance with communications equipment, sensors and navigation suites to ensure precise insertion of the special units towards their objectives. The Americans were already reviewing their own requirements for their special forces troops, and out of those deliberations for clandestine insertions came a new breed of midget submarines that will undoubtedly take their place in the twenty-first century. First trialled in the USA in 1998, they are 19.8 metres long, have a crew of two and can carry a special forces squad to the very edge of their target area. The mini-subs are piggybacked by a host SSN and then unloaded to carry the military or surveillance team on the final leg of its journey into hostile territory and bring it out by the same means.

The whole question of what Britain's submarine force would look like in the first decade of the new millennium came under review as the Polaris squadron, along with the remaining British fleet submarines of the Valiant and Swiftsure classes, approached the end of their time. The Valiant and Churchill boats were decommissioned in the first half of the 1990s, followed by the Resolution class that carried Polaris. That left the service with 12 nuclear-powered fleet submarines. The five Swiftsure class had proved to be excellent boats, although one of them, class leader *Swiftsure*, was subsequently laid up under the 1992 budget cuts. The remainder, with weapons upgrades and refits, would need replacing between 2003 and 2006. The seven Trafalgar submarines would remain in business until at least the end of the first decade of the twenty-first century.

The Trident strategic-missile squadron, moving in to replace Polaris between 1994 and 2001, loomed large at the top of the family tree. Military analysts were agreed that the volatility of Russia would not necessarily be cured by a change of leadership but more likely held back by financial constraints. At best, the accelerator pedal could be eased up a touch, but the Trident programme remained the big story in terms of British military and naval history. Delivery of the first boat in 1994 saw the end of a 14-year research, development and production programme that dwarfed Polaris.

The project began back in 1980 when the American Congress agreed to sell Britain the Trident D5 missile, a three-stage solid-fuel rocket approximately 13 metres long, 2 metres in diameter and each weighing 60 tonnes. It had a range of over 6,000 kilometres. Each missile was capable of carrying up to 12 nuclear warheads and delivering them on to different targets supposedly with incredible accuracy. As with the Polaris agreement, Britain would build her own warheads and the submarines that carry them. The warheads were designed by the Atomic Weapons Research Establishment at Aldermaston, and it would require the largest submarine ever built in the United Kingdom to accommodate this collection of city-flatteners, with 16 missiles in each submarine.

The boat is more than 150 metres in length and over 16,000 tonnes, more than twice the displacement of the Polaris submarines of the Resolution class. To get an idea of its size, which is difficult to picture even when only half-submerged, *Vanguard* is slightly smaller than the *Invincible* aircraft carrier. Yet she carries a crew of only 132 officers and men, compared with a Polaris submarine's 149. This is possible because of increased automation in a number of the systems. The 16-tube missile compartment was based on the design of the 24-tube system used by the United States navy's Ohio-class Trident submarines. The *Vanguard* submarine is capable of carrying 192 warheads, although Britain has a policy of limiting its boats to no more than 96 deployed at any one time; the power, however, is still exceedingly potent.

As with Polaris, extensive support facilities were needed at Faslane, the home of the strategic nuclear deterrent force, and at the Royal Naval Armament Depot at Coulport, although this time the missiles themselves were to be returned to the United States Strategic Weapons Facility at Kings Bay in Georgia for reprocessing at periodic intervals. The first submarine, *Vanguard*, was commissioned on time in December 1994, followed by *Victorious* in 1995, *Vigilant* in 1997 and *Vengeance* in 1999.

Vanguard started sea trials in October 1992. The first missile was fired on 26 May 1994 on the American test range, with the updated version of Trident now installed, and the first operational patrol was completed early in 1995. At the time, the missiles could be made ready to fire within 15 minutes of the order, but in the Strategic Defence Review in 1998 readiness to fire was relaxed 'to days rather than minutes'. In addition to its responsibility for the United Kingdom's nuclear deterrent force, the Royal Navy continued to plan around the three core capabilities provided by nuclear-powered submarines, aircraft carrier task groups and amphibious forces.

Although vastly bigger in every respect, the space for crew in *Vanguard* barely altered. Operational areas are still cramped and, as ever, miles of internal cabling and pipework run through the boat like continuous giant graffiti on the ceilings and walls. Every available space has been utilised for the network of electronics and consoles. The rest of the spare space is filled with boxes of food in the early days of a patrol. Although around 75 per cent of the crews are volunteers who wouldn't swap their life, some are conscripted from general service to make up the numbers and are less keen on the idea of spending weeks at sea in an environment in which privacy remains an unattainable luxury. Many, however, stay on.

Life aboard the Trident boats is much the same as preceding classes, with sleeping arrangements for the ratings that were never designed to accommodate the larger male form. Hot-bunking, where men coming off duty take over the bed of one going on, remains a fact of life, especially when trainees are on board and the daily routine of the officers and men differs little from that of the Polaris boats. They operate in shifts around the clock; although many of the monitoring tasks are now automated, the crew still need to confirm the computers' self-diagnosis and to check the dials of the nuclear reactor and watch and listen to the sonar stations for any activity.

Drills to test emergency procedures for fire, damage and escape are regularly performed. They are challenging and noisy, as if in a real alert, and are designed to keep every level of the boat's crew safe and on top form. There are good recreation and keep-fit facilities and, of course, the chefs work wonders in a galley that is the size of a kitchen in an average-sized home. The missile compartment is a spectacular, if frightening, sight, with the 16 heavyweight missiles poised for dispatch if Armageddon ever arrives. The very sight of them reinforces the need for careful selection of the men who are to work in this clinical, pristine environment with the ceaseless hum of the nuclear reactor a constant reminder to all on board of its great power.

Those who have not volunteered may find the life stressful to begin with, although most generally get used to it and enjoy the camaraderie. It does occasionally happen, however, that the claustrophobic atmosphere, the time spent under water and never seeing daylight, the thought of the missiles and concern about their families on shore or other personal troubles can combine to have an unsettling effect.

Wives and partners of non-volunteers are also more likely to find the prospect of their menfolk being away for perhaps three months with no real contact except in true emergencies difficult to come to terms with. They feel it most when untoward incidents occur, such as the loss of the Russian submarine *Kursk* with all hands, or reports of defects on Britain's nuclear boats, which became prevalent at the end of the 1990s. For the most part, Trident crews slip into the routine without a hint of disquiet about their increased firepower, and the implications had been well discussed in advance, both in training and in the messes. If their reason for being is ever questioned, those whose lives and careers are tied to nuclear boats will still recite the message back, loud and clear: 'Who knows for sure that the Russians will remain peaceful? These missiles are the best insurance policy we've got against attack. Their predecessors stood us in good stead, and we've gone for half a century without a single nuclear incident. Now, we live in more dangerous times – there are a few madmen about who might not be so restrained.'

That is a reference to the modern age of rogue dictators and pariah states who are striving for nuclear capability, along with an increasing number of developing countries buying submarines from which to fire newly acquired weapons. The prospect that it may be necessary to put on a show of menace by the nuclear boats if some overambitious nation prepares to start flinging their stuff around is never far from their thoughts.

Nor was Trident enough. A new line-up of fleet submarines to replace the Swiftsure and Trafalgar classes was ordered in March 1997 when the Ministry of Defence announced a £2 billion contract for the new class, to be known as the Astute. They were given the names *Astute*, *Ambush* and *Artful* and were promised to be the largest, quietest, fastest and most powerful hunter-killer submarines ever built by the Royal Navy. The Astute class, eventually expected to be ten strong, is 40 per cent larger than the Trafalgar design and loaded with Spearfish torpedoes and Harpoon anti-ship missiles and are able to carry Tomahawk land-attack cruise missiles. They are powered by Rolls-Royce PWR2 nuclear reactors. The boats are being built by BAE Systems at their Vickers yard in Barrow, and the MoD reckoned that 7,000 jobs were secured as a result of this order at a variety of locations across the UK. The Astute class also has a new tactical weapon system which was first fitted to the Trafalgar-class boats as part of an extensive upgrade programme.

The purchase of the Tomahawk cruise missiles required the dispensation of the US Congress, and the first British submarine to receive the Tomahawk was *Splendid*, which travelled to America for its test-firing off the coast of California in November 1998. Within five months, *Splendid* was using them for real – in the first-ever offensive using cruise missiles launched from a British nuclear submarine, and the first weapons fired in anger since *Conqueror* sank *Belgrano*. The action came during the Kosovo crisis, when *Splendid*, under the command of Commander Richard Baker, joined US submarines in the NATO bombing operations against Yugoslavia in March 1999. Commander Baker was subsequently awarded the OBE, while Petty Officer Lee Goldhill, Chief Petty Officer Robert Newbitt and Petty Officer Andrew Newney were awarded MBEs in the 2000 New Year's Honours List.

The cruise missile attacks were among the most controversial of the bombing campaign against Yugoslavia and were used in the strike against the building which housed the Serbian television station and the party headquarters of President Milošević in Belgrade. Sixteen civilians were killed in the attack and twenty were injured. According to US officials, the property was targeted specifically to 'maximise the domestic and international propaganda value of seeing such a high-profile building in the Belgrade skyline under fire'. Planners assessed which parts of the building were most likely to contain the controls for fire alarms and sprinkler systems, and the missiles were targeted directly into the sixth floor and on to the roof to increase the chance that any fire they caused would spread.

According to a summary of the cruise attacks published in *Jane's Defence Weekly*, *Splendid* fired 20 Tomahawk cruise missiles during the war, 17 of which hit their targets. US ships and submarines fired 218 cruise missiles at 66 targets, and 181 reached their 'intended aim-points' according to US naval officers. The attack on the television building was strongly criticised by US human rights groups and Amnesty International, but NATO's supreme commander at the time, General Wesley Clark, and his British counterparts insisted that the building was a legitimate military target because it was used to pass information to Serbian military units in Kosovo and to promote Serbian propaganda.

British submarines also launched the first strikes against the Taliban regime in Afghanistan as the war on international terrorism opened up after the atrocities in New York on 11 September 2001. The submarines *Triumph* and *Trafalgar* played their full part in the attack launched by the naval battle group hastily assembled by America and Britain in response to the terrorist attacks on America. They targeted Taliban military positions and Osama Bin Laden's terrorist bases using Tomahawk cruise missiles launched from the British and

American submarines and destroyers in the Persian Gulf and Arabian Sea. *Trafalgar* was already in the region as part of the huge British military exercise, Saif Sareea II, in Oman and *Triumph* was moved into position at the end of September. The Royal Navy's Tomahawk land attack missile, known as T-Lam, was the Allies' weapon of choice for precision strikes on ground targets. Each missile costs about £300,000 and can carry a 1,000lb high-explosive warhead or large numbers of combined-effect bomblets that pepper the target. During the initial days of the campaign, seaborne cruise missiles were fired at 31 targets inside Afghanistan. Three were in Kabul itself, and four against large settlements. The remainder were fired at Taliban air installations, aircraft, early warning radar systems, military positions and Bin Laden's terrorist training camps.

This initial bombardment neutralised the Taliban air defences, paving the way for the massive Allied airborne attacks that ensued over the next nine weeks. 'We were generally pleased with these early results,' said General Richard Myers, chairman of the US joint chiefs of staff. He reported that the demolition job by the submarines on airfields and the Defence Ministry building in Kabul in these attacks proved invaluable to the swift progress of the war against the Taliban regime. Other areas targeted by the submarines included the northern city of Jalalabad, where Osama Bin Laden had a number of bases, and on the Taliban's spiritual home, Kandahar, in the south. In all, 50 Tomahawk cruise missiles were fired by the British and American navies in the first round of attacks.

The use of submarines in the kind of operations that engaged them for Kosovo and Afghanistan was a significant departure from the established pattern of patrols and surveillance. It also gave a pointer to the future and the kind of situations that might engage the British submarine service in its more global approach. Warning signs of possible future trouble spots were already evident at the dawn of the new millennium. While both Russia and America had reduced their submarine fleets substantially in the previous decade, other nations around the world were beginning to build small but significant submarine flotillas. Some, like China and Israel, were thought to have nuclear warheads.

A clear pattern was emerging: with the Cold War over, a good deal of the hardware produced during that era was now heading for the open market. Manufacturers and agents began looking for outlets for their machines and weaponry now that the more readily available home market had dried up, not just in Russia, but in the USA and across Europe. By the mid-1990s, more than 20 developing countries possessed a variety of diesel attack submarines. North Korea had 25, India 22, Turkey 15, Greece 10, Egypt 8, Libya 6 and Pakistan 8. Two Russian Kilo-class submarines delivered to Iran immediately began sea trials and menacing operations, including torpedo-firing tests, near the Persian Gulf, raising the spectre of future trouble. China was known to have a fairly large force of diesel submarines and five SSNs bought from Russia. Many boats bought by developing nations in the 1980s and 1990s were obsolete, worn out and operated by poorly trained crews. They presented no threat to the navies of the developed world. But by the end of the century the complexion of these submarine flotillas was changing and there was every sign that the trend would continue. Third World nations began to purchase advanced vessels and systems from Russia and Western European countries where traditional markets had diminished.

German manufacturers in particular set up promotional deals to boost sales, which included training packages. This in turn encouraged competition from manufacturers in other countries offering such things as finance and servicing packages. Germany also made manufacturing deals with South Korea, India and Argentina. Russia, desperate for hard currency, sells to all and sundry, including modern vessels to China which, in turn, sold her outdated Romeo-class submarines to North Korea and Egypt. France supplied its Daphne and more modern Agosta models to Pakistan. Sweden sold to Malaysia and launched a marketing drive in southern Asia. In 1996 the US government gave approval for the production of diesel-powered boats in spite of the fact that the US navy runs only nuclear-powered boats, which meant the former could only be sold abroad.

By the end of the twentieth century, submarine salesmen were travelling the globe offering new and used boats and beneficial deals. They were followed by the weapons salesmen. America sold Harpoon missiles to Israel, Pakistan and others. The French aggressively marketed a submarine version of the deadly Exocet missile that caused so much damage in the hands of the Argentinians in the Falklands War. Russia offered a large stock of sophisticated weaponry. Like the arming of Saddam Hussein by Britain and the West in the 1980s, trouble is being stored up for the future.

Worse still are the implications for future terrorist attacks. A wealthy terror group or rogue nation with a half-decent submarine and a clutch of high-powered weapons could make a very nasty dent in London or New York. The Americans are so concerned about this possibility that the CIA and the FBI joined forces with naval intelligence to work out counter-measures to foil any such attempt. The navy told them it was virtually impossible to say with absolute certainty that a determined submarine commander could be prevented from penetrating US defences, and the spectre of *Red October* still existed. Attack submarines in the hands of rogue states or terrorists could also pose a substantial threat to naval and commercial shipping. As *Conqueror* showed when she sank *Belgrano* with Second World War-vintage torpedoes, hi-tech gear is not necessary to wreak havoc and, as with much of the arms industry, the salesmen were out in force while their governments issued doom-laden warnings of the impending upsurge in terrorism.

Safety concerns of another kind were brought to the attention of the European Parliament in a 1998 report and resolution concerning the 'imminent threat to the global environment, safety and security created by nuclear submarines and submarine reactor decommissioning'. These took the form of recommendations about the way in which the West ought to cooperate with Russia in cleaning up its highly dangerous stock of rusting nuclear submarines. First, there were some interesting, and previously unrevealed, statistics about close encounters during the Cold War. In the period between 1965 and 1995, there were 13 direct collisions between United States, Russian/Soviet, French, British and Chinese nuclear submarines or nuclear submarines and military surface ships, 2 of them occurring after the Cold War had ended. In the same period, 7 nuclear reactors were lost at sea when nuclear-powered submarines sank, 43 Soviet and 7 US nuclear warheads were lost at sea, and there were 612 incidents involving US nuclear submarines alone. The figures were not available from Russia.

The report centred on fears already expressed by Alexei Yablokov, chairman of the Russian Ecological Safety Commission and former adviser to President Yeltsin, that many submarines of the Russian navy had become 'floating Chernobyls and environmental catastrophes'. The problem was highlighted by the near meltdown of several nuclear submarine reactors on 20 September 1995 at a nuclear submarine base on the Kola Peninsula, after the electricity supply had been cut off because the Russian navy hadn't paid its bill. The Russian Nuclear State Inspectorate made clear that submarines awaiting decommissioning had become floating spent fuel bins in an unsatisfactory condition and that boats of the former Russian Northern and Pacific fleets had accumulated so much nuclear waste that they had run out of storage space. The report called on the EU and America to cooperate with Russia to avert a real crisis in the management of decommissioned Soviet submarines. At the time of writing, there had been no satisfactory resolution to the problem.

Britain also ran into trouble with concerns over a totally different aspect of safety, resulting in all 12 of the Swiftsure- and Trafalgar-class nuclear-attack submarines being temporarily withdrawn from service in November 2000. The move followed the discovery of a leak in the pressurised water reactor cooling circuits of *Tireless*. Initially, it was thought that the fault was an isolated weld failure, but after closer investigation the Ministry of Defence announced that it could be a generic fault. Initial checks to six boats have revealed similar defects, but no leaks. All the fleet submarines were immediately withdrawn for repairs. The four Vanguard-class Trident ballistic-missile submarines were not affected and remained operational. The repair work was not as simple as first thought, and the submarines were laid up for months. Although other defects had been reported and resolved over the years, this was the first major problem that the Royal Navy had experienced.

There was, on the other hand, a more gratifying statistic that enables us to close this account on a more upbeat note. In the first half of this century of submarine history, wars not included, Britain lost 170 submarines and, in consequence, many hundreds of crew members died. In the second half of the century, only three submarines were lost and all predated the nuclear vessels. Not a single British nuclear submarine has ever been in trouble in spite of their presence at the forefront of a particular kind of war that could have exploded into some great catastrophe at any moment. Yet those same British boats were called into offensive action only twice in 50 years – for the Falklands and Kosovo – the only section of the British forces which, if judged on the strength of weapons fired when compared with other sections of the military, appeared to have been seriously unemployed. That was never the case.

Simply put, the submariners held the line.

APPENDIX

Principal Classes in a Century of British Submarine History

Non-Nuclear Boats

Holland class
Vickers Son and Maxim, Barrow-in-Furness, built 5 boats of the original *Holland* design at a cost of £35,000 each, as described in Chapter One. The first was launced in 1901 and commissioned on 2 February 1903. Displacement submerged: 120–150 tonnes; dimensions: length 19.48 metres, beam 3.64 metres, depth 3.58 metres; crew: 7; propulsion: a single 4-cylinder 250-hp petrol engine and a 74-bhp motor when submerged. Speed: 8 knots (surface), 5 knots (submerged). Torpedoes: 1 × 35.56-centimetre. All were treated cautiously by the Royal Navy after *Holland 1* was damaged by an explosion of petrol vapour a month after delivery, killing 4 of the crew, on 4 March 1903. All 5 were taken out of service by 1912. *Holland 1* sank off Plymouth while being towed to the scrapyard. The boat was found by divers in 1981 and was

subsequently raised and placed on permanent display at the Royal Navy Submarine Museum at Gosport, Hampshire.

A-class

Built to the Royal Navy's own specifications, based on the *Holland* but with the addition of a conning tower and ironing out some of the flaws. The class was also modified during the building programme, and the second version had a displacement submerged of 207 tonnes. Dimensions: length 30.17 metres, beam 3.81 metres, depth 3.5 metres; crew: 14; propulsion: 550-hp petrol engine on the surface and 150-hp electric motor submerged. Speed: 11.5 knots (surface), 7 knots (submerged). Torpedoes: 2 × 45.7-centimetre. Of the 14 that were built, 6 were lost or severely damaged in accidents.

B-class

An improved version of the A-class, although initially still built for use in home waters in a defensive role. Later additions to the class were, however, dispatched to the Mediterranean and the Dardanelles at the onset of the First World War. Displacement submerged: 313 tonnes; dimensions: 41.15 by 4 by 3.6 metres; crew: 13; propulsion: 6-cylinder, 550-hp petrol engine (surface), 180-hp electric motor (submerged). Speed: 12 knots (surface), 8 knots (submerged). Torpedo tubes: 2 × 45.7-centimetre bow tubes. Of the 11 built, 2 were lost. In service from 1904 to 1922.

C-class

Enlarged version of the A- and B-classes, and many changes were made to improve surface operation and seaworthiness.

Even so, submariners led eventful lives. Displacement submerged: 320 tonnes; dimensions: 43.5 by 4 by 3.5 metres; crew: 16; propulsion: 600-bhp petrol engine (surface), 200-bhp electric motor (submerged). Speed: 13 knots (surface), 8 knots (submerged). Torpedoes: 2 × 45.7-centimetre. In service from 1907 to 1923, 10 of the 38 built were either lost or scuttled.

D-class

First British submarine with diesel engines and twin screws. Displacement submerged: 620 tonnes; dimensions: 49.3 by 6.2 by 3.3 metres; crew: 27; propulsion: 1,200-bhp Vickers diesel engine (surface), 550-bhp electric motor (submerged). Speed: 14 knots (surface), 10 knots (submerged). Torpedo tubes: 2 bows, 1 stern. *D4* was the first submarine to carry a gun, and the class was the first to have wireless communication. In service from 1908 to 1921, 4 of the original 8 were lost.

E-class

A further improved and enlarged version of the earlier models but with the added development of internal watertight bulkheads that strengthened the pressure hull and allowed deeper diving up to 60 metres. Built in 2 groups, the largest of which had a displacement submerged of 825 tonnes. Dimensions: 55 by 4.5 by 3.8 metres; crew: 30–33; propulsion: 2 × 1,600-hp diesel engines (surface), 2 × 840-hp electric motors (submerged). Speed: 16 knots (surface), 10 knots (submerged). Torpedoes: 4 × 45.7-centimetre, 2 bow, 2 beam (group 1); 5 × 45.7-centimetre, 2 bow, 2 beam, 1 stern (group 2). Of the 56 built, 28 were lost or scuttled. In service from 1914 to 1921, when the majority were scrapped or sold. Also, 2 E-class were built for the Royal Australian Navy; both lost.

F-class
Displacement submerged: 525 tonnes; dimensions: 46 by 4.8 by 3.2 metres; crew: 18; propulsion: 2 diesel engines (surface), 2 electric motors (submerged). Speed: 14 knots (surface), 8.2 knots (submerged). Only 3 were built, towards the end of the First World War, then scrapped; remainder of class cancelled.

G-class
Designed specifically to operate on overseas patrols and in the North Sea against German U-boats in 1915. Displacement submerged: 964 tonnes; dimensions: 57 by 6.8 by 4 metres; crew: 31; propulsion: 2 × 1,600-hp Vickers diesel engines (surface), 2 × 840-hp electric motors (submerged). Speed: 14.5 knots (surface), 10 knots (submerged). Torpedoes: 4 × 45.7-centimetre tubes, 2 bow, 2 stern; 1 × 53.3-centimetre stern tube. Gun: 7.6-centimetre. *G7* was the last submarine to be sunk during enemy action of the First World War. In service from 1915 to 1928, although most were scrapped or sold by 1921. Of the 14 built, 4 were lost.

H-class
Group 1: displacement submerged: 434 tonnes; dimensions: 45.7 by 4.7 by 12.9 metres; propulsion: 2 × 480-hp diesel engines (surface), 2 × 320-hp electric motors (submerged). Speed: 13 knots (surface), 11 knots (submerged). Torpedoes: 4 × 45.7-centimetre bow. Group 2: displacement submerged:

504 tonnes; dimensions: 52 by 4.7 by 4.5 metres; crew: 22; propulsion and speed: same as group 1. Torpedoes: 4 × 53.3-centimetre bow. Group 1: 12 built, 5 lost or scuttled; *H6* was salvaged and commissioned into the Dutch navy. Group 2: 44 built, 5 lost or damaged; several remained in service in the Second World War, noted for use in anti-submarine warfare training of Atlantic convoy escorts and for forming a ring of steel around the German-held port of Brest.

J-class

The largest boat yet built by the Royal Navy, designed for speed. Displacement submerged: 1,820 tonnes; dimensions: 83.9 by 7 by 4.8 metres; crew: 44; propulsion: 3 diesel engines (surface), 3 electric motors (submerged). Speed: 19.5 knots (surface), 9.5 knots (submerged). Torpedoes: 4 bow, 2 beam, 45.7-centimetre. Commissioned in 1916, 7 were built, 1 lost and the remainder transferred to Australia at the end of the First World War. Most were scrapped within 5 years.

Nautilus

Nautilus (*N1*), laid down in 1913 but not completed until June 1917, was an experimental boat designed by Vickers for extended operations in all weather conditions. At the time of original conception her length of 79.2 metres was twice the size of any existing submarine. Displacement submerged was 2,026 tonnes, and a considerable firepower consisted of 2 × 45.7-centimetre bow torpedo tubes, 4 × 45.7-centimetre beam tubes and 2 × 45.7-centimetre stern tubes (with 16 torpedoes carried). The estimated cost of building *Nautilus* was close on £250,000. A 7.6-centimetre high-angle (HA) gun was fitted on the superstructure just forward of the bridge and this was raised and lowered. The boat saw little or no service and was scrapped in 1918, although she provided the confidence for the building of larger K-, L- and M-class boats.

K-class

Successor to the J-class and even larger. Displacement submerged: 2,600 tonnes; dimensions: 103.3 by 8 by 6 metres; crew: 55; propulsion: 2 revolutionary steam turbines (surface), 2 electric motors (submerged). Speed: a remarkable 23 knots (surface), 10 knots (submerged). Torpedoes: 8, 4 bow, 4 beam, 45.7-centimetre. Guns: 2 × 10-centimetre. Considered by many to be an unlucky boat, although, conversely, others had a great affection for her (see Chapter Four). First commissioned in 1916, 18 were built and 7 were lost or severely damaged; most were sold or scrapped in the 1920s.

L-class

Introduced towards the end of the First World War but saw little action. The L-boats were an improved version of E-class submarines, becoming the workhorse between the wars, and were popular with crews. Built in three groups, the largest of which had a displacement submerged of 1,089 tonnes. Dimensions: 72.5 by 7.1 by 3.5 metres; crew: 40; propulsion: 2 × 1,920-hp diesel engines (surface), 2 × 1,150-hp electric engines (submerged). Speed: 17 knots (surface), 10.5 knots (submerged). Torpedoes: 6 × 53.3-centimetre. Of 40 built, 4 were lost, in peacetime. In service from 1918 to 1944, though the majority were scrapped or sold in the 1930s.

M-class

An interesting development, and derived from the K-class, this boat was built as a submersible battleship (see first photographic section), complete with a gun from the Colossus-class battleship. Displacement submerged: 1,950 tonnes; dimensions: 90.2 by 7.4 by 4.8 metres; crew: 60–70; propulsion: 2 × 2,400-hp 12-cylinder Vickers diesels (surface), 2 × 1,600-hp motors (submerged). Speed: 15.5 knots (surface), 9.5 knots (submerged). Torpedoes: 4 × 45.7-centimetre bow. Gun: single 30.4-centimetre Mk XI and 7.6-centimetre disappearing anti-aircraft gun. Only 3 built. *M1* lost with all hands after a collision in 1925; *M2* was converted into Britain's first – and only – submersible aircraft carrier but was lost with all hands in 1932 after hangar door remained open. *M3*, converted into a minelayer, was scrapped in 1930.

O-class

Designed in the mid-1920s for overseas patrols, predominantly on the China station, the East Indies and the Mediterranean, the O-class were the first boats to be given a name rather than a number. Displacement submerged varied through the range to 2,040 tonnes. Dimensions: up to 88.3 by 9 by 5.1 metres; crew: 55; propulsion: 2 × 4,400-bhp diesel engines (surface), 2 × 1,325-bhp electric motors (submerged). Speed: 17 knots (surface), 9 knots (submerged). Torpedoes: 6 bow, 2 stern. Noted for occasionally leaky fuel-carrying ballast tanks, providing an extended range on the surface. Most of the 9 built were being held as somewhat tired reserves at the outbreak of the Second World War, when they resumed operations; 4 were lost on active service, including *Oxley*, mistaken for a U-boat and sunk by one of her own,

Triton. Surviving boats were scrapped or sold in 1946.

P-class

Introduced in the early 1930s, an improved version of the O-boats and again with further extended range for operations in the Far East. Returned en masse to the Mediterranean at the outbreak of war and saw good service. Displacement submerged: 2,040 tonnes; dimensions: 88 by 8.5 by 4.1 metres; crew: 55–58; propulsion: 2 × 4,640-bhp Admiralty diesel engines (surface), 2 × 1,635-shp electric motors (submerged). Speed: 17.5 knots (surface), 8.5 knots (submerged). Torpedoes: 6 bow, 2 stern, 53.3-centimetre. Of 6 built, *Poseidon* sank after a collision off Korea in 1931, although many of the crew escaped, 4 were sunk in enemy action in the Mediterranean, and the only survivor, *Proteus*, which recorded 12 hits on enemy transport ships in the war, was scrapped in 1946.

Porpoise class

Specialist minelayers, launched progressively from 1932. The mine-deck carried 50 mines, using a railway system for delivery, which ran the length of the boat. Displacement submerged: 2,157 tonnes; dimensions: 88 by 7.7 by 4.7 metres; crew: 60; propulsion: 2 diesel engines (surface), 2 electric motors (submerged). Speed: 15 knots (surface), 9 knots (submerged). Torpedoes: 8 × 53.3-centimetre tubes. Of 6 built, 5 were lost in the Second World War, including *Seal*, captured by the Germans after being badly damaged by depth charges. *Porpoise*, depth-charged and sunk while laying mines in the Far East in January 1945, was the last British submarine to be sunk in the Second World War. The minelayers were also noted for some heroic blockade-running activities at the time of the siege of Malta.

R-class

A small, streamlined submarine rushed into production in 1918 specifically to take on the German U-boats. Only 1 saw service, the rest being delivered after the war had ended. Displacement submerged: 500 tonnes; dimensions: 49.6 by 4.8 by 3.5 metres; crew: 22; propulsion: 2 diesel engines (surface), 2 electric motors (submerged). Speed: 15 knots. Torpedoes: 6 × 45.7-centimetre bow. The 10 built were barely used before they were scrapped in the 1920s, only 1 remaining in service beyond 1925. A **second R-class** was produced in 1930, substantially larger and more comfortable, designed for the China station. All 4 were transferred in 1940 to the Mediterranean, where 3 were sunk in enemy action and the 4th was severely damaged off Crete and was scrapped in 1946.

S-class

A popular, smaller submarine noted for her fast diving capability, built on 3 designs and produced between 1930 and 1945 for the North Sea and Mediterranean patrols; 1 of the 3 major classes at the forefront of the Second World War. Group 3, the largest of the class and which was in constant production throughout the war, had a displacement submerged of 990 tonnes. Dimensions: 66.1 by 7 by 3.7 metres; crew: 36; propulsion: 2 × 1,550-hp 8-cylinder diesel engines (surface), 2 × 1,300-hp electric motors (submerged). Speed: 14 knots (surface), 10 knots (submerged). Torpedoes: 6 × 53.3-centimetre bow. In all, 62 were built, of which 18 were lost during the Second World War.

T-class

The second of the three most prominent classes in British submarine operations in the Second World War and with an outstanding record. The class includes some of the most famous names in the illustrious history of wartime submarines. They were also the first British boats to be fitted with radar. Displacement submerged: 1,571 tonnes; dimensions: 83.8 by 8 by 4.4 metres; crew 59/60; propulsion: 2 × 2,500-hp diesel engines (surface), 2 × 1,450-hp electric motors (submerged). Speed: 15.25 knots (surface), 9 knots (submerged). Torpedoes: modified to provide 6 internal and 2 external tubes. This was a hugely successful class, especially in the Mediterranean campaign. The largest class of ocean-going boats, 53 were built and 17 were lost during the war. A number of the T-boats were converted after the war into fast, streamlined submarines in the Guppy configuration; 12 of the class remained in service until the late 1960s.

U-class

The third major element of British submarine warfare between 1939 and 1945, this smaller boat had originally been intended to replace the H-class when building began in 1937. Displacement submerged: up to 740 tonnes; dimensions: 61.8 by 4.8 by 4.1 metres; propulsion: 2 × 615-bhp diesel engines (surface), 2 × 825-bhp electric motors (submerged). Speed: 11.75 knots (surface), 9 knots (submerged). Torpedoes: 4 internal bow tubes, 2 external. A total of 49 were built and again saw excellent service, notably in the

Mediterranean; 19 were lost during the war, 13 of them in the Mediterranean, including, of course, the most famous of the U-class boats, *Upholder*, under the command of Lieutenant-Commander Malcolm Wanklyn, VC. Additionally, 22 **V-class**, of similar design to the U-class, were built in the latter stages of the war, several remaining in service into the 1960s.

X-class

These midgets, whose operations are described in Chapters Ten and Eleven, were designed to be towed by conventional submarines to within 100 miles of the target, notably against the famed German battleship *Tirpitz* and later against Japanese shipping. The crews included a diver who would exit and place high explosives under enemy ships. They came in two models, the X and the XE, with a displacement submerged of 30 and 34 tonnes respectively. The X-craft dimensions were 15.6 by 1.75 by 1.75 metres, which clearly left no room for standing up straight. Powered by a 42-bhp motor, they were capable of 5.5 knots submerged. Approximately 30 were built across the two designs, and they were also used for the reconnaissance of invasion beaches; 9 were lost on operations, 3 were kept in service after the war and the remainder were scrapped. *X24* is on display at the Royal Navy Submarine Museum at Gosport, Hampshire. A **second X-craft** limited edition of four boats (*Minnow*, *Shrimp*, *Sprat* and *Stickleback*) were produced in the early 1950s, intended for a variety of operations, including spying and reconnaissance operations against the Soviet Union; 3 were scrapped in 1965 and *Stickleback* was preserved at the Imperial War Museum, Duxford, Cambridgeshire.

Second A-class
Although designed and in production before the end of the Second World War, the second A-class was overtaken by peace. Originally, 46 were planned, but only 16 were built. Based on the T-class, they had a submerged displacement of 1,620 tonnes. Dimensions: 85.8 by 6.8 by 5.2 metres; crew: 61; propulsion: 2 diesel engines, 2 electric motors. Speed: 18 knots (surface), 8.5 knots (submerged). Torpedoes: 4 bow, 2 stern, 2 external bow, 2 external stern. All were streamlined in post-war years and, apart from *Affray* and *Artemis* (see Chapter Eleven), remained in service until the 1970s. *Alliance* was preserved as a standing exhibit at the Royal Navy Submarine Museum at Gosport.

Second Porpoise class
The first post-war operational submarines in service, they were designed for long patrol endurance and were particularly noted for their submerged speed of 17 knots, achieved from two massive main batteries which developed 5,000 hp. With new snort equipment enabling recharging of batteries submerged, they led the way into the development of boats that could remain submerged for days at a time without surfacing. Displacement submerged: 2,157 tonnes; dimensions: 88 by 7.8 by 4.7 metres; crew: 60. Torpedoes: 8 × 53.3-centimetre tubes. Launched from 1955, remained in service to 1980.

Oberon class
The first British submarine to have a fibreglass casing and the only major order for conventional general-purpose submarines in the second half of the twentieth century, appearing as they did at the time the first nuclear boats were being planned.

Displacement submerged: 2,410 tonnes; dimensions: 90 by 8 by 5.5 metres; crew: 68; propulsion: 2 Admiralty 16-valve diesel engines and 2 electric motors. Speed: 17 knots (submerged). Torpedoes: 6 bow, 2 stern. Between 1959 and 1964, thirteen Oberon-class submarines were built, and had an excellent reputation for reliability and their quiet electric engines. The Oberons replaced the Porpoise-class submarines as Cold War tensions peaked after the Cuban missile crisis when silent approaches were vital for secret missions. One example, *Ocelot*, sailed over 90,000 miles in the first three years of her commission. In the 1980s she and others were given the capability of firing the Tigerfish torpedo as well as the Sub-Harpoon missile. During its time, the Oberon submarine was considered one of the finest in existence and many were sold to overseas navies. The class remained in service until the early 1990s. *Ocelot* was among those sold for scrap in 1992 but was saved by the dockyard that built her, HM Chatham dockyard, now known as the World Naval Base Museum. The dockyard provides guided tours around the submarine, providing a fascinating insight into what was one of the Navy's most elusive weapons of war, as well as the cramped and claustrophobic conditions endured by the crews.

Upholder class

A major leap forward in the technological content of conventional submarines with fully integrated and computerised sonar suite for long-range detection and attack, this class was intended to have a complement of 18 but was overtaken by events, such as the end of the Cold War, cuts in defence spending and the switch entirely to nuclear boats. Displacement submerged: 2,400 tonnes; dimensions: 70.25 by 7.2 by 7.6 metres; crew: 47; propulsion: 2 × 5,400-shp high-speed diesel engines, 2 electric motors. Armaments: 6 bow tubes, sub-Harpoon missiles, wire-guided torpedoes and mines. Only 4 built, commissioned in the early 1990s, then mothballed prior to being sold to Canada.

Nuclear Boats

Dreadnought
Britain's first conventionally armed nuclear-powered submarine, launched by the Queen on Trafalgar Day, 21 October 1960, and commissioned in April 1963, four years in building and costing £18.5 million. Life on board a British submarine would never be the same again. Submerged endurance now counted in weeks rather than days. Displacement submerged: 4,000 tonnes, dimensions: 80.7 by 9.9 by 7.9 metres; crew: 88. US power pack. Speed: 25 knots (surface), 30 knots (submerged). Torpedoes: 6 bow tubes. Capable of diving depth of 305 metres (compared with 30 metres for the *Holland*). Finally laid up in 1983, her nuclear fuel was removed and her equipment stripped out. She was towed to the Rosyth naval dockyard to remain in storage until hundreds of tonnes of radioactive material inside the steel hull has decayed. She will eventually be broken up or sunk deep in the Atlantic, although the disposal of all nuclear boats remains to be resolved.

Valiant, Churchill, Swiftsure and Trafalgar classes
Valiant led the way for the first 'all-British' nuclear boats based on *Dreadnought*, but slightly larger. Displacement submerged: 4,500 tonnes; dimensions: 86.8 by 9.8 by 8.2 metres; crew: 103; propulsion: Rolls-Royce nuclear steam-raising plant and other specifications as *Dreadnought*. Successively built between 1963

and 1993, 18 boats that made up these classes were classified as fleet submarines, or more commonly known as hunter-killers. Their role was to protect the nation's squadron of nuclear-armed submarines (see below), to undertake surveillance and the monitoring of manoeuvres of hostile nations, but specifically tracking the submarines and shipping of the Soviet Union throughout the Cold War, and to participate in both anti-submarine warfare and attacks on surface ships and terrain should the need arise. Only 2 of the 18 boats ever fired in anger up to 2001: *Conqueror* sank *General Belgrano* in the Falklands War, and *Splendid* sent cruise missiles hurtling into Belgrade during the Kosovo crisis. At the end of September 2002, however, *Trafalgar* and *Triumph* moved into position to join the Allied bombardment of 31 targets inside Afghanistan in response to the terrorist attack on New York on 11 September. The earliest of the hunter-killers began to reach the end of their life in the late 1980s, eventually to join *Dreadnought* in decontamination storage at either Rosyth or Devonport. It is said that it will be at least 16 years from decommissioning before they can be safely scrapped.

Resolution class

The beginning of the strategic submarine era with the first British nuclear-armed squadron of Polaris-carrying submarines whose sole task was to roam the seas to provide round-the-clock cover so that a British second-strike deterrent 'remains totally credible at all times'. *Resolution* was the first of the four (the others were *Repulse*, *Revenge* and *Renown*) to be commissioned in 1967. Displacement submerged: 8,400 tonnes; dimensions: 109.7 by 10 by 9.1 metres; crew: 141. They carried 16 Polaris missiles and nuclear warheads. They fulfilled their mission until the early 1990s, when they were progressively taken out of service, with a formal decommissioning ceremony arranged by the then defence secretary, Michael Portillo, in 1996.

Vanguard class

Successor to the Polaris squadron as keeper of the nuclear deterrent, the Vanguard class carried the more potent Trident missiles. Built by Vickers, the new strike force consisted of *Vanguard*, *Victorious*, *Vigilant* and *Vengeance*, which were delivered between 1993 and 1999. Bigger still, with a massive displacement submerged of 15,900 tonnes, with a power plant based on second-generation Rolls-Royce reactors, the boats have the capacity to circumnavigate the globe 40 times without refuelling, developing 27,500 shp, a submerged speed of 25 knots, manned by a crew of 135. The Trident missiles bought from the USA at a cost of $30.9 million apiece have a delivery range of 4,000 nautical miles and are equipped with the latest multiple independently targetable re-entry system.

Astute class

Much of the technology developed for the Trident boats was included in the new breed of hunter-killers, a £2 billion package to provide 3 new submarines – *Astute*, *Ambush* and *Artful* – for delivery by BAE Systems at Barrow-in-Furness in the first half-decade of the twenty-first century. A further 2 will almost certainly be added later, at a cost of an additional £1 billion. They replace the ageing Swiftsure and Trafalgar boats and will be employed in anti-submarine warfare, anti-surface-vessel warfare and land attacks. The power plant will allow them to complete a life span of 25 years without refuelling.

Displacement submerged: 6,000 tonnes; dimensions: 91.7 by 10.4 by 10 metres; Rolls-Royce reactors, GEC turbines, developing 15,500 shp. Armaments: 5 missile tubes for 38 weapons, including sub-Harpoon missiles, Spearfish torpedoes, Tigerfish torpedoes, Tomahawk cruise missiles and mines.

Websites
A full and detailed list of all losses and accidents suffered by the submarine service has been compiled by the research team at the Royal Navy Submarine Museum at Gosport in Hampshire. It can be viewed, along with a great deal of other information, articles and photographs, on the museum's website: www.rn-submus.co.uk. The museum itself, of course, contains outstanding collections and exhibits on the entire history of the Royal Navy's submarine service and is open daily to the public.

Among numerous websites consulted in the course of research for this book, the author strongly recommends the following.

Submariners Association (Barrow branch):
www.submariners.co.uk

A complete history of every Royal Navy submarine and much more on: www/geocities.com/j_d_holt

Complete history, fates and articles on U-boats:
www.uboat.net

Excellent and wide-ranging articles, charts, recollections and links on British military history: www.british-forces.com

The Royal Navy's own website: www.royal-navy.mod.uk

The nuclear situation and the submarine deterrent, compiled by John Pike, website coordinator for the Federation of American Scientists: www.fas/nuke/guide/uk/index

Modern-day nuclear submarines:
www.shima.demon.co.uk/poseidon.htm

INDEX

Now you can buy any of these other bestselling non-fiction titles from your bookshop or *direct from the publisher*.

FREE P&P AND UK DELIVERY
(Overseas and Ireland £3.50 per book)

Other titles in this series by John Parker published by Headline

SBS: The Inside Story of the Special Boat Service £7.99
A fascinating exploration into this small, highly trained marine force, the naval equivalent of the SAS, normally shrouded in secrecy.

The Gurkhas: The Inside Story of the World's Most Feared Soldiers £7.99
An exhaustive study into the mysterious gurkha regiments, showing above all their incredible bravery and ferocious allegiance to the British monarchy.

Commandos: The Inside Story of Britain's Most Elite Fighting Force £7.99
An in-depth investigation into the history of the Commandos, Britain's first-ever special forces, formed using the best of all three forces.

Also by John Parker, published in hardback in September 2002

Strike Command: The Inside Story of the RAF's Warfare Heroes £18.99
A gripping, behind-the-scenes look at the RAF's finest fighter-bomber pilots, the 'top-guns' of the Strike Command.

TO ORDER SIMPLY CALL THIS NUMBER
01235 400 414
or e-mail orders@bookpoint.co.uk
Prices and availability subject to change without notice.